Evolutionary Economics and Social Complexity Science

Volume 14

The Japanese Association for Evolutionary Economics (JAFEE) always has adhered to its original aim of taking an explicit "integrated" approach. This path has been followed steadfastly since the Association's establishment in 1997 and, as well, since the inauguration of our international journal in 2004. We have deployed an agenda encompassing a contemporary array of subjects including but not limited to: foundations of institutional and evolutionary economics, criticism of mainstream views in the social sciences, knowledge and learning in socio-economic life, development and innovation of technologies, transformation of industrial organizations and economic systems, experimental studies in economics, agent-based modeling of socio-economic systems, evolution of the governance structure of firms and other organizations, comparison of dynamically changing institutions of the world, and policy proposals in the transformational process of economic life. In short, our starting point is an "integrative science" of evolutionary and institutional views. Furthermore, we always endeavor to stay abreast of newly established methods such as agent-based modeling, socio/econo-physics, and network analysis as part of our integrative links.

More fundamentally, "evolution" in social science is interpreted as an essential key word, i.e., an integrative and /or communicative link to understand and re-domain various preceding dichotomies in the sciences: ontological or epistemological, subjective or objective, homogeneous or heterogeneous, natural or artificial, selfish or altruistic, individualistic or collective, rational or irrational, axiomatic or psychological-based, causal nexus or cyclic networked, optimal or adaptive, micro- or macroscopic, deterministic or stochastic, historical or theoretical, mathematical or computational, experimental or empirical, agent-based or socio/econo-physical, institutional or evolutionary, regional or global, and so on. The conventional meanings adhering to various traditional dichotomies may be more or less obsolete, to be replaced with more current ones vis-à-vis contemporary academic trends. Thus we are strongly encouraged to integrate some of the conventional dichotomies.

These attempts are not limited to the field of economic sciences, including management sciences, but also include social science in general. In that way, understanding the social profiles of complex science may then be within our reach. In the meantime, contemporary society appears to be evolving into a newly emerging phase, chiefly characterized by an information and communication technology (ICT) mode of production and a service network system replacing the earlier established factory system with a new one that is suited to actual observations. In the face of these changes we are urgently compelled to explore a set of new properties for a new socio/economic system by implementing new ideas. We thus are keen to look for "integrated principles" common to the above-mentioned dichotomies throughout our serial compilation of publications. We are also encouraged to create a new, broader spectrum for establishing a specific method positively integrated in our own original way.

More information about this series at http://www.springer.com/series/11930

Toshio Yamada

Contemporary Capitalism and Civil Society

The Japanese Experience

Springer

Toshio Yamada
Nagoya University
Nagoya, Japan

ISSN 2198-4204 ISSN 2198-4212 (electronic)
Evolutionary Economics and Social Complexity Science
ISBN 978-981-13-0516-0 ISBN 978-981-13-0517-7 (eBook)
https://doi.org/10.1007/978-981-13-0517-7

Library of Congress Control Number: 2018951060

This Springer imprint is published by the registered company Springer Nature Singapore Pte Ltd.
The registered company address is: 152 Beach Road, #21-01/04 Gateway East, Singapore 189721, Singapore

Preface

The aim of this book is to undertake a critical analysis of contemporary capitalism both in Japan and around the world, while on the one hand revisiting the ideas of civil society developed in postwar Japan and on the other hand adapting and developing the conceptual framework of French régulation theory.

Today, in the 21st century, the world's advanced capitalist economies seem to have taken an abrupt turn away from the Fordism-style growth regime of the past and rushed headlong down the path referred to as "neoliberalism." In doing so they have destroyed the old national growth/welfare regime centered on industry and ushered in a difficult era characterized by globalization, deindustrialization, financialization, growing inequality and social cleavage. The Japanese economy, which passed through the first few decades after the war with rapid growth and an export offensive, is no exception. After its bubble economy burst at the beginning of the 1990s, Japan descended into "long-term stagnation," and with an economy unable to respond to the "new social risks" created by the ongoing transformations of capitalism, lifestyle insecurity among the general population and social inequality are continuing to grow.

Regarding the various risks and the inequality created by these changes in the economy, there are demands for the voices of ordinary citizens to be reflected in politics through the democratic system and for these problems to be solved. Unfortunately, however, democracy is in significant decline and is facing its own crisis. In the name of "democracy," populist and xenophobic emotions have taken center stage, while behind the scenes plutocratic lobbyists maneuver to make politics their private possession. The crisis of democracy is not unrelated to the immaturity of "civil society" in some countries and its decline in others. Capitalism must be democratized, and to this end it must be supported by a strong and sound civil society.

The Western term "civil society" or *bürgerliche Gesellschaft* has a long history and has inevitably acquired many connotations. Several definitions come to mind. First, from Aristotle to Hobbes and Locke, it has referred to the "body politic." Second, it has been used to refer to economic society as seen by Hegel and Marx (a system of division of labor and exchange constructed out of self-interested individuals). Third, from Tocqueville to Habermas' "Zivilgesellschaft," it has been used to describe "intermediary groups" or *corps intermédiaires* and the public sphere they form.

In postwar Japan, however, the term "civil society" (*shimin shakai* in Japanese) followed a fixed path; beginning with a Marxist or Hegelian definition, the connotation of "commercial society" as described by Adam Smith was added, and a wholly original and unique normative concept was developed around this definition. The resulting civil society theory then went on to play an important role in postwar Japanese democratic thought. This book is an attempt to bring this unique Japanese concept of civil society to bear on a critical understanding of contemporary capitalism. This is what is meant by its title, "Contemporary Capitalism and Civil Society." Its subtitle is "The Japanese Experience," and this refers not only to the Japanese experience of capitalism but also to our experience of this concept of civil society.

This book includes eleven chapters divided into three parts.

Part I "Postwar Japan and the Theory of Civil Society" includes three chapters. After presenting an overview of general trends in political economy in postwar Japan, I consider the unique civil society thought that blossomed in this country during this period, with a focus on two of its leading figures.

In Chap. 1, "Political Economy in Japan After World War II," I look back at the state of the social sciences, and political economy in particular, in Japan during the postwar period, and discuss the historical and social-scientific context in which Japanese civil society theory was developed. This chapter is based on the essay "Economic Development and Economic Thought After World War II: Economic Development and Marxian Political Economy," included in Shiro Sugihara and Toshihiro Tanaka, eds., *Economic Thought and Modernization in Japan*, Cheltenham and Northampton: Edward Elgar, 1998, but I have made extensive additions to the original text for this book.

In Chap. 2, "Yoshihiko Uchida and His Thoughts on Civil Society: Between Equality in Exchange and Equality as Human Beings," I analyze how the concept of civil society inherent in Yoshihiko Uchida's thought was deepened by this leading proponent of civil society theory in postwar Japan. This process of deepening is presented in the form of civil society *as* capitalism, civil society that is *extruded from* capitalism, and civil society that *passes through* capitalism. Uchida's true vision lies where his concept of civil society finally came to rest, and I have tried to convey to the reader this preeminent achievement of Japanese civil society theory. This chapter was written for this book.

In Chap. 3, "Kiyoaki Hirata and His Thoughts on Civil Society," I discuss Kiyoaki Hirata, who came after Yoshihiko Uchida and developed a theory of civil society through a new interpretation of Karl Marx. Hirata's scholarship led him to study Quesnay, Marx, and ultimately Gramsci and régulation theory, and in this chapter I trace how his concept of civil society was created, developed, and changed over time. This chapter is based on "Hirata Kiyoaki and His Thoughts on Civil Society," included in *The History of Economic Thought* (The Japanese Society for the History of Economic Thought), 56(1), July 2014, with a few minor additions.

Part II "The Rise and Fall of Contemporary Japanese Capitalism" includes four chapters. Here I analyze Japanese capitalism from the postwar period to the present day using the methodology of French régulation theory. The keyword in this analysis is "companyism" rather than "Fordism."

Chapter 4, "The Introduction of Régulation Theory in Japan," is a new essay. In the 1970s the "golden age of capitalism" had passed, and a new era of confusion and unemployment in developed countries was beginning. In this environment, Japanese capitalism made great strides by taking up the weapon of aggressive exports, and in the 1980s Japan even reached the point of being recognized as a "great economic power." In the face of such transitions, existing economics lost its persuasiveness in Japan just as it did in other countries. It was under these circumstances that the régulation theory created in France began to attract attention, and in this chapter I examine the nature of the works through which this theory was presented in Japan.

Chapter 5, "Postwar Japanese Capitalism and Companyist Régulation," attempts an analysis of postwar Japanese capitalism inspired by régulation theory. Japan's mode of régulation, which cannot be fully grasped using the régulationist keyword "Fordism," is understood instead in terms of the concepts of "companyism" and "the companyist compromise," and the key to understanding the postwar Japanese economy is sought in the fact that this "companyism" is effective in guiding investment-led and export-led growth regimes. The examination of companyism, looked at in another way, is in fact the examination of civil society. This chapter is based on "Japanese Capitalism and the Companyist Compromise," included in Robert Boyer and Toshio Yamada, eds., *Japanese Capitalism in Crisis: A Regulationist Interpretation*, London and New York: Routledge, 2000, with extensive revisions and additions.

Chapter 6, "The Collapse of Companyism and Today's Post-Companyist Transformation," traces the transformation the Japanese economy has undergone from the collapse of the bubble at the beginning of the 1990s to the present. During this period Japanese companies undertook striking overseas expansion and multinationalization. In the process, the Japanese mode of régulation characterized as "companyism" was clearly to a large extent destroyed. That being said, it is not as though at present a vigorous new mode of régulation and growth regime have been established. I refer to this current state as the "post-companyist transition" and compare it with the "companyism" it has succeeded. This chapter is based mainly on sections I contributed to two previously published articles, "How Has the Japanese Mode of *Régulation* Changed?: The Whereabouts of Companyism," coauthored with Yasuro Hirano and included in Robert Boyer, Hiroyasu Uemura and Akinori Isogai, eds., *Diversity and Transformations of Asian Capitalisms*, London and New York: Routledge, 2012, and "Multinationalization of Japanese Firms and Dysfunction of Companyist *Régulation*," coauthored with Yasuro Hirano and presented at the International Conference on Research & Regulation 2015 held at the Université Paris Diderot in June of 2015.

Chapter 7, "Analyses of Japanese Capitalism Based on the Régulation Approach: An Overview of Thirty Years of Research," is a survey of 30 years of Japanese economics research based on régulation theory. The main topics it addresses are as follows. (1) Was the high growth in the 1950s and 1960s Fordist? (2) How was Japan as an economic power in the 1970s and 1980s régulated? (3) What type of crisis has the Japanese economy been in during its long stagnation since the 1990s? (4) How is Japan situated in relation to other Asian countries? This chapter was written by adding content to "Analyses of Japanese Capitalism Based on the *Régulation* Approach: An Overview of Twenty Years of Research," a paper presented at the Yokohama-MFJ International Conference held in Tokyo at the Maison Franco-Japonaise in August of 2008.

Part III "Theoretical Considerations of Contemporary Capitalism" includes four chapters. In them I consider several theoretical topics with a focus on the diversity of capitalism in the modern world, the dominance of neoliberalism, and the current state of affairs in countries with transition economies. Through this I anticipate the development of the régulation approach and further maturation of civil society.

In Chap. 8, "Stage Theory or Typology?: Methodological Reflections on the Comparative Analysis of Capitalism," I consider methodological questions that must be taken into account when discussing diversity in modern capitalism and the unique character of capitalism in Japan. Are the differences between capitalism in each country differences in these countries' stage of historical development, or differences in their tracks or types? How should the temporal and spatial variance in each country's capitalism be understood as a whole? My discussion of these questions is based on "Methodological Reflections on the Comparative Analysis of Capitalism," an article previously published in *The Journal of Comparative Economic Studies* (The Japanese Society for Comparative Economic Studies), 10, March 2015.

In Chap. 9, "Economic Crises and Growth Regimes," I attempt a theoretical examination of the dynamics of capitalism in time and space based on the régulation approach. In engaging in a historical/structural analysis of the modern world, I elucidate the importance of what are called the "comparative approach" and the "growth regime approach." The chapter was written by substantially expanding my article "Economic Crises and Growth Regimes," previously published in Hideko Magara, ed., *Economic Crises and Policy Regimes: The Dynamics of Policy Innovation and Paradigmatic Change*, Cheltenham and Northampton: Edward Elgar, 2014.

In Chap. 10, "The Neoliberal Regime and Its Possible Crisis: A Reflection from the Viewpoint of Institutional Change," I elucidate the strengths and weaknesses of neoliberalism in the current era, while giving an overview of the potential for crisis through, on the one hand, synthesizing growth regime and policy regime theories and, on the other hand, analyzing the mechanisms of gradual institutional change. Focusing in particular on the ways in which neoliberalism is destroying democracy, I emphasize the need to counter this by activating the "society principle" and invigorating civil society. This chapter was written by making extensive additions to "Institutional Change and Regime Crisis: A Critical Viewpoint on Neoliberalism," previously published in Hideko Magara, ed., *Policy Change Under New Democratic Capitalism*, London and New York: Routledge, 2017.

In Chap. 11, "Transition Economies and State Capitalism," I address the fact that in recent years there has been a strengthening trend toward "state capitalism" in the socio-economies of nations transitioning from socialism to capitalism (particularly Russia and China). I attempt to understand this state capitalism as a particular type of mode of régulation – one arising out of the immaturity of civil society. Here this analysis is presented for the first time in English.

On many occasions, including international conferences held in Paris, Grenoble, Turin, and many cities in Japan, I have received useful comments and helpful suggestions from a considerable number of friends and colleagues. In particular, I wish to express my deep gratitude to Robert Boyer, Hiroyasu Uemura, Hideko Magara, Bruno Amable, Nanako Fujita, Robert Chapeskie, and the Japan Association for Evolutionary Economics.

I would also like to thank the publishers and editorial boards of the books and journals cited above for allowing previously published texts to be reproduced in this book.

Nagoya, Japan
July 1st, 2018

Toshio Yamada

Explanatory Notes

1. Unless otherwise noted, all emphasis has been added by the author.
2. Words in square brackets ([ ]) in quotations have been added by the author.
3. Ellipses (…) in quotations indicate text has been omitted by the author.
4. Citations in the body of text include the name of the author, year of publication, and page(s) on which the cited text appears. For example, "Uchida (1953:34)" refers to a quotation from page 34 of a text by Uchida published in 1953. Full citations are given at the end of each chapter.
5. Throughout this book, the French word "régulation" (for the most part written without italics) is used with its French spelling (acute accent on the "é") to distinguish it from the English "regulation" which has a slightly different connotation.

Contents

Part I
Postwar Japan and the Theory of Civil Society

Chapter 1
Political Economy in Japan After World War II

1.1 An Overview of Japan's Postwar Political Economy

As a necessary prelude to examining the theory of civil society in postwar Japan, in this first chapter I will begin by discussing how Japanese political economy viewed economic development and contemporary capitalism in the postwar era. As is well known, postwar Japan, emerging from the military defeat of World War II, realized an astonishing level of economic development and became a "great economic power." From today's point of view, this is obviously one of the major events in world history. But for the economists present during these historical events, what were the main issues in Japanese economic development, in which direction did they want to guide the Japanese economy, and how did they develop their own economic thought and theories? Examining these questions will illuminate the historical and theoretical background against which civil society thought was developed in the postwar era.

Our focus in this review will be on Marxian political economy. Of course, during the period we examine there also existed Keynesian and post-Keynesian schools of political economy that attained significant results. But Marxism held greater sway in the field of economics in Japan than in Western countries until at least the 1960s. We may cite several reasons for its strong influence: first, its demonstration of analytical power in the "debate over Japanese capitalism" in the 1930s (discussed below); second, the prestige it accrued as a science directly and unflinchingly confronting poverty and war; and third, the great distance between the realities of Japanese society and the theoretical world of American neoclassical economics.

The success of Marxian economics, however, was confined to universities and labor movements, its historical view was not necessarily supported by the general public. On the contrary, as early as the 1950s, Japanese Marxian economics had begun to lose its capacity for scientific analysis and its popular support due to various conflicts and splits within the international communist movement and the

T. Yamada, *Contemporary Capitalism and Civil Society*, Evolutionary Economics and Social Complexity Science 14,
https://doi.org/10.1007/978-981-13-0517-7_1

Japanese Communist Party (JCP). This meant that Marxian economists had begun to lose both the desire and the ability to participate in formulating economic policies. In this way Marxian political economy, having in many respects lost interest in actual political concerns entirely, became an abstract discourse of criticism of capitalism in general; it defended itself by turning its back on the actual circumstances of the era.

In the postwar period, Japanese Marxian economists were also indifferent to, or actively withdrew from, international academic society. Japanese scholars had of course been very sensitive to the world's latest academic trends and translated into Japanese many Marxian texts such as those of Paul M. Sweezy, Maurice H. Dobb, and Eugen S. Varga. But these "international interchanges" were only instances of scientific "importation," not of reciprocal contribution and debate. Consequently, until the 1970s Japanese Marxian political economy developed in isolation, cut off from trends in the rest of the world. And as a result of this isolated development, "(rather like some fragment of a biological species which is cut off from others by geographical circumstances) their [Japanese Marxists'] theories began to evolve in a number of distinctive directions" (Morris-Suzuki 1989: 104). The two most prominent of these "distinctive directions" were systematization into grand theories and a flourishing of exegetical studies of Marx's texts.

Speaking more precisely, postwar Japanese Marxian political economy can be divided into three schools: the orthodox school, the *Uno* school, and the civil society school. While the *Uno* school is a descendant of the prewar *Rōnō* school, the other two constitute two types of successors to the *Kōza* school that took part in the so-called debate over Japanese capitalism (*nihon shihonshugi ronsō*) that unfolded in the 1930s. It is therefore useful to give a brief account of this debate before moving on.

In the 1920s, Japan saw the publication of the first Japanese language translation of Marx's *Capital*; however, the capitalist world depicted in *Capital* differed greatly from Japan's socioeconomic realities at the time. The biggest issue was how to evaluate the remnants of feudal or semi-feudal systems, which at that point still existed to a considerable extent throughout Japan. Were they transitory features that would disappear along with the capitalist development of Japan or structural features that would necessarily survive as long as Japan remained capitalist? Were they a result of Japanese backwardness in terms of stages of capitalist development or necessary elements peculiar to Japanese capitalism? In other words, it was also a debate over how to evaluate the nature and possibility of civil and modern socioeconomic elements within a Japanese context. These questions provoked a great number of disputes that comprised the "debate over Japanese capitalism" among Japanese Marxists in the 1930s.

At the same time, this debate was also closely related to political strategies for socialist revolution. The *Rōnō* school considered feudalism a product of Japan's backwardness in terms of its stage of development, insisted that its socio-economy would converge on that of other advanced capitalist nations as its capitalist development progressed, and asserted that the coming revolution must be socialist. This school included, among many others, Tamizō Kushida (1885–1934) and Itsurō

Sakisaka (1897–1985). On the other hand, the *Kōza* school, led by Moritarō Yamada (1898–1980) and Eitaō Noro (1900–1934), stressed the impossibility of dissolving feudalism under capitalism; they asserted that its survival was inevitable, that it would result in a specific type of Japanese capitalism, and that Japan required two revolutions: first bourgeois and then socialist. This debate thus included many creative ideas on how to analyze the capitalist economies of the day outside of a Western context.

In postwar Japan, however, Marxism underwent a general decline, primarily because it remained wedded to the "general crisis theory of capitalism" in the midst of an era of rapid growth. This is aptly stated by Furihata: "While modern theory [for example, that of the neo-classical synthesis] was shown to be in error by the end of [the period of] high growth, Marxian political economy had already collapsed as a result of high growth itself" (Furihata 1983: 6). Most of the Marxian economists fled from the analysis of actual economies, turning to textual critiques of Marxian manuscripts, the study of which expanded to an abnormal extent during the high-growth era (Takasuka 1985). Japanese Marxian economics thereby became turned in on itself and fell into its own crisis. This crisis was further amplified by the successive collapses of the socialist countries beginning at the end of the 1980s. It can also be said, however, that this crisis gave birth to a fruitful new approach that made more flexible use of Marxian ideas.

In short, we can summarize the Japanese Marxian political economy in the last half of the 20th century as a period in which this approach to economics, despite enjoying a heritage of high level discourse created during the debate over Japanese capitalism before the war, failed to adjust to the conditions of postwar Japan. But we cannot grasp the full import of Japanese postwar political economy by noting only this general trend. Because of the historical and critical perspectives the Marxian perspective alone could provide, Marxian political economists, especially those of the *Uno* and civil society schools, proposed a number of insightful ideas concerning the issues of postwar economic development. Here we will consider these ideas by dividing the so-called postwar era into three periods: the economic reconstruction period, the rapid economic growth period, and the post-oil shock period.

1.2 Directions of Economic Reconstruction

The main issues concerning economic development in the period of recovery (1945–1955) immediately after the war centered around the fundamental direction of economic reconstruction. The Japanese economy and its citizens' livelihoods had been utterly destroyed by the war. But democratic reforms of the Japanese economy were then carried out under the direction of the American Occupation Force. These included land reform, dissolution of the *zaibatsu* financial cliques, and the emancipation of trade unions. From 1950 onward, aided by the special procurements of the US military during the Korean War (1950–1953), the Japanese economy began to recover.

But no one believed that the purpose of reconstruction should be to reproduce the Japan of the prewar era. What form, then, should the new Japanese economy take? Marxists joined the debate over the nature of this new era. And to their advantage, Marxists alone enjoyed the benefit of having inherited their own discourse from the prewar debate over Japanese capitalism. Japanese Marxian political economy was at the height of its influence in the period of economic recovery, during which prototypes of the representative Marxian schools of postwar Japan were formed.

1.2.1 The Theory of State Monopoly Capitalism

The orthodox viewpoint typical of postwar Japanese Marxism is presented by Inoue and Usami (1951). Taking up the definition of Japanese capitalism as "militarist and semi-feudal imperialism" as proposed by the prewar *Kōza* school, they point out its insufficiency and introduce the concept of "state monopoly capitalism" (SMC) that had first been conceived by V. I. Lenin. With the establishment of the Soviet Union in 1917, capitalism had entered, they argue, an era of "general crisis," in addition to the crises of the world wars and the Great Depression. Under such intense pressure, monopoly capitalism became unable to sustain itself without transforming itself into SMC. Thus SMC reveals "the last aspect" of capitalism and implies that those seeking the establishment of socialism have "taken the high ground."

Here we observe an erroneous schema of history: general crisis → SMC → collapse of capitalism → socialism. This is, however, the very schema of capitalist development on which orthodox Marxism insisted in postwar Japan. According to orthodox Marxism, capitalism will collapse before very long, and therefore there will be no room for ongoing economic development under a capitalist system. Today we can easily point out Marxism's errors, but we must not forget that for at least two reasons it was very persuasive at the time. First, capitalism in the 1930s and 1940s was in what seemed to be its final crisis. Second, the notion of SMC correctly posited the growing role of the state in advanced capitalist countries both during and after the war. This is why postwar Japanese Marxian theories of contemporary capitalism and economic development were in most cases constructed upon the concept of SMC. Indeed, "this is … quite crucial to an understanding of the controversies of the postwar Japanese left" (Morris-Suzuki 1989: 122).

Based on these general conceptions of history, Inoue and Usami (1951) argue that Japanese capitalism was an instance of SMC that constituted the last phase of capitalism and at the same time a form of capitalism that was structurally integrated with semi-feudal elements. The wartime economy had deepened these structural contradictions, objectively creating the necessity of land reform through dissolution of the semi-feudal system of landholding and the liberation of tenant farmers. According to Inoue, however, the land reform carried out under the control of the Occupation Force beginning in 1946 only "reorganized" the feudal system, allowing the semi-feudal system of landholding to survive unchanged. Consequently, what was needed was a struggle for "the complete overthrow of the semi-feudal system" (Inoue et al. 1953).

In short, there was no possibility of ongoing economic development, not only because Japan was in the midst of the general historical phase of SMC but also because Japanese capitalism in particular preserved semi-feudal elements from the prewar era. According to this orthodox Marxian view, Japanese capitalism still retained its structural contradictions in spite of the postwar reforms and existed as an extremely weak capitalism in comparison to Western models. Inoue suggests that as a result the reconstruction of the Japanese economy could not be achieved without transforming it into a socialist system. In his view, only a socialist revolution could lead to economic development.

1.2.2 Modernization Theory

There was, however, another group which, although it succeeded the same *Kōza* school, established a different theory. This approach was referred to as "modernization theory," though not in the Rostowian sense. This group was not necessarily composed of Marxists alone. Even those of its members who were close to Marxism addressed Marx in relation to Adam Smith or Max Weber and did not elevate Marx alone in their analysis. Here we will examine one such thinker, Hisao Ōtsuka (1907–1996), who was remarkably active in this period.

His point of view on the development of the Japanese economy can be summarized as follows (Ōtsuka 1946). What is most important for the reconstruction of the Japanese economy is the creation of a "modern type of human being." The objective conditions this requires are a liberation of the peasantry "from below" (general formation of an independent and self-sustaining peasantry) and the creation of a domestic market before the creation of foreign markets that was being insisted upon by the government. In other words, it is only on the basis of these two conditions having been met that a modernized population can be formed in Japan, a population made up of a "modern type of human being" that will then constitute one of the most powerful "productive forces" in the reconstructed Japanese economy.

Ōtsuka's approach is based upon his earlier studies of European economic history conducted both before and during the war, and its result is an original and influential doctrine called "Ōtsuka Historiography." Calling into question the driving forces that had brought modern capitalism into existence, Ōtsuka (1951, 1964) sharply criticizes the accepted theory of the German Historical School that had located these forces in the "development of commerce" and proposes a new theory that situates them in the formation of a "mediocrity of fortune" (intermediate producers' stratum) and its subsequent polarization. According to Ōtsuka, while the "path from above," or the progression from commercial capital (antediluvian capital) to industrial capital, was seen primarily in Prussia, the "path from below," or the progression from yeoman capital (intermediate producers' stratum) to industrial capital, was most evident in Britain and America. The "path from above" could not be truly revolutionary in the birth of capitalism. On the contrary it was the "path from below" that constituted a pure and civilized capitalism sustained by modern type human beings and modern productive forces.

From Ōtsuka's perspective, the direction of development for postwar Japan should be one in which peasants become landed farmers by liberating themselves from semi-feudal relations and in which a broad domestic market is built up on the bases of both the public wealth (*Volksreichtum*) in the hands of farmers and the division of national labor between agriculture and industry. What was critically important at that moment was that working people be molded into a "modern type of human being" and thereby become vehicles of "modern productive forces." While orthodox Marxism insisted on the impossibility of capitalist development and the great potential of socialist development, Ōtsuka, despite having inherited the same *Kōza* school theory, emphasized that the authentic path of economic development consisted in a "from below" approach supported by a modern type of human being, regardless of whether Japan adopted a capitalist or socialist system.

1.2.3 Uno Theory

We have so far followed two theories stemming from the tradition of the *Kōza* school, but postwar Japan also had an excellent political economy framework developed by the *Rōnō* school, the other prewar school of Japanese economic thought. The political economic thought of Kōzō Uno (1897–1977), which came to be called "Uno Theory," attracted many followers who formed the influential "*Uno* school." Uno's works are, it can surely be said, among the greatest achievements in postwar Japanese economics (see Barshay 2004: Ch. 4). His political economy is constructed in a very systematic way from a pure and abstract theory to a concrete analysis of the real world. Though the domains that Uno himself studied are situated on the level of pure theory ("general principles"), his methodology not only originated from his own reflection on the debate over Japanese capitalism in the interwar period but also is deeply related to debates on the direction Japan was to take in its reconstruction. Before we examine his system of political economy, therefore, we will first briefly review what he wrote about economic reconstruction.

The reconstruction of postwar Japan, Uno (1946) argued, should be based mainly on the establishment of capitalist agriculture and large enterprises, rather than on landed farmers and industrial capital, so that farm and factory workers will have the organizational basis to develop democracy. In short, Uno stressed that economic democratization had to be founded on industrial socialization, and he predicted the emergence of socialism in Japan based upon industrial socialization and a widening economic democratization.

Uno Theory, which emphasizes capitalist management of agriculture and socialization of industry, contrasts sharply with Ōtsuka Historiography, which stresses a broad formation of small commodity producers. Uno presents a new conception in which economic democratization in contemporary Japan should be achieved, in contrast to the case of England, for example, on the basis of industrial socialization. Uno's novel insight lies, in short, in the recognition that a backward country does not simply imitate and repeat the historical processes of advanced countries; its capitalist development may end up taking a different form in accordance with the historical stage of world capitalism in which it starts its development. This view formed the basis of his own methodology and system of political economy.

Any system of Marxian political economy, Uno (1962) argued, has to be divided into three progressive levels: general principles, stage theories, and analysis of actual conditions. The first level, that of general principles, is a field in which, assuming for methodological purposes a pure capitalist society, we define the most fundamental economic laws of capitalism. The second level, that of stage theories, is a field of research addressing the particular contents of different stages of capitalist development, such as the stage of commercial capitalism (exemplified by the mercantilist policies of the 16th and 17th centuries), the stage of industrial capitalism (exemplified by liberal policies after the Industrial Revolution), and lastly a stage of finance capitalism (exemplified by the rise of imperialism beginning in the late 19th century). And it is only on these foundations of general principles and stage theories that we can undertake analyses of the actual conditions of capitalism in a particular country during a particular period, such as, for example, postwar Japan. Analysis of actual conditions constitutes the third and last level and also the ultimate goal of all economic studies.

To be sure, the pure capitalism that is presupposed in the postulation of general principles has never existed. But a methodological supposition of pure capitalism is, Uno says, neither arbitrary nor unreasonable, because capitalist societies, especially that of England, manifested, from the 17th century to the middle of the 19th century, a tendency to evolve toward pure capitalism. It is on this real and historical basis that one can construct the general principles of political economy. From Uno's point of view, Marx's *Capital* is clearly a text of pure theory or general principles of capitalism, but as such is insufficient and incomplete; one finds there a careless mixture of pure theory with a number of propositions that do not belong at the level of general principles, for example, those concerning the pauperization of the working class, primitive accumulation, and so on. According to Uno, the pauperization thesis, for example, describes a characteristic particular to English capitalism, especially during the first half of the 19th century, and thus a phenomenon whose study ought to belong to the level of stage theory or of the analysis of actual conditions.

If all capitalist countries always moved toward pure capitalism, it would be enough for us to have, as disciplines of political economy, merely general principles and the analysis of actual conditions. In reality, however, the self-purifying tendency of capitalism was reversed with the historical appearance of finance capital at the end of the 19th century. This is why the general principles, by themselves, are not sufficient and a stage theory is required. Uno distills these reflections from the debate between the *Kōza* and *Rōnō* schools. Both schools, he claims, made the same mistake of attempting to apply Marx's *Capital* directly to the actualities of Japanese society at the time. As a result the *Kōza* school overestimated the distance between *Capital* and Japanese society, while the *Rōnō* school erred in the opposite direction.

The essential task both schools had overlooked was the construction of a theory of the stage of imperialism as a basis for the analysis of the Japanese economy of their era.

Even as he was devising the above methodology of political economy, Uno devoted himself to the completion and perfection of his own general principles (Uno 1950/1952). Uno Theory is typical of postwar Japanese thought in its construction of a grand theoretical system and is a great achievement of which postwar Japanese Marxian political economy deserves to be proud. Furthermore, in advocating "the separation of science from ideology," Uno was an early critic of Stalinism and also opposed the interference in academic studies of particular political parties or sects. Uno's most important book has been translated into English (Uno 1980), his ideas are often introduced in texts written in English (Mawatari 1985), and we can also find English works making use of his ideas (Albritton 1986, 1991). Although the historical limitations and defects of Uno Theory are obvious when we consider it from the viewpoint of the 21st century, viewed in its original context it still shines, side by side with Ōtsuka Historiography, as an exemplary achievement of social science in postwar Japan.

1.3 High Economic Growth and Its Significance

In the 1950s and 1960s, the advanced capitalist world experienced a long period of prosperity called the "Golden Age of Capitalism" or the "Fordist Era." In Japan, too, in 1956, just one decade after the country's military defeat, the *White Paper on the Economy* claimed, "we are no longer in the postwar period." In fact, in the previous year, 1955, the GNP of the Japanese economy had recovered to the highest level of the prewar era. By 1956, the period of economic growth under postwar reconstruction had ended. The new expectation was for growth through the modernization of technology and the economy. Although a pessimistic view prevailed both inside and outside of Marxism, the Japanese economy thereafter enjoyed, contrary to all forecasts, an average annual real growth rate of around 10% for some 20 years, an exceptionally high rate of economic growth. This period (1956–1973) is often referred to as the "era of high economic growth." During this period the rural population decreased sharply, the real wages of workers increased, new consumer goods became popular, and people's lifestyles and values changed drastically.

In general Marxian political economists were either critical of high economic growth or viewed it impassively. But high growth raised serious questions for Marxism. The first was how to explain the emergence of this high economic growth itself, not only in Japan but also in advanced capitalist economies in the age of the so-called "general crisis of capitalism." The second was how to understand why the particular mechanisms of rapid growth in this country existed in Japan and nowhere else. Next we will examine the struggles of Marxian economists as they grappled with these questions.

1.3.1 The Socialization Theory of SMC

As we have seen, postwar Japanese Marxists consecrated "State Monopoly Capitalism" (SMC) as a paradigmatic concept for the analysis of contemporary capitalism. Two suppositions are implied in this conception of capitalist evolution: first, that SMC is a product of the general crisis of capitalism (crisis theory of SMC) and second, that economic stagnation will persist for a long time under SMC (stagnation theory). These theoretical suppositions necessarily result in treating the fact of high economic growth as an "exception" to the basic tendency toward stagnation of 20th-century capitalism. In short, according to the dogmatic view of postwar Japanese Marxism, high economic growth was in the end an exceptional phenomenon.

However, a new group then began to confront the fact of high growth, finding that structural changes had altered the nature of capitalism from what it had been in the prewar period. One member of this group was Takuichi Ikumi (1901–1995). Drawing heavily on the work of Kurt Zieschang (1957) of East Germany, this group set out to explain SMC not in terms of a general crisis of capitalism but rather the "socialization of productive relations." They held that as the "socialization of productive forces" develops in a capitalist system, productive relations must also inevitably become socialized. This socialization is expressed in the formation of joint-stock companies and monopoly corporations, and SMC constitutes the ultimate stage of this development. So SMC is not a product of the crisis of capitalism, but a product of a certain degree of capitalist development (Ikumi 1958).

This view is often called the socialization theory of SMC. However, the basic explanatory conception is nothing but historical materialism, according to which productive relations must develop (socialize) themselves in proportion to the development (socialization) of productive forces. This explanation is a product of direct and immediate application of abstract formulae of historical materialism to contemporary economies and has no relevance as a theory of capitalist development. While in this sense the theoretical approach taken by this group was flawed, they nevertheless attempted to earnestly address the realities of the development of productive forces within contemporary capitalism and its long-term prosperity.

So although this group perceived the fact of high economic growth clearly, their new theory of SMC failed. Reflecting on this failure over time, the advocates of the socialization theory of SMC eventually realized that its roots lay in the very concept of SMC itself. "SMC" is inseparable, by virtue of its origin in the thought of V. I. Lenin, from a historical schema of "increasing contradictions and a final collapse of capitalism." The sustainable growth of 1960s capitalism could not be well understood using the antiquated concept of SMC, and as a result they soon declared that they would cease employing this term (Kishimoto 1975; Tamagaki 1976). The paradigmatic concept of postwar Marxism began to be called into question.

1.3.2 The Crisis Theory Approach to SMC

Alongside the trend toward abandoning the theory of SMC, there appeared another movement intended to revise and restructure it. This was a theory of SMC proposed by Tsutomu Ōuchi (1918–2009). As one of the leading followers of Uno, his objective was the construction of a foundation for the analysis of actual conditions that Uno had left incomplete. This was what motivated his approach to SMC. Ōuchi (1970) explains the essence of SMC as control of the economy by the state through fiscal policies based on a managed currency system. As he indicates by naming his doctrine the "crisis theory approach," the ultimate objective of the state under SMC consists in escaping from crises, and the principal method for doing so is reducing real wages through inflationary measures. Ōuchi thus explains SMC not simply by resorting to the idea of general crisis alone, but by paying attention to the modifications in capital–labor relations in capitalist countries it precipitates.

In spite of these positive contributions, Ōuchi's theory has a fatal flaw: it is incapable of explaining high economic growth because it accepts the theories of general crisis and chronic stagnation. For him, Japan's high rate of growth was, in the end, an abnormal phenomenon (Ōuchi 1962). This rapid growth was to be explained exclusively by the "backwardness" of the Japanese economy and the "postwar factor." He considered "backwardness" to be primarily "an abundant existence of low-wage labor" and the "postwar factor" to be new possibilities for the expansion of investment and the domestic market owing to the end of the war. However "backwardness" and the "postwar factor" of Japanese capitalism were only temporary phenomena which would disappear before long, and rapid growth based upon these particular conditions was nothing but an "abnormal," "particular," "temporary," and exceptional phenomenon. From the vantage point of the present, it is clear that in this he was quite mistaken.

We have examined two new versions of SMC theory. The story of their development is a valuable record of the ways in which the theory of SMC, which was born during an era of difficult conditions for capitalism, endeavored to transform itself in the face of the fact of high economic growth. One approach rejected the crisis-oriented character of the theory so as to start from the fact of rapid growth and prosperity but failed to establish a positive economic theory. The other was successful in building a refined economic explanation based on Uno theory but was unable to explain rapid growth, retaining the crisis-oriented character of the original theoretical framework. Both are ultimately unsuccessful theories. But these two approaches played the important role of "negative intermediate" in leading postwar Japanese political economy to finally abandon the paradigmatic concept of SMC and later accept new concepts concerning contemporary capitalism, for example, that of "Fordism."

1.3.3 Civil Society Theory

A view of economic development that did not adopt any position on SMC also emerged in Japanese political economy. This was Yoshihiko Uchida's "civil society theory." Beginning in the early postwar period, Uchida (1913–1989), through reflection on the debate over Japanese capitalism, made an ongoing effort to address questions concerning the particularity of Japanese capitalism and the direction of social reform. He had learned much from Ōtsuka Historiography, an approach from which he borrowed, for example, the concepts of a "modern type of human being" and a "mediocrity of fortune," which he then expanded into a conception of "civil society."

In the context of this discussion, let us for the moment define "civil society" in an abstract and transhistorical sense as "a system of equivalent exchange and productive forces" or "a society with freedom and human rights." (We will examine Uchida's discourse on civil society in greater detail in the next chapter.) Based on this concept of civil society, Uchida pointed out the problems with capitalist development in Japan and criticized the Japanese form of high economic growth (Uchida 1967, 1981). According to Uchida, the establishment of capitalism in Japan was achieved not through the creation of liberated and equal individuals, but rather through the incorporation of feudal and premodern elements. This claim, advanced by the *Kōza* school in the prewar period, led Uchida to posit "the distinguishing of civil society from capitalism" and finally to characterize Japan as "capitalism without civil society." Of course, conditions were very different before and after the war. In the postwar era, especially in the era of high economic growth, we cannot deny a certain degree of development of civil elements. But can we really say that the unprecedentedly high rate of economic growth resolved the issue of civil society in Japan? Or was it precisely thanks to the weakness of civil or modern elements in Japanese society that the economy was able to develop so rapidly?

Uchida (1967) blamed the weakness of the civil elements vis-à-vis the power of capital on the fact that people's lives and collective consciousness were still organized around the logic of capital; the power of capital is robust, in contrast to the weakness of human rights, as was demonstrated in the problems that arose concerning education and pollution. In the 1960s Uchida criticized the Japanese form of high economic growth by citing Hajime Kawakami's (1879–1946) older comparison of Japan and Europe: "In Europe, God created human rights, and afterwards man created the rights of the state. Conversely in Japan, God first created the rights of the state, and then the state created human rights" (Kawakami 1911, 1982: 119). In the Japanese model of economic development, only the power of capital and that of the state manifested themselves, while human rights and civil society remained immature. It was precisely for this reason that Japan was able to develop so rapidly.

Uchida's conception provides, beyond a mere criticism of Japan in the period of high growth, a critical perspective on Japan as an "economic power," that is, on Japan, as it found itself in the 1970s and 1980s, in the vanguard of ultramodernization and under the sway of catchphrases such as "high-tech society" and "information-oriented society." In this way, Uchida's view of Japanese capitalism crystallized into an "articulation of the premodern with the super-modern." In other words, he believed that "something pre-modern that underlies the Japanese economy or society does not work in the direction to prevent Japan from developing, but to realize excessively high growth or to create the super-modern without the modern" (Uchida 1981: 11). However paradoxical it may seem, says Uchida, Japanese capitalism is developing through the weakness of civil society (see Yamada 1986, 1987).

It is obvious that the question of a country's economic development must not be reduced to a mere realization of industrialization or a high growth rate. High economic growth may indeed resolve unemployment and material poverty. In Japan, however, growth was realized not by strengthening human rights and civil society, but by suppressing them. In this sense Japanese capitalism has gone hand in hand with new forms of discrimination and poverty. Japan is thus in no sense a model to be followed by, for example, other Asian countries.

1.4 Universalities and Particularities of Japanese-Style Capitalism

With the onset of the first oil shock in 1973, Japan's period of high economic growth came to an end. Economic growth came to a halt not only in Japan but in all advanced countries; following this shock, economic indices in all of these other nations also continued to worsen for a long period of time. Advanced countries were afflicted by stagnation, which brought on an era of long-term global depression. Contrary to most predictions, however, Japan's economy, one of the most severely damaged by the oil price shock, recovered relatively quickly. Japan returned to growth by rapidly introducing microelectronic technologies and transforming its industrial structure, but perhaps the greatest key to its recovery was the cooperation of the working class in this transformation. By the early 1980s, the Japanese economy was again relying on export demand as it developed into a global power. At the end of that decade Japan then experienced the speculation-driven "bubble" economy, followed by an ongoing depression after the bubble burst in the early 1990s.

In the post-oil shock period of the last quarter of the 20th century, that is, in the third period of the postwar Japanese economy described in this chapter, the traditional theories of general crisis and SMC completely lost their validity and were practically abandoned by almost all Marxian economists. In general, Marxian political economy found itself marginalized within the world of economics. At the same time, however, new theoretical approaches appeared that were not predetermined by traditional views. In this period, there were two major questions to which economics was expected to provide answers. First, what were the causes and mechanisms of the long-term global depression? Second, stemming from the desire to understand the secrets of Japan's economic success, what were the universalities and particularities of this country's economic system? The most interesting answers given by political economists were provided by scholars affiliated with the *Uno* school.

1.4.1 Long-Term Global Depression

The shift from sustained growth to long-term depression in the early 1970s was a great challenge to the entire field of economics. How could economists explain the change from growth to crisis and show us the way out of the depression? Makoto Itoh (1936–) wrestled squarely with these questions.

Itoh (1988, 1990) begins by pointing out four major factors or conditions for the sustained economic growth of the postwar capitalist world: the economic hegemony of the United States and its dollar expenditures, a long wave of technological innovation, relatively cheap primary products (especially crude oil) from third world countries, and the availability of relatively low-wage workers. The underlying cause of the crisis that began in the 1970s lies, according to Itoh, in the fact that these conditions began to erode during the continuous period of high economic growth. In particular, this erosion "simultaneously contained the more fundamental difficulty of overaccumulation of capital in relation to the inelastic supply of both the laboring population and primary products from Third World countries, so squeezing the rate of profit throughout the capitalist world" (Itoh 1990: 45). In other words, the cause of the crisis lay in the fact that capital accumulation, which had greatly increased in advanced countries throughout the sustained growth period, became excessive in comparison not only to the supply of domestic labor but also to that of primary products from the third world. In short, Itoh argues it was the overaccumulation of capital that caused the crisis.

For Itoh, an adherent of Uno Theory, this indicates the direct validity of Uno's crisis theory (excessive capital theory), which had been proposed at the level of general principles, in explaining the post-oil shock depression, which had to be analyzed in terms of actual conditions. In other words, the process that had given rise to a global depression in the 1970s and 1980s was very similar to that behind the classical crises in the 19th century described, for example, in Uno (1953).

Furthermore, for Itoh this also means that capitalism is now revealing its own difficulties at the level of general principles, or that capitalism today is, to a surprising degree, once again approaching the theoretical world of general principles. While Uno acknowledged a historical reversal of the self-purifying tendency of capitalism at the end of the 19th century, at the end of the 20th century Itoh observed a new reversal of capitalist development over the preceding 100 years and a "flowing backwards" of capitalism. This is typically manifested in three facts: a shift of capital investment from heavy and large-scale to lighter and smaller-scale industrial plants and equipment, a weakening of the role of trade unions, and a reduction of the economic role of the state (contrary to the theory of SMC). The current recomposition of Fordism into post-Fordism and the rise of neoliberalism are rooted, says Itoh, in this flowing backwards of capitalism.

What about Japan? In this period one heard the mantra "learn from Japan" all over the world. But Japanese capitalism cannot be a model for workers around the world to study and follow. In fact, although the Japanese trade surplus increased enormously in the period after the oil shock, underlying it we have seen deteriorating circumstances for workers: a stagnation of real wages, an increase in precarious employment, worsening labor conditions, and so on. Itoh argues that in this sense Japanese capitalism leads to a flowing backwards *à la* post-Fordism.

1.4.2 The Japanese-Style Economic System

There was great deal of discussion of the "Japanese-style economic system" in the post-oil shock period, driven mainly by a desire to elucidate the secrets of Japan's "success" in the 1970s and 1980s. This was followed by a series of debates over issues like the closed nature of the Japanese economy and its failure to observe rules, as reflected in frequent corporate scandals, and in doubts about the relevance of the postwar economic system in the midst of the long depression that began in the 1990s. Marxian political economy also began to move beyond its traditional focus on capitalist or socialist systems and devote more attention to comparative institutional analysis. Many hypotheses regarding Japanese capitalism were put forward, among which the "companyism" hypothesis of Hiroji Baba (1933–2011) stirred the greatest interest.

According to Baba (1991, 1997a, b), we can enumerate the characteristics of Japanese companies (at least until the 1990s) as follows: weak stockholder control, a small gap between various classes and ranks within companies, the active engagement of employees in their jobs, and a strong awareness among employees of being members of their companies. Baba terms this company-centered attitude or consciousness "companyism." These facts themselves had already been pointed out many times in discussions of Japanese-style management, but Baba's originality lies in reconsidering companyism from a historical point of view.

First, Baba argues, companyism emerged in the high-growth era and provided the Japanese economy with strong guidance in the period after the oil shock, giving rise to the strong performance of the postwar Japanese economy.

Second, companyism is "the most suitable organizational form that one can think of for elevating productive forces." "Effective" companyism has helped make Japan the world's most productive country. Moreover, companyism, being "the greatest mechanism for the development of productive forces," possesses a worldwide universality. While thus emphasizing the historical efficiency and universality of companyism, Baba also points out that its excessive elevation of productive forces has also brought forth many negative phenomena.

Third, as a theorist of the *Uno* school, Baba attempts a critical reconstruction of Uno's stage theory. Reexamining Uno's definition of the stage of finance capital, Baba finds in it a development from managerial capitalism *à l'américaine* (the post-war period) to companyism *à la japonaise* (the post-oil shock period). Companyism is not only an extreme form of finance capital but also, says Baba, the participation of workers in management means that it is the most advanced stage of capitalism, a form that goes beyond even managerial capitalism. Finally, he finds in companyism "a penetration of socialism into production centers" or "a creeping socialism."

In short, Baba presents the historical context of companyism, acknowledges its efficiency, universality, and advanced character, and finds in it "socialist" elements. To be sure, his discourse contains some clear exaggerations and errors. But his principal intention is not to boast about the efficiency, universality, and advanced character of Japanese capitalism. His true message is that it is very important for humankind to seriously consider what awaits us beyond the current model of economic growth under capitalism, a system capable of engendering even something as extreme as companyism. Baba illustrates this through a concept referred to as "mass overenrichment" or "excessive affluence" (Baba 1986, 1997a, b; Barshay 2004: 146).

Evidence of excessive affluence is not only evident in the fashionableness of dieting and jogging in advanced countries but is also suggested by the well-known calculation that the earth would at once become an unlivable planet if its entire population attained living standards or income levels equal to those of advanced countries. The index of mass overenrichment is, according to Baba, a per capita GDP of $5000 (in 1982 dollars), which corresponds to a living standard characterized by the popularity of cars, a declining increase in caloric intake, and 30% of Engel's coefficient. The so-called advanced countries had already attained this level by 1970.

The ultimate outcome of this capitalist development is the destruction of communities and the natural environment. These two forms of destruction imply of course an existential crisis for humanity. And it is only by reversing economic growth and reducing living standards in advanced countries that humankind will be able to survive it. This requires an escape, argues Baba, from capitalism. His warning about capitalist development is thus issued using his own concepts of companyism and excessive affluence.

Baba's argument provoked great debate, and many of the criticisms made of him were quite passionate. Some rejected him on an emotional basis (Lie 1987). It is true that today, in the first quarter of the 21st century, we must reexamine his discourse in a new context featuring a relative decline of Japanese capitalism in global terms and the restructuring of Japanese companies in a manner that strengthens the power of shareholders while weakening that of workers. But it must be admitted that the questions he asks are very provocative and important, whatever one may think of his answers. First, he has called into question the economic growth and economic systems of our era from a historical point of view. Is it not indeed a task appropriate to political economists like Baba to raise questions with such a long time-frame? Second, he has upended almost all of the debates and perspectives of postwar Marxian economics by turning from the state to the company (critique of the SMC theory), from stagnation theory to growth theory (critique of general crisis theory), from pauperization theory to excessive affluence theory (critique of the theoretical model rooted in the 19th century), and from a theoretical approach to Japanese capitalism emphasizing its particularities and backwardness to an approach emphasizing its universalities and advanced character (critique of the debate over Japanese capitalism). Whether or not they agree with Baba, political economists must seriously consider these changes in perspective if the discipline is to remain relevant in the 21st century.

1.5 Defining Characteristics and Problematic Aspects of Marxian Theories of Contemporary Capitalism in Postwar Japan

1.5.1 State Monopoly Capitalism and Uno's Three-Level Theory

In the preceding sections, we have traced the achievements and problematic aspects of Marxian economics in an examination of postwar Japan divided into three periods. In this section we will attempt to extract the characteristic ideas seen in Japanese Marxian economics throughout all three periods by focusing on the methodology of the analysis of modern capitalism. To examine this methodology is at the same time to ask in what sort of "logical system" Marxian economics ought to be developed. Both the orthodox school and *Uno* school consciously developed theories of contemporary capitalism based on economic methodologies and economic systems, so here problematic aspects of this approach will be addressed with a focus on these two schools.

As discussed above, orthodox Marxism was based on a framework of an understanding of contemporary capitalism called "state monopoly capitalism" (SMC). This theory, which spread from countries that were socialist at the time to the rest of the world, described SMC as a product of the response of capitalism to the "general crisis of capitalism" (the emergence and expansion of socialist nations). In Japan, however, the argument that SMC was in fact the product of the internal contradictions of monopoly capitalism itself had at last begun to gain traction (Kitahara 1977). At the same time, the history of capitalism came to be understood as a progression from the stage of free competition (the era of Marx in the 19th century) to the stage of monopoly capitalism (the era of Lenin from the end of the 19th century to the beginning of the 20th century) and the stage of SMC (from the 1930s onward, or the modern era from the end of World War II to the present). It was also asserted by some Marxian economists that SMC was a "sub-stage" within monopoly capitalism. In any case, SMC is a regime in which the state intervenes to come to the aid of weakened monopoly capitalism and has been historically positioned as the "final stage of capitalism" and "gateway to socialism."

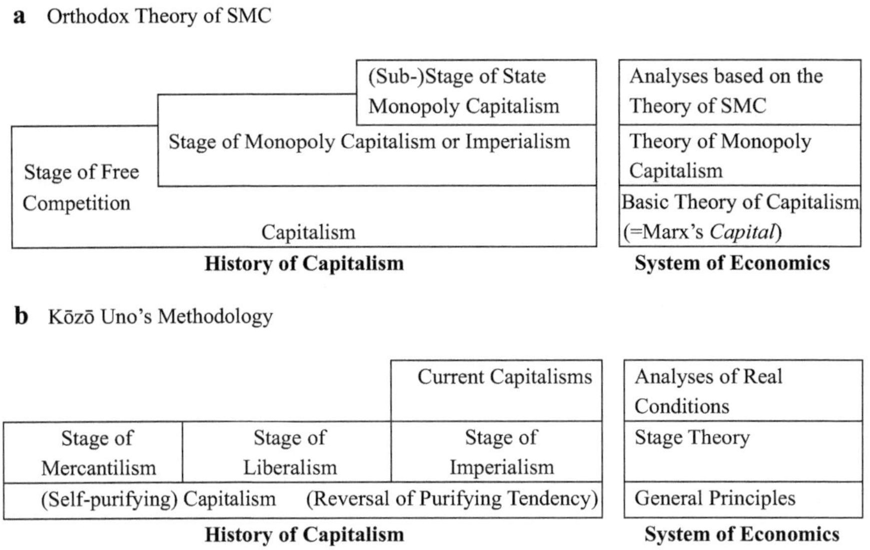

Fig. 1.1 History of capitalism and system of economics: (**a**) orthodox theory of SMC, (**b**) Kōzō Uno's three-level methodology. (Source: Author)

This kind of historical understanding inevitably led to a particular view regarding the "system" of Marxian economics. Specifically, it was claimed that economics had to begin by placing a general theory of capitalism (Marx's *Capital*) at its foundations, then on this basis address monopoly capitalism (using a theoretical approach based on Lenin's *Imperialism, the Highest Stage of Capitalism*), and finally construct atop these earlier levels of analysis a theory of state monopoly capitalism. It was thought that the analysis of contemporary capitalism only becomes possible when these three logical levels are layered on top of each other (Fig. 1.1a).

The economics of Kōzō Uno stood in sharp contrast to these ideas of the orthodox school. But in certain respects his system also closely resembled its broad tendencies. As we have already noted, Uno's economic methodology and economic system is known as a "three-level theory." In this view economics is a field of study that should begin by laying a foundation of general principles (a purification of *Capital* toward a theory based on "capitalism's trend toward purification"), construct a stage theory (an analysis of economic history and policies at each stage of capitalism's development) on top of this foundation, and finally reach the point of using this stage theory as a basis for analyzing actual conditions in the present era.

Capitalism is seen as passing through three historical stages, mercantilism (infancy), liberalism (maturing period), and imperialism (overripe period), and the capitalism of the current era is thought to belong for the most part to the stage of imperialism. This imperialist stage began in the early 20th century, has been positioned as capitalism's "final period" or "period of collapse," and has been understood to be capitalism's "final stage." In this stage of imperialism, the trend toward purification capitalism had shown (movement in the direction of the generalization of capitalist production of goods, tripartite class division, and so on) is "reversed," and as a result contemporary capitalism cannot be understood by relying solely on general principles (that are based on this trend toward purification). A specific theory of the imperialist stage is required. Only once this is adopted as a foundation does an analysis of the current state of affairs, the "ultimate goal of economic inquiry," become possible (Uno 1962: 57). Uno himself devoted his career to the perfecting of general principles and left behind only a few suggestions regarding stage theory and the analysis of actual conditions. In Uno Theory, too, ultimately the theory of contemporary capitalism must be developed on the basis of layering or piling up the three logical levels: general principles, stage theory, and analysis of the current state of affairs (Fig. 1.1b).

1.5.2 Layering the Three Levels and Privileging the 19th Century

As we have seen, whether pursued by the orthodox school or the *Uno* school, Marxian theories of contemporary capitalism developed in Japan share a common strength in their remarkable efforts to not simply understand the current era as the current era but instead come to grips with the present as an era arising out of a specific historical structure, or, in other words, a present that is a part of history. At the same time, however, this goes hand in hand with a major weakness. It goes without saying that the historical view of the present era as capitalism's "final period" or "period of collapse" was off the mark. But what must also be viewed as problematic is the methodology of layering three levels or dimensions in order to understand the present era, whether it be "general theory – monopoly capitalism theory – state monopoly capitalism theory" (the orthodox school) or "general principles – stage theory – analysis of actual conditions" (the *Uno* school), and the positioning and treatment of Marx's *Capital* that lies at its foundations.

What we see here is a methodology in which *Capital* or its revised adaptations (Uno's "General principles") is put in place as the underlying logic of the system as a whole, and an attempt is then made to understand 20th-century (and later 21st-century) transformations of capitalism by layering on top of it new historical stage theories involving monopoly capitalism (imperialism) and state monopoly capitalism. This can be described as a methodology of "three-level layering." Behind this methodology lies a tacit understanding that "pure" or "normal" capitalism is 19th-century free competition capitalism, and this is what is given a fundamental theoretical treatment in Marx's *Capital*. From the 20th century onward, however, capitalism has undergone major changes: monopoly capitalism that does not lead to free competition has emerged, and the trend toward purification has been reversed.

How were the new realities of capitalism to be reconciled with Marx's *Capital* written in the 19th century? Here the "transformation of capitalism in stages" approach was brought in, and the analysis of particular aspects of these new stages became the theories of monopoly capitalism and imperialism. *Capital* was thus evacuated to a safe location and preserved unchanged as a general theory of capitalism, and arguments that found deformed or distorted versions of its general laws in the new stages of capitalism were layered on top of it. In the case of the orthodox school, another layer of arguments concerning the transition to state monopoly capitalism from the middle of the 20th century onward was then added. The result was a perspective in which, no matter what changes the actual circumstances of capitalism might undergo, the *system as a whole* of *Capital* is always retained as that which elucidates the general laws (general principles) of capitalism, and this *Capital* system is to be used as the *foundation* of any analysis.

The characteristic understanding of this view was that *Capital* was not a theory that merely analyzed 19th-century capitalism, but a theory that analyzed capitalism in general. Since 19th-century capitalism was a capitalism of free competition, and since free competition was the "normal" or "pure" form of capitalism, this analysis of 19th-century capitalism formed the foundation upon which a general theory of capitalism ought to be constructed. To put it another way, this view understood capitalism from the 20th century onward to be a "deformation" or "distortion" of its normal form, an "abnormal capitalism," so to speak, and through this understanding became consistent with the hopeful view of Marxists that capitalism's days were numbered.

For at least two reasons, however, this understanding became a major impediment to the analysis of capitalism. First, by treating *Capital* as a general theory of capitalism and not merely an analysis of 19th-century capitalism, the status of this text was elevated from that of a "classic" that should be studied in the present to a sacred, inviolable "holy book." This closed off the path to learning from valuable theoretical results obtained outside of Marxism. Second, if *Capital* is taken as the general theory of capitalism, then today, 150 years after this text was written, the path to constructing new theoretical elements on the basis of this historical experience is also barred. To insist that our fundamental theory must be based on 19th-century capitalism is both anachronistic thinking and theoretical negligence. Here a state of "privileging the 19th century" (Shiozawa 2002: 167) when it comes to theory, a bizarre situation that would be unthinkable in other schools of economics, arose in Japanese Marxism.

In this way, postwar Japanese political economy, not in every instance but throughout its main schools, trod the path of "systemization" in the form of privileging the 19th century when it came to theory, employing a logic of three-level layering, and adopting *Capital* as the foundation undergirding all of its efforts. This was a systemic understanding very much particular to Japan, and from an international perspective may well have been a kind of "Galapagos evolution." Nonetheless, the economic system that emerged here was, at least as a methodology, grand and even in a sense "beautiful." Unfortunately, however, it was perhaps too "grand," and in practice no one was able to complete its formulation as a coherent system. Worse still, its methodology of constructing a three-level system led to the estrangement of economic "theory" and the "analysis of actual conditions" and ultimately to a bifurcation of economic research into a description of reality without theory and theoretical research without an analysis of actual conditions.

1.6 Concluding Remarks

I will conclude with a summary of the outstanding features of Japanese Marxian political economy with regard to postwar economic development and contemporary capitalism.

When it comes to economic development and contemporary capitalism, the history of postwar Japanese Marxism has been one of conflict between the theory of SMC based on the general crisis theory and attempts to disengage from this framework. As we have seen, the theory of SMC was proposed in the early postwar period and taken up by many Marxian economists in the high growth period. At the same time, however, an effort by some Marxian economists to free themselves from this theoretical framework was also launched early on in the form of the "socialization" version of the SMC theory, and in the period after the oil shock almost all first-rate analyses were in fact critical of SMC theory, which subsequently underwent a complete collapse. This meant that Japanese Marxists had at last begun to accept the growth and development of the Japanese economy as undeniable facts.

Concerning the system and methodology of economics, too, there was a particular perspective that underpinned postwar Japanese Marxian political economy. This point of view held that the construction of a "grand" theory covering everything from a fundamental theory of economics to the analysis of present-day capitalism was required and that an economic system based on a "three-level" theory should be conceived. The fundamental understanding underlying this approach, while acknowledging that capitalism had undergone major changes since the era of Marx's *Capital*, at the same time maintained that the *system as a whole* described in this text (or partially revised versions of it) could live on, and indeed had to be preserved, as the fundamental theory of capitalism. The result was a strange state of affairs in which it was believed that the fundamental theory of economics should be constructed on the basis of 19th-century capitalism. Through this "privileging of the 19th century" in theory, the analysis of current conditions and theoretical research underwent a bifurcation in practice, and the path toward an accurate theory of contemporary capitalism was blocked.

The issue upon which Japanese political economy has maintained an unceasing focus is that of the "universalities and particularities of Japanese capitalism." This was also, of course, the central issue in the debate over Japanese capitalism in the interwar period. The *Kōza* school saw in Japan a "type" of militarist imperialism based on a semi-feudalistic system of landholding and emphasized its particularities and weakness as a form of capitalism. The *Rōnō* school, on the other hand, considered so-called semi-feudalism as a form of backwardness generally seen in capitalist "late bloomers"; according to the *Rōnō* school, Japanese capitalism would inevitably acquire the universalities of capitalism as its development progressed. This debate continued well into the postwar period. Both camps agreed, however, on recognizing the backwardness (and specific qualities) of Japanese capitalism. Beginning in the 1970s, with the rise of Japan as an "economic power," some

Marxists began to propose different arguments in which they emphasized the advanced character and universality of Japanese capitalism. This was a major volte-face in the Marxian economists' view of the Japanese economy and Japanese capitalism.

Another change of position on economic development and contemporary capitalism can be seen in the shift from theorizing about grand systems to theorizing about institutions. Until the 1970s, political economy often operated in the broad framework of a choice between two systems: capitalism or socialism. It has since gradually transitioned into a more elaborate framework centered on institutions and organizations. From this point of view, it is easy to understand that "institutions" are better studied in the framework of Marxian theory than in that of a neoclassical perspective that is fundamentally based upon a theory of market equilibrium (Yagi 1993).

Political economic studies in postwar Japan have adhered so stringently to theoretical consistency, methodological strictness, and exegetic exactness that they have neglected the creative and flexible analysis of real economies and bold theoretical development. The *raison d'être* of political economy today must consist not in adherence to exegetic studies or excessive methodological discussions, but rather in explaining, from a long-term historical point of view as well as from an institutional perspective, the realities and objective outcomes of today's capitalism governed by neoliberal policies and globalization.

References

Albritton, Robert (1986) *A Japanese Reconstruction of Marxist Theory*, London: Macmillan.

——— (1991) *A Japanese Approach to Stages of Capitalist Development*, London: Macmillan.

Baba, Hiroji (1986) *Huyūka to Kin'yū Shihon* (*Mass Enrichment and Finance Capital*), Kyoto: Minerva Shobō.

——— (1991) 'Gendai Sekai to Nihon Kaishashugi' (Contemporary World and Japanese Companyism), in Tokyo Daigaku Shakaikagaku Kenkyūjo (Institute of Social Science, The University of Tokyo) ed., *Gendai Nihon Shakai* (*Contemporary Japanese Society*), vol.1, Tokyo: Tokyo Daigaku Shuppankai.

——— (1997a) *Shin Shihonshugi-ron* (*A New Theory of Capitalism*), Nagoya: Nagoya Daigaku Shuppankai.

——— (1997b) 'Japanese Companyism and the End of Cold War,' in Junji Banno ed., *The Political Economy of Japanese Society*, vol.1: *The State or the Market?*, Oxford: Oxford University Press.

Barshay, Andrew E. (2004) *The Social Sciences in Modern Japan: The Marxian and Modernist Traditions*, Berkley, Los Angeles and London: University of California Press.

Furihata, Setsuo (1983) *Kaitai-suru Uno Gakuha* (*The Uno School in Collapse*), Tokyo: Ronsōsha.

Ikumi, Takuichi ed. (1958) *Kokka Dokusen Shihonshugi* (*State Monopoly Capitalism*), Tokyo: Ōtsuki Shoten.

Inoue, Harumaru and Seijirō Usami (1951) *Kiki ni okeru Nihon Shihonshugi no Kōzō* (*Structure of Japanese Capitalism in the Crisis*), Tokyo: Iwanami Shoten Publishers.

Inoue, Harumaru et al. (1953) 'Nōchi Kaikaku to Han-hōkensei' (Farmland Reform and Semi-feudalism), in Iwanami Shoten Publishers eds., *Nihon Shihonshugi Kōza* (*Symposium on the Japanese Capitalism*), vol.5, Tokyo: Iwanami Shoten Publishers.
Itoh, Makoto (1988) *The Basic Theory of Capitalism: The Forms and Substance of the Capitalist Economy*, London: Macmillan.
——— (1990) *The World Economic Crisis and Japanese Capitalism*, London: Macmillan.
Kawakami, Hajime (1911) 'Nihon Dokutoku no Kokkashugi' (An Etatism Peculiar to Japan), *Chūō Kōron* (*Central Public Opinion*), March; in *Kawakami Hajime Zenshū* (*Complete Works of Hajime Kawakami*), 6, Tokyo: Iwanami Shoten Publishers, 1982.
Kishimoto, Shigenobu (1975) *Shihonsei Keizai no Riron* (*A Theory of Capitalist Economy*), Tokyo: Nihon Hyōronsha.
Kitahara, Isamu (1977) *Dokusen Shihonshugi no Riron* (*A Theory of Monopoly Capitalism*), Tokyo: Yūhikaku Publishing.
Lie, John (1987) 'Reactionary Marxism: The End of Ideology in Japan?,' *Monthly Review*, 38(11).
Mawatari, Shohken (1985) 'The *Uno* School: A Marxian Approach in Japan,' *History of Political Economy*, 17(3).
Morris-Suzuki, Tessa (1989) *A History of Japanese Economic Thought*, London: Routledge.
Ōtsuka, Hisao (1946) 'Kindaiteki Ningen Ruikei no Seiritsu' (Creation of a Modern Type of Human Being), *Daigaku Shinbun* (*University Journal*), 11 April; in *Ōtsuka Hisao Chosaku-shū* (*Collected Works of Hisao Ōtsuka*: *CWHO*), 8, Tokyo: Iwanami Shoten Publishers.
——— (1951) *Kindai Shihonshugi no Keifu* (*Genealogy of Modern Capitalism*), 1, Tokyo: Kōbundō; in *CWHO* 3.
——— (1964) 'The Market Structure of Rural Industry in the Early Stages of Capitalism,' *Second International Conference of Economic History in Aix-en-Provence 1962*, 2, Paris.
Ōuchi, Tsutomu (1962) *Nihon Keizai-ron* (*On Japanese Economy*), vol.1, Tokyo: Tokyo Daigaku Shuppankai.
——— (1970) *Kokka Dokusen Shihonshugi* (*State Monopoly Capitalism*), Tokyo: Tokyo Daigaku Shuppankai.
Shiozawa, Yoshinori (2002) *Marukusu no Isan: Aruchusēru kara Fukuzatsukei made* (*Inheritances of Marx: From Althusser to Complex Systems*), Tokyo: Fujiwara Shoten Publisher.
Takasuka, Yoshihiro (1985) *Marukusu Keizaigaku no Kaitai to Saisei* (*Collapse and Renaissance of Marxian Economics*), Tokyo: Ochanomizu Shobō.
Tamagaki, Yoshinori (1976) 'Kokka Dokusen Shihonshugi-ron no Konponteki Hansei' (Fundamental Reflections on the Theory of State Monopoly Capitalism), *Gendai no Riron* (*Theories Today*), 144.
Uchida, Yoshihiko (1967) *Nihon Shihonshugi no Shisō-zō* (*Intellectual Portrait of Japanese Capitalism*), Tokyo: Iwanami Shoten Publishers; in *Uchida Yoshihiko Chosaku-shū* (*Collected Works of Yoshihiko Uchida*: *CWYU*), 5, Tokyo: Iwanami Shoten Publishers.
——— (1981) *Sakuhin to shiteno Shakaikagaku* (*Social Science as a Popular Work*), Tokyo: Iwanami Shoten Publishers; in *CWYU* 8.
Uno, Kōzō (1946) 'Keizai Minshuka to Sangyō Shakaika' (Economic Democratization and Industrial Socialization), *Shinsei* (*Renaissance*), December; in *Uno Kōzō Chosaku-shū* (*Collected Works of Kōzō Uno*: *CWKU*), 8, Tokyo: Iwanami Shoten Publishers.
——— (1950/1952) *Keizai Genron* (*Principles of Political Economy*), 2 vols., Tokyo: Iwanami Shoten Publishers; in *CWKU* 1.
——— (1953) *Kyōkōron* (*Theory of the Crisis*), Tokyo: Iwanami Shoten Publishers; in *CWKU* 5.
——— (1962) *Keizaigaku Hōhōron* (*Methodology of Political Economy*), Tokyo: Tokyo Daigaku Shuppankai; in *CWKU* 9.
——— (1980) *Principles of Political Economy: Theory of a Purely Capitalist Society*, Translated by Thomas T. Sekine, Sussex: Harvester Press & New Jersey: Humanities Press.

Yagi, Kiichirō (1993) 'Seido no Keizaigaku to shiteno Marukusu Keizaigaku' (Marxian Economics seen as an Economics of Institution), *Keizai Riron Gakkai Nenpō* (*The Bulletin of Japan Society of Political Economy*), 30.

Yamada, Toshio (1986) 'La théorie de la société civile: Un nouveau marxisme au Japon,' *Critiques socialistes*, 1.

——— (1987) 'Les tendances du marxisme japonais contemporain,' *Actuel Marx*, 2.

Zieschang, Kurt (1957) 'Zu einigen theoretischen Ploblemen des staatmonopolistischen Kapitalismus in West Deutschland,' *Jahrbuch des Instituts für Wirtscahftwissenschaften*, 1.

Chapter 2
Yoshihiko Uchida and His Thoughts on Civil Society: Between Equality in Exchange and Equality as Human Beings

2.1 The Life and Works of Yoshihiko Uchida

In this chapter I focus on Yoshihiko Uchida (1913–1989), one of the leading scholars of civil society in postwar Japan, and examine how the concept of "civil society" was understood and developed in his works. As pioneers of Japanese thought concerning civil society preceding or distinct from Uchida, putting aside whether they employed the technical term "civil society" itself, others to which one can point include Zen'ya Takashima (1904–1990), Kazuo Ōkōchi (1905–1984), Hisao Ōtsuka (1907–1996), and Masao Maruyama (1914–1996). In the sense that he was the thinker who most consistently addressed and deepened the inquiry surrounding civil society, however, I would like to position Yoshihiko Uchida at the starting point of postwar civil society theory.

I will begin by briefly introducing Uchida's life and works (cf. Fujiwara Shoten Henshūbu 2014). He was born in Nagoya the year before WWI broke out and spent his childhood and youth until entering university in Hyōgo Prefecture's Okamoto Village (now part of Kōbe city). While studying at Kōnan High School, he made many friends who would go on to have careers in the fields of drama, film, and literature. Not having been blessed with a healthy constitution, Uchida himself was forced to leave school for a total of more than 4 years during his boyhood to receive treatment for tuberculosis, and he waged an ongoing battle against esophageal cancer from his diagnosis shortly after turning 60 years old until the end of his life.

During Uchida's adolescence Japan rushed headlong from the invasion of China into WWII, and in a country dominated by militarism and nationalism, the freedoms of speech, thought, and academic inquiry were suppressed one after another. In this environment, Uchida, then a student at Tokyo Imperial University, continued to search for "proof of being alive." At university he was particularly influenced by the economic history of Hisao Ōtsuka, but his interest extended to a wide range of

T. Yamada, *Contemporary Capitalism and Civil Society*, Evolutionary Economics and Social Complexity Science 14,
https://doi.org/10.1007/978-981-13-0517-7_2

subjects such as literature, drama, music, and technology and was not narrowly confined to economics or the social sciences.

In 1946, after Japan's defeat in the war, the then 33-year-old Uchida obtained a position at Senshū University and remained at this institution, teaching mainly courses on "the history of economics," until reaching retirement age. Uchida's academic activities becoming serious pursuits, too, occurred during this postwar period. He left behind a large number of writings, but Uchida himself highlights *The Birth of Economic Science* (Uchida 1953) and *Social Science as a Popular Work* (Uchida 1981) as pivotal texts within his own body of work.

The former was Uchida's first book and is still read as a landmark text in the study of Adam Smith. It reexamines the emergence of Smith's economics not from within the mainstream of post-mercantilist British economics but rather in the context of the civil society thought of figures such as Hobbes, Locke, Rousseau and Hume, and portrays Smith as a thinker critical of mercantilist "modernization from above" (cf. Uchida 2017). The latter can be described as a work that relates the intellectual achievements of Uchida himself as he pursued his studies of Smith and modern Japanese social thought in the midst of an environment of rapid economic growth in postwar Japan. In it Uchida simultaneously asserts, as can be surmised from the title, both the need for ordinary citizens to develop an understanding of social science in order to solve their own individual problems and the importance of expert social scientists not restricting themselves exclusively to the creation of the "production goods" of texts written for other specialists but also seeking to produce scholarship as a "consumable good" that answers the everyday questions of laypeople. Uchida's other works include, inter alia, *The World of* Capital (Uchida 1966), *Intellectual Portrait of Japanese Capitalism* (Uchida 1967), and *Steps of Social Awareness* (Uchida 1971a). Uchida's thoughts on "civil society" continued to mature throughout all of these texts.

One more thing I should say here to lay out a blueprint for the main text to follow is that the concept of "civil society" in Yoshihiko Uchida's thought, while it starts out as something originating in Europe, gradually moves away from the connotation of a direct connection to history itself and is then abstracted, idealized, and made normative. At the same time, it is also inseparable from the deepening of Uchida's critical view of Japanese capitalism and human history. In other words, the concept of civil society in Uchida's thought is not tied down to a single, fixed connotation, but rather something that evolved in the midst of working back and forth between reality and its conception and in conjunction with the deepening of Uchida's own understanding of society/history. Ultimately this gaze was then turned toward the deepest aspects of human history. As this unfolded, however, the former connotation of the concept was not simply discarded, but rather wrapped up in a new, additional connotation. In this way the concept of civil society was fashioned into several layers or levels, each of which was then propelled downward to illuminate the deepest elements of historical societies. Taken together as a whole, they constitute Uchida's thoughts on civil society.

2.2 Civil Society as Pure Capitalism

There is a 1944 note by Yoshihiko Uchida entitled "Theory of production. Memo." It is a study note written during a time when a young Uchida, under the wartime restrictions on speech that did not allow for academic freedom or freedom of expression, wandered in search of an academic foundation he could fully understand and accept while enduring the suffering of illness and the anxiety of not having a steady job. On the whole it is a fascinating text that suggests Uchida had absorbed much from thinkers such as Hisao Ōtsuka and Kazuo Ōkōchi, and, after examining "the question of self-interest in Smith," Uchida penned the following section entitled "two facets of self-interest, an economic concept and an ethical concept":

> Morality exists where self-interest, through laissez-faire, is joined to the interests of the whole, but here we must pay attention to the manner in which these two sets of interests are brought together. … Whether the liberation of sense [sentiment/intuition]… is virtuous or not is a matter of chance, so to speak, and was a reality during the period of the formation of British *civil society*. (… In addition, it should be noted separately that at its start the establishment of *civil society* was not a liberation of sense, but [occurred in] a society, Germany, that demanded a different self-denying affirmation from the bourgeoisie….). (Nozawa and Sakai 2002: 24–25)

Uchida's observation here is that whether or not the self-interest Smith discusses is a principle that liberates people from old societies depends on the model or type of capitalism that is adopted. Britain and Germany are used as a specific comparison. In Britain self-interest signifies the "liberation of sense," and this is connected to the formation of civil society as a system of productive forces through the invisible hand. To this extent self-interest is "virtuous." In Germany, however, this kind of invisible hand was not in effect, and as a result self-interest was directly connected to neither productive forces nor civil society. The formation of civil society in Germany had to be mediated, not by the liberation of sense, but by "rationality," which Uchida characterized as "self-negating affirmation." Uchida would later reaffirm that "Smith believed that self-interest becomes (for the first time) a lever for social good when the monopolies established by feudal political structures and mercantilist regulations are broken up" (Uchida 1967: 261).

Uchida's pressing interest in the topics of Smith and self-interest grew out of a critical view of Japan's controlled economy in which this "invisible hand" and the ethics that came with it possessed no validity whatsoever. Putting that aside, what is most interesting to us here is the first appearance – or at least a very early appearance – of the term "civil society" in the writings of Yoshihiko Uchida. As can be seen from its use in the phrase "the period of the formation of British civil society," here "civil society" seems to have been understood as an actual historical phenomenon, or, more specifically, something very close to "formational period British capitalism." At the same time, this British capitalism can also be said to have been viewed as a representation of the "normal" or "typical" form of capitalism, or what might be termed "pure" capitalism.

This conception of it as pure capitalism was Uchida's initial understanding of civil society. But while it might be described as "pure," the degree of abstraction toward this "purity" was not great, and it amounted to a capitalism represented by something close to the early British capitalism that had emerged as an actual historical phenomenon. And to the extent that the civil society being discussed here was "capitalism," historically speaking it was created out of opposition to "feudalism" or "feudal society." By the time of his most important work, *The Birth of Economic Science*, in regard to the significance of Smith's *Wealth of Nations* as part of his history of the formation of British civil society, Uchida had indeed come to position civil society as a society liberated from feudalism.

> In this second line of research, classical political economy is seen as part of the history of the formation of society, and the formation and development of classical political economy is examined from the perspective of what sort of problems emerged when *civil society tried to liberate itself from feudal society*, and how political economy responded to them. ...It was the mercantilists who played the role of *demolishing feudal society and erecting modern civil society*.... (Uchida 1953:34)

To the extent that civil society is capitalist, it is also a society that includes within itself exploitative relationships and conflicts between the capital and wage labor classes. In the "civil society = capitalist society" conception based on Smith, however, to the extent that each class (landowners, capitalists, laborers) was the owner of its own commodity (land, capital, labor), all of them stood on an equal footing; a Smithian civil society was a society in which overall wealth is more predominant than class inequality, and in which class inequality, while it does indeed exist, is not sharpened into radical confrontation. In this sense "civil society" is a much more natural and appropriate expression to use for a Smithian society than "capitalism."

> In his [Smith's] view... a society in which each class [landowners, workers, owners of stock] loses its exclusive or privileged position, and [the classes] interact with each other only as level traders, is civil society as a natural society. This is indeed a civil society, a society governed by its citizens. (Ibid. 207)

This concept of civil society formulated by Uchida is of course not distinctively Japanese, but can be seen as belonging to the genealogy of Hegelian/Marxian "bourgeois society" or Smithian "commercial society."

2.3 Civil Society as a Society That Upholds the Law of Value

If we take the phrase "a society in which each class loses its exclusive or privileged position, and [the classes] interact with each other only as level traders" from the preceding quote one level deeper, it describes a society in which not only "each class" but indeed "each person" loses their exclusive or proprietary position, and these people then interact with each other as level human beings. Here an "exclusive or proprietary position" refers to receiving, for example, rights or benefits from special feudal, status-based, or personal characteristic-based privileges or connections. A civil society is one in which these kinds of feudal or "insider connection" human relationships are eliminated, and individuals deal with each other as level traders. It is a society in which people are bound together only by their ability to have reified control over the goods they own, and in which human relationships are distilled into relationships of value. Officially it is a society governed by equality under the law. It is assumed that in such a society the exchange of goods between individuals will be conducted in the fair form of "exchanges of equivalents" (exchanges in accordance with value). It is the world of "equality in exchange," so to speak. This is what Uchida calls a "one-good one-price civil society" (Uchida 1967: 71).

> Apart from the "force propre" possessed by goods, all social bindings disappear, and on this foundation the singular rule of capital is established. This *society thoroughly permeated by the law of value* is a civil society. (Uchida 1953:97)

> Modern civil society, in Smith, is viewed as a *one-good one-price economy society*... (Uchida 1967:67, emphasis Uchida's)

This kind of "one-good one-price" society that upholds the law of value is, at the same time, a society in which "productive forces" are liberated and develop, and in this sense a civil society is also a system of productive forces. The prevalence of the law of value and the liberation of productive forces are understood as forming a set. This kind of civil society as a law of value society, while in one aspect being connected to British capitalism as an historical actuality, in another aspect is abstracted *to a certain extent* away from a real historical actuality and demonstrates a tendency toward an idealized society. In order for exchanges of equivalents between level human beings without privileged positions to be established in such a society, "free," "equal," and "fair" human and legal relationships liberated from feudal or old community bonds must be realized (here "equal" means only quantitative equality in terms of exchanges of equivalents, nothing more). Each person is taken to be free and independent as a subject who owns goods and a fair person who will not violate the "justice" of exchanges as a subject who interacts with others.

This kind of society is, so to speak, a "society created out of free, equal, and independent individuals." Stated more assiduously, it is "a society formed through equitable relationships that are voluntarily entered into by free and independent persons" (Imai 2001). Or, to borrow Zen'ya Takashima's classic phrasing, it is a society dominated "politically by the spirits of liberty, equality, and fraternity, legally by the concepts of justice and contracts, and economically by the ideas of equivalence and free competition" (Takashima 1974: 23). A civil society that upholds the law of value exists as this kind of society. And normally when we speak of Uchida's civil society theory, it is understood as having this kind of connotation. Moreover, since postwar Japanese civil society theory in general is also understood to have more or less this sort of content, it is often criticized as an approach that idealizes "Western modernity" and a "simple commodity production society."

As already noted, this "society created out of free, equal, and independent individuals," while it is connected to specific societies as historical actualities, also becomes estranged from them. This "connection" exists because "freedom and equality" are indeed concepts that arose along with the modern era as a historical development and were legally and formally recognized in this context. It becomes "estranged" from them in two senses. First, because even if we postulate a "purely capitalist" society, liberty and equality will only ever exist formally; in actuality they will become their exact opposites (see Sect. 2.5). Second, because in the great majority of actual capitalist systems that do not become "pure" capitalism, violations of people's liberty and equality and infringements of the law of value remain a daily occurrence just as they were in the past. Taking this reality into account, the concept of a civil society as a free and equal society (a society that upholds the law of value) is indeed something that is extracted from within western modernity as a historical period, but ultimately it has been transformed into an idea or norm that transcends this historical specificity.

Looking back at research on the history of economic doctrines conducted during the war, Uchida states, "civil society was initially understood as an orientation toward *pure capitalism*, but gradually it came to be recognized as an *abstract civil society*" (Uchida 1967: 92), and at the same time this was also the path taken by Uchida's own thoughts on this subject. Uchida's "civil society as an abstract concept" must first be understood in terms of the above implication. As we shall see later, however, deepening his inquiry beyond this framework was a characteristic that distinguished Uchida from other scholars.

2.4 The Buying and Selling of Labor Power Commodities and Civil Society

It directly concerns theories of civil society based on the law of value, but as an important point regarding both the formation of Uchida's civil society theory and the work of modern economics, here I would like to examine a problem surrounding the application of the law of value to labor power commodities. The core of this problem is that "the progress of one good, one price and the progress of capital/wage labor relations are not necessarily parallel" (Uchida 1967: 71). In other words, the progress of capitalism itself does not bring about "one good, one price" regarding labor power commodities, and as a result we cannot expect so-called market logic alone to reform wage labor relations on the model of a civil society.

Exchange in accordance with value must naturally extend to labor power commodities, too. Civil society relations must also be carried through to the buying and selling of labor power. The law of value extending into labor power commodities means that after labor power has been bought, sold, and used (labor power has been consumed), it is once again normally reproduced. Here reproduction is not only the physical/mental and social/cultural reproduction of individual laborers but also includes the continuous reproduction of generations of laborers. To this end special conditions that differ from those for general commodities must be imposed among the usage conditions for labor power, and wages, too, must satisfy the conditions required for labor power reproduction in the broad sense stated above.

The reality of capitalism, however, has been a succession of situations that do not allow for the normal reproduction of labor power, such as excessive lengthening of the working day, arbitrary domination and harsh overuse of labor power, poor and unhygienic working environments, and the reduction of wages below the value of labor (low wages), and this continues to be the case today. Marx's *Capital* accurately describes this state of affairs in terms of 19th century British capitalism, and Kazuo Ōkōchi incisively expresses it as "primitive labor relations" in Japanese capitalism from the Meiji era onward. Uchida learned a great deal from Ōkōchi during the war, but as Japan was barreling toward a militarist system in the 1930s, the latter, asserting that "war is the driving force behind the development of social policy," wrote as follows:

> That war is the driving force behind the development of social policy is a point that does not seem to have been given adequate consideration. Since the Meiji period, our national deficiencies in normal laborer protection – preservation of labor power – have accumulated, leading to an overall wearing down of "labor power" and thus a decline in the physical strength of our citizens, with a result that should cause concern regarding national defense… But the same fact also brought to the fore the difficulty of procuring "healthy" labor power for the expansion of military production, and in response necessitated "labor force cultivation" and "training of skilled workers" as social policies. This need for social policy is something that had been submerged only latently within peacetime economic society, and war has in a single stroke made it manifest and visible. Long term war and the ongoing economic construction it enforces… will surely necessitate a policy of rational preservation regarding "labor power" as a comprehensive *national policy*. (Ōkōchi 1938 [1969: 344–345], emphasis Ōkōchi's)

In other words, a wartime economy requires healthy and capable soldiers and labor power, and a Japanese capitalism that needed to develop a high level of military production had to become more advanced both in terms of its industrial structures and its productive powers. In this way the execution of the war, through the promotion of social policies for the sake of "preserving" and "cultivating" labor power, could not help but insert the law of value into the buying and selling of labor power commodities. The advancement of capitalism without the dissolution of "primitive labor relations" was inconceivable, and a wartime economy would achieve this dissolution in a single stroke. Here, while it was limited to labor power commodities, a paradoxical and problematic – but not dismissible out of hand – "civil" argument developed which asserted that a controlled economy would give rise to civil society. This was the topic to which Yoshihiko Uchida addressed himself immediately after the war. He writes as follows:

> During wartime, when even assertions of a social democratic nature were not permitted, on what grounds did assertions that war achieved social policy acquire a certain practicality – at least in one aspect – and a certain progressivity, albeit within a limited scope? …In the name of productive forces, Professor Ōkōchi sought the sweeping away of *antediluvian*, primitive labor relations, and the preservation of labor power as physical bodies from military or antediluvian devouring, through the buying and selling of labor power "in accordance with value" that is "intrinsically" demanded by the *advancement* of capitalism itself, creating a kind of protest against the times. (Uchida 1948 [*CWYU* 10:113, 116], emphasis Uchida's)

Here Uchida, from the perspective of the formation of a law of value society, evaluates Ōkōchi's argument as a critique of wartime Japanese capitalism. There is indeed room for this kind of assessment, but is it really sufficient? In fact, this essay of Uchida's was criticized for focusing only on the development of productive forces and ignoring relations of production. While in one sense accepting this criticism, on the whole Uchida did not believe his critics were correct and submerged himself in the study of Adam Smith in search of a solution to the problem. The result was his most important work, *The Birth of Economic Science*.

The problem lay in how a "civil society" forms and ultimately was connected to the question of what a "civil society" is. Even if Ōkōchi's theory included "civil society" assertions, was it not a "civil society" seen as having to be formed "from above" and as a "national policy" from the "perspective of total capital"? Did it not end in a theory of the law of value that relied on war and control? These questions seem to have been thorns in Uchida's side.

Uchida would eventually pose these questions in various settings. But he didn't address them in reference to Ōkōchi himself, reformulating them instead with Marx as his primary resource. The issue of the necessary development of social policy (to begin with, the buying and selling of labor power in accordance with its value) Ōkōchi saw in wartime economies in fact shares a common foundation with the issues surrounding the necessity of factory laws Marx saw in 19th century British capitalism. Marx's comments on laborers' fight for a shorter working day and factory laws that legally regulate the working day in *Capital* are well known, but Uchida breaks them down further and focuses on two distinct inevitabilities: the "inevitability of factory laws being introduced in the legislature" and the "inevitability of proposed legislation that has been introduced being watered down by capitalists" (Uchida 1971a: 191–192). Underlying "factory laws" was the existence, to some degree, at least, of a civil society demand – labor power being penetrated by the law of value. The civil society movement that attempted to secure, in the face of primitive devouring of labor power, the normal reproduction of labor power in the form of factory laws inevitably arose as what might be termed a "natural historical process" in the era of the large industry system. The realization of this, however, was prevented by the interests of capitalists, and this too was another inevitable occurrence. While extracting this from his reading of Marx, Uchida presented his own perspective as follows:

> As for the question of whether the *realization* of factory laws *automatically* emerges from the material foundation of the development of the large industry system, the answer is that it does not. It is introduced in the legislature but inevitably watered down. Then a fight breaks out over the realization of factory laws. Marx uses a truly profound expression when he says that factory laws are "the product of a long civil war," and here his view wonderfully unifies the class struggle and productive forces views of history. (ibid. 192, emphasis Uchida's)

Rephrasing this in terms that tie into our present topic of interest, the movement to implement the law of value in labor power emerges with natural inevitability in the form of "factory laws" within the context of the large industry system, but this natural inevitability is not "automatically" realized. A "long civil war" and "struggle" undertaken by laborers are absolutely indispensable to this "realization." The law of value is not realized without conscious and subjective effort on the part of laborers. The "productive forces" inevitability is not realized without the mediation of "class struggle." In other words, in Uchida the development of the law of value does not emerge as a simple external or objective fact, but is understood in connection with the conscious, subjective actions of individuals taken for the sake of its realization (Sugiyama 2012: 22; Tanaka 2013: 122). The terms "struggle" and "civil war" are used, but expressed in today's context they signify the imposing of social and political frameworks on markets and their institutionalization. It is only when labor markets are subjected to social *régulation* that they can be brought closer to civil relationships.

Here the Uchida who had somewhat positively evaluated Ōkōchi's theory that "war achieves social policy" is gone. The law of value is not something that can be given "from above," nor, in fact, is it something that can easily be obtained from the "perspective of total capital," much less from the "perspective of individual capital." Nor again is it something that can be realized by clinging to objectivity; while being undergirded by objectivity and a productive forces foundation, it is realized and maintained through a bottom-up, subjective effort and struggle. Reaching a turning point at this issue of labor power commodities, Uchida's theory of civil society orients itself toward "subjective" social formation "from below."

2.5 Civil Society as Appropriation in Accordance with Ability

A commodity economy is perfected when not only ordinary products but even labor power is commoditized. Similarly, a civil society based on the law of value is perfected when "one thing, one price" is implemented not only among ordinary commodities but also among labor power commodities. But a society in which labor power has been commoditized is in fact a society in which capital/wage-labor relations have been established, or, in other words, a capitalist society. And the process of capitalist accumulation, when viewed from the perspective of "property" (and "distribution"), is one in which, through appropriating surplus labor, capitalists ultimately have access to new appropriation of others' labor (new surplus value) based on the past appropriation of others' labor (laborers' surplus labor). Even if capitalists start out with "property based on their own labor," within repetitions of the capital circuit the products of their labor are converted into the products of others' labor, and a system of "appropriation of others' labor based on others' labor" is established. Labor no longer grounds property, and on the contrary property is grounded in property itself, with surplus value being doubly or triply transformed into unearned income. Marx called this the "inversion of the law of appropriation" and explains it in *Capital* (Book I, Chapter 24, Section 1).

What this means is that the implementation of the so-called law of value gives rise to disparity and a gap between ownership and non-ownership, and the free and equal relations between human beings are transformed, in their substance, into relations that are neither free nor equal. A civil society is transformed, in its content, into capitalist class rule. Capitalism strips away the content from inside the form of a civil society, leaving it hollow. Civil society as "property based on labor" inevitably turns into a capitalism of "property based on property." The application of the law of value to labor power commodities makes civil society more completely what it is, but at the same time also gives rise to a capitalism that is "extruded from" civil society and which, since it is "extruded from" this society, also, in a sense, "negates" it. It gives birth to capitalism as property.

> In the end capitalist appropriation [property based on property] is formed through the mediation of one thing, one price/the law of value. ...Pure *capitalism* is a society in which the requirement of income *in accordance with ability* is ultimately obscured in the form of a transformation from property through labor to *capitalist appropriation* mediated by the law of value. In this sense, the question of whether a capitalist society can really be called a civil society immediately arises. The part that is *in accordance with ability* (not connections or status) is pushed out, and as a result civil society becomes tinged with an abstract character and is extruded from *pure capitalism*. (Uchida 1967: 92–93, emphasis Uchida's)

As noted above, the "connections and status" mentioned here are factors that stand in the way of the law of value, and which must be overcome by a civil society. Civil society had already been conceived as "one-thing one-price" relations between "level traders" in contrast to connection/status-based relations, but here these "level traders" are newly defined from the perspective of ownership or property: they are people who obtain property in accordance with their own "ability." Here the concept of a civil society is deepened to encompass a society composed of the type of human being who "appropriates in accordance with ability." This conception of a civil society is indeed different from that of a capitalism of property based on property. Uchida's theory of civil society is "extruded from pure capitalism."

"Civil society" being abstracted and distinguished from "capitalism" poses the following as a problem with Japanese capitalism. "Even if Japanese capitalism is capitalism in the second sense [capitalist appropriation], it is not a civil society in the first sense [the law of value]" (ibid. 93). Here Japan is characterized as "capitalist appropriation without the law of value," that is, "capitalism without a civil society," and the distinctive structure and pattern of Japanese capitalism are called into question; having become tangled up in "premodern" elements, does Japanese capitalism differ from so-called pure capitalism? And this questioning does not stop at the problem of Japanese capitalism, but broadens to present an analytic perspective of "capitalism and civil society" concerning capitalism in various other countries. Nor indeed did this concept of civil society stop there, instead going as far as to pose the problems of "socialism and civil society" and "civil society in socialism" (ibid. 100) in regard to the socialist countries of the day whose negative aspects had become evident.

So an abstract civil society as "appropriation in accordance with ability" means a society in which individuals obtain property in accordance with their labor, effort, and talent. Here "obtaining property" includes not only material/economic income or ownership but also an individual's social evaluation in broad terms. This is, more than anything else, an opposing concept to appropriation through premodern connections or status or feudal ownership or privilege (the so-called category of "rent"), but at the same time is also a concept critical of capitalism (as displayed in the inversion of the law of appropriation and the category of "capital interest"). In other words, an "ability-based" principle of appropriation becomes the fundamental principle of a civil society, a principle that stands in contrast to "property based on property," whether premodern or capitalist. To this extent Uchida's theory of civil society accords with the issues of increasing asset inequality and income inequality raised in recent years by Piketty (2013).

Taking a hint from Sohō Tokutomi (1863–1957, journalist and intellectual), beginning in the 1960s Uchida also expressed this "ability-based" type of human being as "industrious-type homo economicus" and invoked it as a concept critical of modern Japanese homo economicus and capitalism. "Is there not a glaring paradox in the young people of the new era who despise old ideas trying to pursue their economic interests while clinging to goodwill? – These were Sohō's words, and using them I established the categories of sycophant-type = connection-type homo economicus and one-thing one-price, industrious-type homo economicus." (Uchida 1967: 95).

Here the "appropriation in accordance with ability" that contrasts with "appropriation in accordance with property" comes into sharper relief as a civil society composed of "industrious-type homo economicus" in contrast with "connection-type homo economicus." As Uchida himself notes when he says, "A civil society composed of purely industrious-type homo economicus is an abstraction, as both a subject and as a conceptual apparatus" (ibid. 100), the "abstract character" of this kind of conception of a civil society is quite strong. Uchida employs it to critically illuminate Japanese capitalism and the type of human being found in it.

> "Connections alone are not sufficient, and if people do not possess real ability they won't be able to develop connections" – This is the logic of the Japanese economy. It is not pure connection-type. But neither is it pure industrious-type. The basic type of Japanese homo economicus is a "pariah industrious-type" who follows the logic of connections having "ability = industriousness" hidden within themselves, and it is through this kind of connection-type homo economicus *in the form of a pariah industrious-type* that Japanese "economic society" has been formed very dynamically. ...Ability is developed through connections, and through ability the sphere of connections is maintained and reorganized. ...Therefore, the more you are thoroughly committed to the industrious-type and try to become a *pure* industrious-type (not a pariah type), the more you will be ostracized from the places where your ability can be displayed, and ultimately you will cease to be an *industrious-type homo economicus*. (ibid. 96, emphasis Uchida's)

To Uchida, Japanese capitalism was not a civil society in which each person's "ability" was developed as ability, and this developed ability was then evaluated in a one-thing one-price manner. In Japan, the mainstream variety of homo economicus was not quite the "connection-type;" it was instead a "pariah industrious-type" in which ability and connections were symbiotically entangled, and a situation in which "pure industrious-type" people are banished from the economy came to be repeated. Taking this view of Japanese capitalism, this observation of Uchida's transcends his own era and exposes the deepest aspects of the problematic nature of today's Japan, and indeed not only the problems in this country but problems occurring in various countries around the world (see Sect. 2.7).

2.6 Civil Society That Must Pass Through History and Be Realized

When he put forward "civil society as an abstract concept" in *Intellectual Portrait of Japanese Capitalism*, Uchida also rephrased it as "civil society as a transhistorical abstract concept" (Uchida 1967:100). So what exactly is this civil society that passes through history?

In fact it is this concept of civil society that undergirds the deepest foundations of Uchida's thought and forms the root of Uchida's unique theory of civil society. This was a concept that, while it was germinated in the second half of the 1960s at the earliest, would be honed and deepened throughout the remainder of Uchida's life. It had nothing to do with the so-called idealization of Western modernity, and its anthropocentrism was relativized. There has not been a careful examination of Uchida's conception of civil society in the past, and as a result it seems to often have been misunderstood, so here I want to give it the attention it requires. This examination will take up the remainder of this section and the section that follows. I have divided it into two sections for convenience, but I should make it clear from the start that in terms of content both are addressing the same issue and differ only in the aspects of it they illuminate.

When Uchida speaks of something that "passes through history," presumably no one would fail to acknowledge that he is describing the "process of metabolism [Stoffwechsel] between human beings and nature." In this sense he is also to a certain extent referring to Marx's *The German Ideology*. Marx says, "The form of intercourse determined by the existing productive forces at all previous stages, and in its turn determining these, is *civil society*. … This civil society is the true focus and theatre of all history." "This conception of history thus relies on expounding the real process of production – starting from the material production of life itself – and comprehending the form of intercourse connected with and created by this mode of production, i.e., civil society in its various stages, as the basis of all history" (Marx and Engels 1976: 50, 53, emphasis in the original).

But in a move that is very characteristic of Uchida, he does not view this process of metabolism ("real process of production" and "form of intercourse") simply as a given, but instead defines "human beings" in this case as people who must become "human beings as actively *free subjects*" or who must mature into "*social* human beings with self-awareness" (Uchida 1966: 116–118). In Uchida's "civil society that passes through history," there is thus an implication of the realization of a *social* process of metabolism with nature carried out by *free* – or freedom-seeking – human beings as the endless work of humanity that emphasizes its subjective and social elements.

Uchida also uses other phrases regarding this kind of transhistorical civil society, such as "something in the form of a *civil society that is realized while passing through all sorts of systems*" (Uchida 1967: 100) and "the growth of *a civil society that passes through societies of various forms*" (Uchida et al. 1967: 208). In other words, he understood civil society not as something static but rather as something that was historically dynamic, something that would be "realized" and "grow" toward humanity's future. The conceptual content of this civil society differed from that of the civil society discussed in the previous sections in the sense that it is not simply "extruded from" capitalism but also "passes through" all sorts of historical systems including capitalism; in addition to being a civil society that sticks out of capitalism, it is also one that passes through it in both directions, forward and back.

Uchida's transhistorical civil society exists as something that is formed very slowly in the midst of the long history of humanity, making great strides – in the form of the emergence of the law of value, liberty/equality, appropriation in accordance with ability, or at least the formation of these concepts, and the ensuing development of large industrial production powers and its contradictions – in the current "final stage of humanity's prehistory" that is modern capitalism, while at the same time being distorted and held in check in actual capitalist societies, and as a form of society that in the future, while experiencing diversions and distortions, will gradually be perfected in human history as it continues to unfold. As Barshay says, "For Uchida, civil society possesses a virtually transhistorical status. More abstract and with a longer history than just that of the 'modern West,' civil society is a slowly and painfully built-up 'society composed of self-aware individuals.'" (Barshay 2004: 188–189)

What is this realization and growth directed toward? Broadly speaking, it is the ceaseless "rationalization" of the process of social metabolism. "As a whole it rationally undertakes metabolism of human beings and nature" (Uchida 1971a: 200) and the creation of "a rational system for the management of nature" (Uchida 1966: 204). To this end the development of science and technology is needed, and the reform of management organizations and social systems is also indispensable. But on top of these elements – or indeed as something that must be present at their foundations – there is something else of great importance. This is the pursuit of democracy and liberty.

Let us begin with democracy. For Uchida himself, as seen in statements such as "the emergence and development of democracy is something that runs through various forms of society" (Uchida 1971b: 216), democracy, as something dynamic that must pass through history and mature, was an important pillar in the construction of a civil society. Immediately after Japan's defeat in the war, a young Uchida displayed a newly awakened understanding of democracy in the following passage:

> The essence of the formation of the social will under democracy does not lie in the opinions of the general public being socialized and unified through elections. It is something more dynamic. It is something that lies, on the contrary, in members of the public with various perspectives seeing with their own eyes and thinking with their own heads, as active subjects with responsibility for themselves, while the views from these various perspectives are freely mixed and deepened by being permeated by each other, and the general public itself forming a *giant, social compound eye*. (Uchida 1945 [*CWYU* 10: 20–21])

Today it is perhaps clear to anyone that democracy is not merely electoral democracy, parliamentary democracy, or decisions being made by the majority. Under the cover of parliamentary democracy, political decisions are swayed by plutocratic lobbying activities, the will of the people is not reflected in politics, and this in turn is inevitably accompanied by rampant distrust of democracy and political indifference among the general public. Facing this reality, Uchida's now more than seventy year-old claim that the essence of democracy is the public itself forming a "giant, social compound eye" causes us to once again come to grips with democracy's origin point. It is presumably through the formation of a "giant, social compound eye" by the public that social metabolism is "from below" and "subjectively" placed at the foundation of principled administration. This is where the task that must be realized by a civil society passing through history lies. "For Uchida, as long as 'production' is carried through science in a form in which the 'natural environment' and 'life' may coexist, and in addition this is developed democratically without monopolization by the state, then the society in question is socialist and a "civil society" (Onodera 2015: 113).

In addition, civil society as the development of human freedom, parallel to democracy, is also something that must pass through various eras of history and be realized. Uchida sees the image of humanity working toward freedom subjectively in humanity's striving toward rational control of the process of metabolism. In the words of Marx, it is tracing a path toward the "development of human energy which is an end in itself, the true realm of freedom" (*Capital*, Book III, Chapter 48). The process of rationalizing metabolism, along with being undertaken and realized by human beings seeking freedom, is a process that itself creates free human beings and indeed cannot help but do so. The "development of human energy which is an end in itself" may be a dream of "somewhere far away," but whether or not we hold it up as a "goal" *right now* creates a decisive turning point. It creates a turning point because our goal regulates our "approach to addressing the problems we are facing" (Uchida 1971a: 201–202). And because we must behave as if the "actions of the present have a future meaning *in the present tense*" (Uchida 1974: 313); it is by thinking and acting with this as our compass and our course that there is maturation toward a civil society. This point is one that Uchida often reiterated in later years, as can be seen, for example, in the phrase "civil society that passes through history to be established in the distant future, but which *as work to be done right now*, in the present, gives direction to people's consciousness and actions" (Senshū University Institute for Social Science 1982: 50). Civil society might be something that belongs to the "distant future," but at the same time it must also be something that exists "presently."

In this section we have seen that the transhistorical civil society Uchida describes is one that rationalizes metabolism and brings into range the freedom and democracy that are both demanded by and derived as a result of this process. But Uchida saw that something more is required in order for the rationalization of metabolism to develop as part of a set with human freedom and democracy, and conversely for the people who demand freedom and create democracy to take up the rationalization of metabolism. It is where the inquiry is deepened to this extent that the heart of Uchida's theory of civil society is to be found. So what is it?

2.7 A Civil Society Rooted in the Absoluteness of Being Alive

In the "Conclusion" to his 1971 book *Steps of Social Awareness*, Uchida writes as follows. The passage is quite long but I quote it here because it is indispensable if we are to speak of the most profound part of Uchida's civil society.

> I think of a person *living in a manner befitting a human being* as an end in itself. Not, of course, as an isolated individual. Human nature (das menschliche Wesen) includes interaction with society. Human beings are entities that constitute societies, and entities that create societies. *Living in a manner befitting a human being*, including this [social aspect], is indeed an end in itself. Within this act of living, there is of course *engaging in inquiry*. And not only academic inquiry, but all of the various domains of culture are included. When "development of human energy which is an end in itself" is spoken of, it includes all of these sorts of things. …
>
> I repeat myself, but if we do not have the development of human energy which is an end in itself as our far off goal, then we will be unable to see how capital is eroding humanity in the present. And if we are unable to see this, we will also be unable to see, in its truest sense, even the object of social science. It is by grasping the *weight and meaning of being alive itself* that we are able to see the problems that social science must solve. (Uchida 1971a: 202)

Human beings "living" as human beings is an end in itself, and "academic inquiry" is an inseparable part of this "living." In order for this inquiry to be inquiry in a true sense and not merely spinning its wheels, academic inquiry must be deeply rooted in the importance of human beings "being alive" in and of itself. Here Uchida is emphasizing that awareness of the absolute importance of each person's life itself and the manner in which academic inquiry (to begin with, social science) is to be conducted are inextricably linked. What Uchida's civil society theory ultimately envisions is a society in which this "living" and "engaging in inquiry" circulate back and forth between each other.

Uchida asks, "Won't the discovery of the current themes needed to make academic inquiry truly socially significant never be made unless [this inquiry] is connected to the absolute meaning of each individual person being alive?" Within Uchida as he poses this question, there is a reflection on the question of why, whether it is environmental pollution or chemical or pharmaceutical poisoning, we do not recognize such problems when the first – ostensibly small – signals are sent out. Isn't our not accepting these signals as signals perhaps because there is an underlying mentality at work that says, "If one or two wild birds or one or two individual human beings die, how important is that from perspective of *the immensity of the world?*" (Uchida 1974: 357–364, emphasis Uchida's) In other words, we ignore "one or two wild birds, or one or two human beings" or view them as exceptional cases, and do not take to heart the absolute significance of the fact of each individual person's being alive itself. On the contrary, we avert our eyes from it. This is why the tasks that should be taken up by academic inquiry cannot be seen as what they are. We then also lose the ability to discover "truly socially significant" academic themes and the path to human freedom and principled metabolism.

We must also bear in mind that the "concept of *human equality* as living creatures" (Uchida 1967: 348) only arises on the basis of "each human being engaged in the business of living and the absolute meaning this possesses" (ibid. 363). In the final chapter of *Intellectual Portrait of Japanese Capitalism*, Uchida extolls the pivotal importance to modern Western history of the emergence of the assertion "those who do not work should not eat" out of the sympathy between fellow working people on the side of laborers in opposition to the view of property as sacred (predominance of property). He then says, "Precisely because [it was] a view of human equality and solidarity based on *sympathy as human beings who work*, at the same time a sympathy with human beings who cannot eat even though they work (or who cannot work) was also operating… [and] the right to life, the idea that human beings have the right to live for the simple reason that they are human beings, emerged supported by this view of solidarity that comes out of sympathy between fellow human beings who work" (ibid. 349, emphasis Uchida's; cf. Uchida 1970). What is asserted here is that a sympathy and solidarity as human beings created by rejecting the predominance of property must form the foundation of society, but precisely because of the origins of this sympathy it will then also be extended to "human beings who cannot eat even though they work (or who cannot work)."

The starting point is the perspective of "sympathy as people who work," but the implication is not only "people who work" in a narrow sense. The range of this sympathy extends to human beings who "cannot work" and then to "ordinary human beings." Each of these "ordinary human beings" placing themselves in the "absoluteness of being alive" is synonymous with the formation of the concept of "*human equality*" or "*equality as human beings*." Here the idea emerges that all people, as long as they are alive, are equal as human beings. In other words, to be rooted in the absoluteness of being alive is to stand on the foundation of equality as human beings.

This perspective also leads to criticism of the fact that the rapid economic growth in postwar Japan was at the same time accompanied by large-scale destruction of the environment. Uchida makes the following criticism while pointing out that there was a "weakness of awareness of human rights, along with faith in science" in Japan during this period of high growth. "[Japan] must not be a country in which the weight of speech and human rights [that belong to all people] simply because we are human beings, in other words, personhood, is so ignored, and these disparities are growing ever larger." (Uchida 1981:187).

What is important here is that a "human equality" (equality as living beings) is being perceived that transcends "exchange equality" (equality in terms of the law of value, i.e., "one thing, one price"). In the same vein, a principle of "appropriation in accordance with need," transcending "appropriation in accordance with ability," is being put forward. "Human beings have the right to live for the simple reason that they are human beings," and in terms of distribution this is the world of the "principle of necessity." It could also be called the world of "reciprocity," but in either case it is a world untethered to ableist discrimination. This is the last thing Uchida discerned within a civil society that is passing through history and gradually being realized. A civil society running through various forms of society and gradually being realized as it passes through history is something which, based on the concept of equality as human beings (in other words, the absoluteness of being alive), constitutes democracy as a giant compound eye formed by people who seek freedom through the medium of engaging in inquiry, and in this way controls the social metabolism between human beings and nature.

What we must be mindful of here, however, is that Uchida's settling on this civil society as human equality did not mean a complete rejection of his older conception of civil society as exchange equality. *While in the end he positioned equality as human beings (the idea of the right to life) at its foundation, there are ways in which Uchida's civil society theory was constructed as one in which individuals were to embrace a tense coexistence between this principle and that of equality in exchange (respect for labor/ability) in their daily lives.* In assessing utopian socialism, for example, Uchida says, "Even here, the idea of the *right to life* and the fact that human beings must be evaluated in accordance with their *labor* emerge simultaneously" (Uchida 1967: 350); elsewhere he describes this as "one of the fundamental problems of modernity." "There is an aspect in which a human being only becomes a human being through *labor*, and another aspect in which human beings possesses a subtle appeal and raison d'être just by *being alive*, even if they lack the ability to work. And this problem, while a problem of religious reform in intellectual history, as a problem arising within actual history is not one that has already been solved, and is indeed one of the fundamental problems of modernity." (Uchida 1974: 311) As can be seen in this passage, Uchida perceived a world in which the "right to life" and "labor" coexist, along with "being alive" and "work," albeit sometimes in tension with each other. Citizens in Uchida's civil society were beings that must themselves embrace and work to maintain the tense coexistence of human equality and exchange equality. This can also be described as a civil society with a welfare society at its foundation.

As is clear from the above without any need for further reflection, Uchida's civil society theory, while beginning from an image close to foundational period British capitalism (pure capitalism), was eventually conceptualized toward bourgeois equality (fairness in terms of equal value exchange) and an ability-based society (criticism of the category of rent), and was ultimately then deepened, in the form of perceiving a hidden current flowing through history, to the control of metabolism being birthed by free people engaged in inquiry and equality as human beings (absoluteness as living beings). Simply speaking, his thought on civil society was deepened from civil society *as* capitalism to civil society that is *extruded from* capitalism and finally to civil society that *passes through* capitalism just as it has passed through other socioeconomic systems. If we look back from the depths thus reached and try to extract the essence of Uchida's civil society theory, it can be found first in the idea of the social institutionalization (social régulation) of the market in order to activate the principle of "ability" in opposition to the principle of "property," and second in the idea of human equality (the right to life) that serves to prevent the principle of "ability" becoming absolute and to position the principle of "welfare" at the foundation of a civil society.

2.8 In Closing—From "Each Person"

The point at which Uchida's theory of civil society described above ultimately arrives is perhaps a kind of utopia. As I have already noted, however, Uchida says that whether or not we have this utopia as our compass right now is of critical importance; as human beings who do not lean on history but subjectively participate in it, our "present behavior" is scrutinized in terms of its "future meaning."

Looking back, it was from his struggles with Ōkōchi's social policy theory that Uchida firmly adopted the stance of a "subjective" and "from below" approach to the formation of a civil society. Within Smith's theory, he drew Smith toward the "middle and lower social strata" (Uchida 1967: 261), and in regard to academic inquiry stated this in a form that pushed a "synthesis of social sciences from below" in contrast to a "synthesis from above" (Uchida 1971a: 195–198), or "social science as a popular work" (Uchida 1981, 1985) engaged in by citizens in contrast to science as a specialized field dominated by experts. More than "from below," however, Uchida became fond of using the phrase "from each person." This point, while it is particularly notable in *Steps of Social Awareness*, is not inconsistent with *Social Science as a Popular Work*. Here are just a few examples:

> A human being is not an isolated entity, but neither is he or she simply a component of a group. This is where the meaning of *each person* effectively engaging in academic thinking is to be found.
>
> I want to think about why social science has become something so unrelated to us, and by what method we can foster social scientific understanding in *each one of us*.…
>
> I think the word "participate (*sanka*)" becoming a Japanese term that includes all sorts of meanings from everyday occurrences to extreme situations is not a separate issue from fostering a social science inclination within *each of our nation's citizens*; in other words, I think that *each person* becoming a human being who participates in society as a stakeholding subjective entity and *each person* making social understanding their own and taking possession of intellectual and social scientific terminology as part of the vernacular are not separate issues and indeed share the same root. (Uchida 1981:4, 15, 37)

He no longer uses the terms "from below" or "individual," but says instead "each person." This is the "thought of each person," so to speak. This expression is not related to social class or rank, nor does it echo the aloof, distant tone of "individual," but instead seems to be impressing upon each person, as a being that lives and learns, an awareness and responsibility for decision-making that belongs to them alone.

At the same time, it is also a word that admonishes us against forming groups through facile, lip-service participation and then burying ourselves in them. More than that, it is a word that carries the importance of "a human being who participates in society as a stakeholding subjective entity" that ought to lie at the root of the formation of groups and organizations. When it comes to numerous social problems, Uchida says we must solve them "for the time being and to a certain extent as one person" but clarifies that "in this case, 'for the time being and to a certain extent as one person' does not mean in the present. In the future, too, I think this is in essence how things will always be" (ibid. 36–37).

Of course, Uchida is not rejecting so-called civic, social, or political movements, nor is he rejecting the formation of groups for the pursuit of such activism. On the contrary, his active acknowledgement of their necessity is clear without even having to cite the examples of pollution and chemical poisoning issues mentioned above. As can be seen in passages such as "Each person is a subject engaging in academic inquiry. Or they may come together to form a *group*" (Uchida 1971a: 197) and "Each person is to learn science, and through this *joint effort* properly rebuild the Japanese economy" (Uchida 1981: 188), the need for the formation of "groups" or "unions" was within Uchida's field of view. It was on the basis of looking closely at these kinds of popular movements and the formation of groups that he was so adamant about the importance of "each person." He believed we must put "each person" at the origin or starting point and then socially unite on top of this foundation. Looking at the last several decades, we see that civic consciousness and movements with "each person" as their starting point have indeed been fostered even in Japan, mediated by the spread of the Internet during this period.

We often hear the criticism, "There are no politics in Uchida." But what Uchida was concerned with was the awareness and decision-making of "each person" and the academic inquiry (social science as a popular, non-academic work) that would effectively facilitate this that ought to lie at the root of "politics," or indeed at the root of the formation of a "civil society" as a whole. "Each human being should engage in academic inquiry; every member of society, each person, should include inquiry as part of the work of living" (Uchida 1971a: 3). It is by doing this that we move one step closer to the development of freedom and human energy as an end in itself and foster the growth of democracy as a social, compound eye. Metabolism, too, will then be régulated by civil society.

Yoshihiko Uchida's transhistorical civil society was one that must be formed through this kind of awareness and academic inquiry of "each person." In his later years, Uchida came to address the so-called theory of academic inquiry as his main theme, but in the sense outlined above, this theory of academic inquiry was Uchida's answer to the question of how a civil society was to be formed (Yamada 1991). His theory of academic inquiry should more than anything be understood as his theory of the formation of civil society.

In recent years, "new civil society" theory in Europe and America has above all come to mean the positioning of civil society as a third domain in addition to – and distinct from – "markets" and "states," and the conception of this domain as a public space formed by a series of autonomous groups or "intermediary associations." Habermas (1990) calls "non-state, non-economic associations based on free will" "Zivilgesellschaft" and offers associations such as churches, cultural circles, academic societies, debate clubs, and organizations for civil activism as examples. The defining characteristic of "new civil society" theory is its positioning of "civil society" as a distinct space – differing from both "political society" (the state) and "economic society" (the market) – and on this point it differs from the theory of civil society in postwar Japan in which "civil society" was understood as one aspect of society as a whole. But in Uchida's writings, at least since his middle period, denunciation of the negative aspects of modern industrialism (the market) and authority (the state) intensified, and in this sense his approach shared a common underlying understanding with new civil society theory. In this regard Hajime Shinohara is surely correct in saying that "their [Yoshihiko Uchida and Kiyoaki Hirata's] theory has much in common with new civil society theory" (Shinohara 2004: 102). If Uchida's civil society theory has anything more to suggest to "new civil society" theory, it is the fundamental importance of the participatory consciousness of "each person" that should lie at the foundation of the formation of all "groups" and "associations," whether they are "intermediary" or of any other kind.

References

Barshay, Andrew R. (2004) *The Social Sciences in Modern Japan: The Marxian and Modernist Traditions*, Berkeley and Los Angeles: University of California Press.

Fujiwara Shoten Henshūbu (Editorial Department of Fujiwara Shoten Publishers) ed. (2014) *Uchida Yoshihiko no Sekai* (*The World of Yoshihiko Uchida*), Tokyo: Fujiwara Shoten Publishers.

Habermas, Jürgen (1990) *Strukturwandel der Öffenlichkeit: Untersuchungen zu einer Kategorie der bürgerliche Gesellschaft*, 2. Aufl., Frankfurt am Main: Suhrkamp Verlag.

Imai, Hiromichi ed. (2001) *Shin Shiminshakai Ron* (*New Civil Society Theory*), Tokyo: Fūkōsha.

Marx, Karl and Friedrich Engels (1976) *The German Ideology* (Written in 1845–1846), in: *Karl Marx – Friedrich Engels Collected Works*, vol. 5, Moscow: Progress Publishers.

Nozawa, Toshiharu and Susumu Sakai eds. (2002) *Jidai to Gakumon: Uchida Yoshihiko Chosakushū Hokan* (*The Age and the Academic Inquiry: Supplementary Volume of the Collected Works of Yoshihiko Uchida*), Tokyo: Iwanami Shoten Publishers.

Ōkōchi, Kazuo (1938) 'Shakai Seisaku to Tōsei Keizai' (Social Policy and Controlled Economies); *Ōkōchi Kazuo Chosakushū 5: Shakai Seisaku no Kihon Mondai* (*Collected Works of Kazuo Ōkōchi, vol.5: Fundamental Problems of Social Policy*), Tokyo: Seirin Shoin Shinsha, 1969.

Onodera, Kenta (2015) *Sengo Nihon no Shakai Shisō Shi: Kindaika to "Shiminshakai" no Hensen* (*The History of Postwar Japanese Social Thoughts: Modernization and Changes in "Civil Society"*), Tokyo: Ibunsha.

Piketty, Thomas (2013) *Le capital au XXIe siècle*, Paris: Seuil.

Senshū Daigaku Shakaikagaku Kenkyūjo (Senshū University Institute for Social Science) ed. (1982) *'Sakuhin' he no Henreki: Uchida Yoshihiko Osaragi Jirō Shō Jushō Kinen Kōen* (*Wandering toward 'Works': Lecture to Commemorate Yoshihiko Uchida Receiving the Jirō Osaragi Prize*), Tokyo: Jichōsha.

Shinohara, Hajime (2004) *Shimin no Seijigaku: Tōgi Demokurashii toha Nani ka* (*Political Science for Citizens: What is Deliberative Democracy?*), Tokyo: Iwanami Shoten.

Sugiyama, Mitsunobu (2012) '"Kindaika" to "Futatsu no Michi": Uchida Yoshihiko no "Shiminshakai" Saikō' ("Modernization" and the "Two Paths": A Reconsideration of Yoshihiko Uchida's "Civil Society"), *Meiji Daigaku Shinrishakaigaku Kenkyū* (*Meiji University Journal of Psycho-sociology*), 8.

Takashima, Zen'ya (1974) *Adamu Sumisu no Shiminshakai Taikei* (*System of Civil Society in Adam Smith*), Tokyo: Iwanami Shoten Publishers.

Tanaka, Hideo (2013) *Keimō no Shatei to Shisōka no Tabi* (*The Range of Enlightenment and the Journey of Thinkers*), Tokyo: Miraisha.

Uchida, Yoshihiko (1945) 'Shimbun to Minshushugi' (Newspapers and Democracy), *Daigaku Shimbun* (*University Newspaper*), 44; *Uchida Yoshihiko Chosakushū* (*Collected Works of Yoshihiko Uchida*: *CWYU*), 10, Tokyo: Iwanami Shoten Publishers.

——— (1948) 'Senji Keizaigaku no Mujunteki Tenkai to Keizai Riron' (Contradictory Development of Wartime Economics and Economic Theory), *Chōryū* (*Trend*), 3(1); *CWYU* 10.

——— (1953) *Keizaigaku no Seitan* (*The Birth of Economic Science*), Tokyo: Miraisha; *CWYU* 1.

——— (1966) *Shihonron no Sekai* (*The World of* Capital), Iwanami Shoten; *CWYU* 4.

——— (1967) *Nihon Shihonshugi no Shisō-zō* (*Intellectual Portrait of Japanese Capitalism*), Iwanami Shoten; *CWYU* 5.

——— (1970) 'Japan Today and *Das Kapital*,' Translated from the Japanese by Patricia Murray, *The Japan Interpreter*, 6(1), Spring.

——— (1971a) *Shakai Ninshiki no Ayumi* (*Steps of Social Awareness*), Iwanami Shoten; *CWYU* 4

——— (1971b) *Yomu toiu koto: Uchida Yoshihiko Taidanshū* (*"Reading": Collected Conversations with Yoshihiko Uchida*), Tokyo: Chikuma Shobō; *CWYU* 7.

——— (1974) *Gakumon he no Sansaku* (*Rambling toward Academic Inquiry*), Iwanami Shoten; *CWYU* 6.

——— (1981) *Sakuhin toshite no Shakai Kagaku* (*Social Science as a Popular Work*), Iwanami Shoten; *CWYU* 8.

——— (1985) *Dokusho to Shakai Kagaku* (*Reading and Social Science*), Iwanami Shoten; *CWYU* 9.

——— (2017) '*Wealth of Nations* as a Critique of the Old Imperial System,' Translated from the Japanese by Robert Chapeskie and Toshio Yamada, *The History of Economic Thought* (The Japanese Society for the History of Economic Thought), 58(2).

Uchida, Yoshihiko, Kazuji Nagasu and Saiichi Miyazaki (1967) 'Keizaigaku' (Economics), in Toshoshimbunsha (The Book Review Press) ed., *Zadankai Sengo no Gakumon* (*Symposium on Postwar Academic Inquiry*), Tokyo: Toshoshimbunsha.

Yamada, Toshio (1991) 'Uchida Yoshihiko Ron Nōto' (Notes on Yoshihiko Uchida), *Keizai Kagaku* (*The Economic Science*), 38(2).

Chapter 3
Kiyoaki Hirata and His Thoughts on Civil Society

3.1 Life and Works of Kiyoaki Hirata

Kiyoaki Hirata (1922–1995) was a historian of economic thought who played a prominent role in Japanese society in the latter half of the 20th century and was known as a "renovator" of Marxism. Above all, however, he was a theoretician of civil society. Born in Tokyo, he studied under Zen'ya Takashima (1904–1990) at the Tokyo College of Commerce, the predecessor of Hitotsubashi University. Following graduation, after having received some teaching experience in various universities, he became a professor of economics at Nagoya University and then Kyoto University. He died suddenly in the middle of his tenure as president of Kagoshima Keizai University, the predecessor of the International University of Kagoshima. For his *curriculum vitae* and profile, see Souzou-no-kai (1996).

Analyzing Hirata is indeed very difficult; his writings are both hard to understand and voluminous (for an idea of their scope, see Asai and Wakamori 1983; Yagi 1986; Nozawa 2008). Throughout this wide body of work, however, he generally focuses on three key pillars: the thought of François Quesnay, Karl Marx, and Antonio Gramsci. In referencing each of these three thinkers, we can also divide his intellectual activities into three distinct periods during which his thinking on civil society gradually formed, matured, and then underwent a significant transformation.

The first of these periods took place between Japan's defeat in World War II and the early 1960s. During this period, Japan saw an upsurge in movements promoting democracy and socialism, and, beginning in the mid-1950s, a high and durable rate of economic growth. This was the period during which the prototype of Japanese postwar capitalism was built. Young Hirata wrote many articles on classical British and French political economy as well as on Marx. He also translated some books written in French, including Marx's *Misère de la philosophie*. These early writings were later brought together in a lengthy tome, *Creation of Economic Science* (1965).

T. Yamada, *Contemporary Capitalism and Civil Society*, Evolutionary Economics and Social Complexity Science 14,
https://doi.org/10.1007/978-981-13-0517-7_3

The second period, from the late 1960s to the early 1980s, was an era of great political upheaval around the world. In the capitalist world, the previous golden age of capitalism finally came to an end in the stagflation crisis of the 1970s; in the socialist world, we saw the dark side of this system manifest itself in the Sino-Soviet split in the 1960s, the Russian invasion of Czechoslovakia in 1968, and the stagnation experienced by socialist economies. Amidst these upheavals, Hirata vigorously developed a civil society theory based on his investigation of Marx's texts, resulting in severe critiques of the realities of both Japanese capitalism and socialist countries. This was the most fruitful period of Hirata's career, and he garnered much attention in Japan. Works representative of this period are *Civil Society and Socialism* (1969) and *Political Economy and the Philosophy of History* (1971).

I will add a bit more about this second period before moving on (cf. Yamada 1987). In the world of postwar Marxism, an intellectually monolithic characterization of Marx and Lenin – and in some cases Marx, Engels, Lenin, and Stalin – was emphasized under the rubric of "Marxism-Leninism," and this view was then employed in defending the legitimacy and historically advanced character of Soviet socialism and communist parties in other countries. But times changed. In the capitalist world the influence of socialism waned alongside strong postwar economic growth, and in the socialist world the negative factors described above became manifest. In such an era, could the existing "Marxism-Leninism" model of Marxism still be considered the defender of freedom and equality and the liberator of humanity? Was this truly the model Marx himself had conceived? With such questions in mind, Hirata, one of those who continued the legacy of Yoshihiko Uchida's theory of civil society, set out to create a new field he called "Marxology." Along with another of Uchida's successors, Seiji Mochizuki (1929–), Hirata came to be referred to as a "civil society school Marxist." Members of this school set out to confirm what Marx had actually said with their own eyes without relying on officially sanctioned doctrinal systems. In doing so they drew attention to Marx's texts that had been almost entirely ignored in the past (the *Grundrisse der Kritik der Politischen Ökonomie*, and *Le Capital*, i.e., the French edition of *Das Kapital*), and brought to light problematic aspects of the editing of *Die Deutsche Ideologie*. This effort to discover and restore the "original Marx" became an influential movement that was often referred to as the "Marx renaissance." This work itself involved the study of the interpretation of Marx and the close reading of classical texts, but what is important is that through this rereading of Marx it also broke down the barriers of entrenched dogmatic systems to uncover deeper possibilities for Marx's thought in the current era, and revealed the true figure of Marx who, when it comes to our present interest in contemporary reality, can be seen as having been more than anything a "civil society" thinker.

The third of Hirata's academic periods corresponds to a roughly 10-year stretch from the mid-1980s to his death in 1995. After having been the envy of the world in the 1980s, as evidenced by the publication of books such as *Japan as Number One*, in 1990–1991 the Japanese economy experienced the bursting of a financial bubble. In Eastern Europe, a series of collapses of socialist regimes was triggered by civil revolutions in 1989, culminating in the dissolution of the Soviet Union in 1991.

During this period, Hirata went beyond the critique of Marx's texts and began to energetically discuss current affairs, addressing a wide range of topics including contemporary capitalism, existing socialism, the European Community, French polity and economy, and the comparative analysis of Japanese and European civilizations. During this period he published *Civil Society and Régulation* (1993), a book in which he presents his original interpretation of Gramsci and French régulation theory.

3.2 Quesnay's *Tableau Économique* and the Circuit of Productive Capital

3.2.1 The Perspective of the Circuit of Productive Capital

Important questions to be examined about Hirata include how these three pillars or periods are related and how they developed and changed over time. In other words, we are interested in how his thinking vis-à-vis civil society germinated, flourished, and eventually metamorphosed. In my view, the key to understanding his thinking lies in his study of François Quesnay's *Tableau économique* and the perspective of the circuit of productive capital discussed in detail in Hirata (1965).

The circuit of productive capital is a form of capital circuit developed in the second volume of Karl Marx's *Capital*. Here, Marx defines the circuit of productive capital ($P...P$) as a form that typically expresses the exchanges between mankind and nature (i.e., the reproduction of everyday life), as distinguished from the circuit of money capital ($M...\ M'$), which exclusively demonstrates the self-valorizing nature of capital, and from the circuit of commodity capital ($C'...C'$), which implies an interrelation with and the reproduction of total social capital. According to Marx, mercantilism understood capitalism as being established on the basis of $M...M'$, the classical school on $P...P$, and the physiocracy of Quesnay on $C'...C'$. While not denying that the *Tableau économique* is ultimately established on $C'...C'$, Hirata stresses that there obviously exists a perspective of $P...P$ at the very heart of Quesnay's thinking and that his economic system comprises an *Aufhebung* of $P...P$ into $C'...C'$. There exist at first, says Hirata, movements in time of productive capital, which then result in an interrelation of circuits of commodity capital or a spatial structure of social reproduction. This was Quesnay's perspective on the eve of the French Revolution, as well as Hirata's in Japan's age of high economic growth. He declares the theme of his own studies in the afterword of his first book as follows.

> Since political processes and economic theory – which had been harmonious for several years just after Japan's defeat in the war – became antagonistic and showed tragic aspects, with a turning point in 1955–1956, the task of revitalizing the philosophy of history by creating a new economic criterion has become, so to speak, a main theme in all of my studies. I sincerely wanted to learn from the classical literature what kind of critical theory had been hitherto acquired by human beings concerning the following point: a structure composed of many processes in which *human beings who live in economic time – or in*

> *historical time that is defined by cycles of turnover of capital* [*i.e., circuits of productive capital*] – through their reproduction of everyday life steeped in ordinary sentiment are *reproducing by themselves social relations as a system that will be reified in a material-industrial structure*. (Hirata 1965: 564)

Japan in 1955–1956 found itself at the start of a period of high economic growth and an enduring and stable political regime governed by conservative forces. From that point on, the Japanese populace became part of a mass consumption and company-centered society. Democratic movements that had arisen shortly after Japan's defeat in the war peaked with the mass movement protesting the Japan–US Security Treaty in 1960 and began to decline. Under these circumstances, how does the reproduction of people's everyday lives (i.e., the circuit of productive capital) construct new material-industrial interrelations (i.e., the structure of reproduction)? This was Hirata's question, and in the process of searching for theoretical criteria for it he became absorbed in the work of Quesnay.

3.2.2 Circuit Theory and Reproduction Theory

Since the interwar period, it has been a characteristic feature of the Japanese study of the history of economic thought to delve into the classical literature of political economy while focusing on the problems inherent in Japanese capitalism. A characteristic unique to Hirata is that he was greatly influenced by Yoshihiko Uchida (1913–1989), an older thinker with whom he became close friends. How should one understand and get the most out of the "debate over Japanese capitalism" (*Nihon shihonshugi ronsō*) that had taken place in the 1930s – especially when it came to the methodology of the *Kōza* school as represented in Moritarō Yamada's (1897–1980) *Analysis of Japanese Capitalism* (1934)? The debate over Japanese capitalism is, as was already explained in Chap. 1 of this book, a controversy concerning how to evaluate the remnants of the feudal system which at that time still existed extensively in Japan. Were they transitory (as claimed by the *Rōnō* school) or structural (as claimed by the *Kōza* school) factors in the course of the development of capitalism in Japan? This question underpins Hirata's aforementioned afterword, the thinking behind which can ultimately be traced back to Uchida.

> [One needs] to *cut* the picture of Japanese capitalism *in a round slice* [*cross-section*]. This succeeds to the way of thinking of the *Kōza* School, especially as embodied in Professor Moritarō Yamada's *Analysis of Japanese Capitalism*… . Of this book there have been many critiques; for example, [it has been pointed out that] there is in it only a typology but never a development… . As a matter of economic theory, such critiques finally stem from the impossibility of understanding Yamada's analytical method of Japanese capitalism, i.e., that of the *application of Marx's theory of reproduction*… . This controversy implies an opposition of two methodologies: one either shows the structure of reproduction by cutting each moment of capitalism *into round slices*, or one shows an outline of a historical stream along with a *flow in time of economic development*. To cut into round slices … means to understand a country's structure of reproduction as a consequence of interrelations among *circuits of productive capital*… . In short, Yamada's method shows historical *movements* in a cross section of any given moment. (Uchida 1967: 85–86, emphasis Uchida's)

The methodology of the *Analysis* – described here as the "application of the theory of reproduction" – is, according to Uchida, to draw a picture of "cross sections" by "cutting into round slices" the "flow in time" of dated history. Cutting a cross section does not mean ignoring the flow of history; rather, it is recognizing how history has been "poured" into a cross section at any given moment. One finds history in a cross section and processes in a structure. According to Uchida, this is the methodology of *Analysis*; as for economic theory, this means that even when one follows the circuit of productive capital (vertical section), one should maintain a perspective of a country's structure of reproduction (cross section) that is objectively formed by an intervolution of the circuits of productive capital. Uchida finds this methodology within Yamada's work; Hirata, following in the footsteps of Uchida, discerned it in the theoretical development of Quesnay's *Tableau économique* from the archetype to the complete form:

> If we thoroughly follow the cycles of the turnover of productive capital, it will necessarily lead to a recognition of the structure of reproduction of the total social capital, and to a jump from $C'...C'$ as a circuit formula of individual capital to a law of reproduction of a society as a whole... . Quesnay was successful, under a "physiocratic deviation" that agriculture alone is productive, in understanding immediately the logical relevance of the circuit, turnover, and structure of the reproduction of capital, and in this way in creating an economic science that centers on the theory of reproduction. (Hirata 1965: 339–40)

A certain circuit theory underpins Quesnay's reproduction theory – it is a reproduction theory that also contains circuit theory. Reproduction theory must be understood in relation to circuit theory. These are Hirata's claims, and in this way he analyzed the formation process inherent in the *Tableau économique* using the logic of *Capital*. Through this work, Hirata simultaneously contributed to (1) a new reading of *Capital*, (2) the development of Uchida's ideas of "flow in time" and "cutting into round slices," (3) the confirmation of the relevance of Yamada's methodology, and (4) the establishment of his own economic criterion for a critical understanding of the postwar Japanese economy.

3.2.3 Germination of Civil Society Thought

What was the significance of the works Hirata produced during his first period regarding the formation of his civil society theory? Of course, he had developed hardly any elements of his own civil society thought during this period. Nevertheless, he did pose some germinal questions on, and demonstrated a theoretical recognition of, civil society even in those early writings. There are three important points to take note of here before moving on.

First, when he was at university he studied under the direction of Zen'ya Takashima, one of the pioneers of civil society thought in Japan. He was also close friends with Yoshihiko Uchida, another pioneer of civil society thought, right from the start of his professional career. When he translated *Misère de la philosophie* he was deeply interested in Marx's distinction between "société bourgeoise" and "société civile" (Hirata 1993: 243–248).

Second, he stressed above all the importance of the circuit of productive capital, rather than that of money capital or commodity capital. The perspective of the circuit of productive capital that opens with production and ends in production, although implying a risk of naturalizing capitalist society, can lead to an understanding of society that comprises people's concrete production and everyday lives. This perspective he chose early on would become a cornerstone of the full-scale development of civil society theory in the second period of his career.

Third, the perspective of "the circuit of productive capital and reproduction" is more broadly developed into one of "process and structure" or "formation and structure." When Hirata (1965) says at various points that a society or history must be understood in terms of a simultaneous understanding of both "a structural (spatial) summary of process (time)" and "a processing (flowing in time) content of structure (space)," he is referring, by using the word "process," to a world where there exist concrete relationships among actual human beings, and, by using the word "structure," to an abstract and reified interrelation lacking concrete realities. This perspective of "process" is characteristic of his later civil society theory.

Looking back at the era of his first book, Hirata says that the sprouting of a new type of capitalism in Japan beginning in 1955–1956 had brought about the first opportunity to pose questions regarding civil society. "The capital circuit/reproduction process and reproduction structure … proceed as metamorphoses of money and commodities. A 'civil society' as such – that is, 'civil society' in the development of capitalism – became problematic in my consciousness for the first time" (Hirata 1977: 112). Among the many civil society theories, Hirata's is original in that it stemmed from the development of capital circuit theory.

3.3 Marx and Civil Society

3.3.1 Property Theory in Grundrisse

Immediately following the publication of Hirata (1965), Hirata started to study Marx in earnest, developing in the subsequent 20 years his own interpretation of Marx as a thinker concerned with civil society. While up to that point in time civil society theory in Japan had considered Marx an opponent of civil society, a concept developed mainly with an eye to Adam Smith or other Enlightenment thinkers, the originality of Hirata's approach consists in his finding civil society thought in Marx's texts themselves. It is for this reason that Hirata's thinking has been said to belong to the "Marxist school of civil society." The Marxian texts to which Hirata attached special importance are the *Grundrisse* (1973) and the French edition of *Capital* (1967). The former is one of the first drafts of *Capital*, as well as new documents that became for the first time generally available in the 1950s. The latter is the last version of *Capital* that was published under the supervision of Marx himself and has been largely ignored in spite of its value as a source to be studied.

Hirata first tackled *Grundrisse*. His analytical approach was, of course, that of circuit theory. While his first article on Marx following the publication of Hirata (1965) had originally been entitled "Political Economy and the Philosophy of History in Marx" (Hirata 1966), the title was changed to "Circuit-Accumulation Theory and the Philosophy of History" on the occasion of its reprinting (Hirata 1971). For Hirata, Marx's system of economic theory was thus born first and foremost out of the construction of a core circuit-accumulation theory. By using this specific terminology, he implies an accumulation theory comprehended in terms of, or extended to, the scope of the capital circuit. Hirata's question is on what theoretical pivot was the political economy of *Grundrisse* established – or, to put it in more detailed terms, how does circuit-accumulation theory relate to the famous description of history entitled "Forms which precede capitalist production"? He summarizes his own answer as follows:

> I have found that the theoretical dimension to which the "Forms" belong is that of the circuit-turnover process as a development of the accumulation process. And I have recognized that this comprehensive understanding of the capital accumulation that was understood in the context of the circuit-turnover of capital would come to be discussed, in the *Capital* of Marx in his later years, in terms of the relationship and distinction between the processes of production and circulation (and appropriation), and that here exists a theoretical focus of Marx's perception of the 19th-century world. What is to be pursued is nothing other than *a comprehensive understanding of the capital accumulation that unfolds as the circuit-turnover of capital*. (Hirata 1971: 5)

Marx's first system of political economy was formed, insists Hirata, not on the pivot of value theory but rather of circuit-accumulation theory. In *Grundrisse*, accumulation theory was developed from the broad perspective of the circuit-turnover of capital. This poses a new problem: property theory. Hirata paid attention to the fact that the circuit-accumulation theory of *Grundrisse* has in it a passage that refers to the "Forms which precede capitalist production." This well-known passage has been frequently cited, mainly in the discipline of economic history; examples include discussions of Asiatic, Roman, and Germanic forms of commune (community). However, according to Hirata, the "Forms" are discussions of the forms of property rather than those of communes. The most important question for him is why this passage on property is inserted only within the theory of circuit accumulation.

For both Marx in his *Grundrisse* and Hirata, the essence of property (i.e., capitalist private property) needs to be clarified precisely with respect to circuit-accumulation theory. The property theory in question is embodied in discussions of the inversion of the law of appropriation – that is, a theory of the inversion of bourgeois property based on one's own labor to the capitalist private appropriation of others' labor based on the labor of still others. This inversion of the law of appropriation is uncovered "only at the *end of the second cycle*" (Marx 1973: 514, emphasis Marx's). In other words, it is precisely in the circuit-accumulation theory that the essence of capitalist private property is to be critically revealed (Hirata

1971: 40). This perspective on the inversion of the law of appropriation becomes, for Hirata, a pivotal one in understanding modern society, and it necessarily accompanies discussions on the theme of civil society (bourgeois property) and capitalism (capitalist private property).

In short, the perspective on the "capital circuit and the structure of reproduction" Hirata had possessed since his study of Quesnay now constituted a part of his Marxology and had developed into an analytical approach: "circuit-accumulation theory and property theory." Through his understanding of the inversion of the law of appropriation, he brought to light the problematic field of "civil society and capitalism." It was precisely on this foundation that his theory of civil society was able to flourish.

3.3.2 Hirata's Concepts of Civil Society

What is Hirata's concept of civil society? It is not necessarily clear. Not only is his terminology ambiguous and polysemous, but both "civil society" and "bourgeois society" (*bürgerliche Gesellschaft*) in European languages are often translated into the same Japanese term, *shimin shakai*. In this book I have generally used the term "civil society" as an English translation of the Japanese *shimin shakai*. In Japan, at least until the 1970s, the concept of *shimin shakai* had been principally used not with the connotation of particular citizens' (as opposed to public/governmental) groups or associations, but rather that of a social formation on the national level, and at the same time with an implication of something modern, Western and positive vis-à-vis the feudal, statist and bureaucratic elements still found in Japan.

In this second period of Hirata's academic life, he uses this word not in relation to the state or politics, but mainly to discuss the ordinary economic lives of people in modern society, that is, with a connotation similar in nuance to *bürgerliche Gesellschaft*. We can see in Hirata's famous book *Civil Society and Socialism* (1969) at least three implications of civil or bourgeois society.

First, a civil society is, according to Hirata, a society that is rooted in the concrete aspects and ordinary lives of its people. "Civil society is first of all a society where ordinary people interrelate to each other as independent people, exchange their products for those of others, and communicate their individual thoughts and desires to each other" (Hirata 1969: 86). Remembering the terms he used in his study of Quesnay, one can see his civil society is a society understood in terms of the "processes of concrete human beings" who are not yet reified in the objective structure, or "a *development* itself *as* an economic and social *process* of the property and division of labor" (ibid. 175, emphasis Hirata's). The perspective of the circuit of productive capital operates underneath his concept of civil society, as shown in his use of the terms "concrete human beings" and "process." Nonetheless, the concept of civil society in this sense is too abstract to be used to specify some aspects of modern society.

Second, his concept of civil society covers a society of private individuals endowed with freedom and equality. "Civil society is one where people communicate one to another as citizens," he says. Here, citizens constitute a real base of juridical subjects with freedom and equality (Hirata 1969: 79). A free and equal person is a product *par excellence* of modern Western societies; it has been born out of the struggles against traditional communes and arises from the aftermath of their destruction. Furthermore, civil society is something to be evaluated positively. When Hirata says that civil society is a society constituted by free and equal private proprietors in the modern West, he recognizes that "civil society" stands in opposition to the "traditional commune." His approach to "civil society and the commune" develops from this starting point into a comparative discussion of civilization in the West and Japan/Asia and a criticism of premodern elements that survive even in present-day Japanese capitalism.

The concept of civil society as such is not necessarily original to Hirata. It has been shared by more than a few Japanese thinkers in the context of something akin to Adam Smith's "commercial society." From this perspective, it is thus appropriate to consider Hirata's concept of civil society as having evolved from an existing concept shared with these thinkers. On this point, the following passage is suggestive. "The Japanese concept of *civil society* is Marx's picture of the early stage of normal capitalism without sharp class antagonisms, but this is superimposed on Smith's civilized or commercial society. In a revolutionary process, what is civil is not to be expunged, but rather to be fully realised." (Mizuta 2006: 120, emphasis Mizuta's).

What is original to Hirata, however, is to be found in the fact that he defined civil society as a society of "individual property" from the viewpoint of property theory. In distinguishing the premodern commune from civil society by virtue of the criterion of the existence or nonexistence of "individual property," he says that:

> … the property of the members of a civil society is, although superficially private and exclusive, individual and non-exclusive at its very essence. What a civil society objectively produces is the "individual," "individual labor," and "individual property." … A civil society, though under a restriction of private exclusiveness, is conscious of the relationship and distinction between the individual and the genus, thus establishing one as an individual. (Hirata 1969: 88–92)

In short, for Hirata, modern civil society is, unlike premodern communities, a society where individual property is established in the guise of private property – in other words, a society in which individual property is created but is then transformed into private property.

The third nuance inherent in his idea of civil society is one that contrasts it with capitalist society – that is, civil society examined within the framework of "civil society and capitalism." According to Hirata, at least in modern Western society, civil society exists at the root of capitalist society; modern society must therefore be understood in terms of two strata: civil society and capitalist society. Civil society represents the primary social formation in modern Western society, and only on this basis can capitalism exist as a secondary social formation. The logic that intermediates between civil society and capitalist society precisely encompasses the theory of the inversion of the law of appropriation. Not only Marx's *Capital*, says Hirata, but Marx's historical materialism in general also assumes the logic of two strata:

> An actual civil society exists in a ceaseless process in which it is transforming into a capitalist society…. This is why Marx implies also capitalist society in using the terms civil or bourgeois society…. There is no original historical stage of civil society as such. Real social formation develops as a constant transformation from the primary formation (civil society) to the secondary formation (capitalist society). (Hirata 1969: 52–53)

In Western Europe, capitalism exists as something that emerged out of a transformation of civil society, i.e., as a secondary social formation. Although civil society actually exists only as something that has transformed into capitalism, the former must be conceptually distinguished from the latter. Traditional Marxism in Japan has ignored this distinction; its use of overly simplistic definitions for civil or bourgeois society and capitalist society has resulted in the conclusion that civil society needs to be expunged. This, however, is not correct. By distinguishing them, we can gain insights into several fresh and important questions. Is Japanese capitalism based on civil society? Has Japan become a capitalist nation lacking a civil society? Has postwar Japan's high rate of economic growth really brought about a capitalism that features a civil society? Hirata's investigation of civil society and capitalism has highlighted these analytical approaches vis-à-vis both prewar and postwar Japanese capitalism.

3.3.3 The Reestablishment of Individual Property

By confirming in this way what is meant by the term civil society, Hirata sharply examines the problems inherent in socialism. As was previously mentioned, the many negative aspects of socialist countries, such as the Sino-Soviet split, the invasion of Czechoslovakia, and the stagnation of planned economies, grew more apparent in the 1960s and 1970s. In the midst of these circumstances, Japanese Marxists continued to focus only on class struggle, ignoring almost altogether questions relating to individuality and human rights. Criticizing this atmosphere, Hirata boldly questioned the nature of Marx's own socialism.

His conclusion is summarized in his assertion that Marxian socialism represents a "reestablishment of individual property." Hirata's analytical approach is that of property theory, and his analytical method is, from start to finish, that of textual criticism. The subject matter on which he focuses is found in several passages on the negation of negation that are included in the chapter or section on the historical trend of capitalist accumulation (Chapter 24, Section 7 of the fourth German edition of *Capital*, volume 1; Chapter 32 of the French and English editions) that also forms part of the conclusion of the same volume. While Hirata underscores the errors made in the Japanese translation of the sentences in question, here we quote them from the English edition; it too shares the same mistakes:

> The capitalist mode of appropriation, the result of the capitalist mode of production, produces capitalist private property. This is the first negation of individual private property, as founded on the labour of the proprietor. But capitalist production begets, with the inexorability of a law of Nature, its own negation. It is the negation of negation. *This does not re-establish private property for the producer, but gives him individual property* based on the acquisitions of the capitalist era: i.e., on co-operation and possession in common of the land and of the means of production. (Marx 1996: 751; cf. Hirata 1971: 485)

Here the English translation states unequivocally, "This does not re-establish private property for the producer, but *gives him* individual property…." As is well known, the last version of *Capital* that Marx himself revised, and for which he was responsible, is the French edition. He directed that on the occasion of new editions the passage in question ought to follow the French edition, in which this passage becomes "Elle *rétablit* non la propriété privée du travailleur, mais sa propriété individuelle…" (Marx 1967: 342). In the third (1883) and fourth (1890) German editions, following Marx's direction, this sentence is correctly translated: "Diese *stellt* nicht das Privateigenthum *wieder her*, wohl aber das individuelle Eigenthum…." In the English edition, however, another verb, "give," is inserted beside "re-establish": "This does not re-establish … but *gives him* individual property." On account of this incorrect insertion, the result is that the reestablishment of individual property in a future society, as is clearly stated in the French edition, is thoroughly extinguished. The French sentence "Elle *rétablit* …la propriété individuelle du travailleur" can be translated into English as "This *re-establishes* …the individual property of workers." This mistake, insists Hirata, is also found in Japanese translations.

This is not, he says, a mere question of mistranslation, but a serious question concerning Marxists' image of socialism. According to the French edition, Marx says that "a *re*-establishment of individual property" will be realized in a socialist society as a result of "the negation of negation"; individual property had already been established in modern civil society, although it took the form of private property. Through the inversion of civil society into capitalism, private individual property has been transformed into private capitalist property (the first negation). Socialism is, by negating again private capitalist property (the negation of negation), nothing other than a reestablishment of the original individual property (Hirata 1978). The individual property to be reestablished is a social relationship in which "the identity of work and property" is realized at the social level (Hirata 1982: 293). "Only by the re-establishment of individual property does the *de facto* social property [which has been formed in the capitalist era] become a real social property" (Hirata 1971: 475).

For Hirata it is therefore obvious that socialism represents more "a succession of civil society" than a breaking away from capitalism. "The individuality, individual labor and individual property of the working class, which have been distorted by the private form, are now going to flourish properly in the socialist society…. Therefore, we have to acknowledge that the revolutionary transition from capitalism to socialism is a gradual succession as well as a clean break in world history. Only those who acknowledge socialism as a succession of civil society have the right to speak of socialism" (Hirata 1969: 104).

His thinking wherein socialism is defined as the "reestablishment of individual property" and the "succession of civil society" radically renovated the Marxism of the time, which had been steeped in the generally accepted idea that "socialism is nothing other than national property." His approach to "socialism and civil society" constituted an important perspective for the criticism of existing socialist countries headed by the Soviet Union as embodying "socialism without civil society." Although his words "the revolutionary transition from capitalism to socialism" ring hollow today, the essence of his civil society theory, as seen in the concept of the "reestablishment of individual property," is worthy of being reconsidered in the 21st century, be it in a capitalist or socialist context.

In short, middle-period Hirata, as an extension of the perspective of the capital circuit, explored the new theoretical pivot of the inversion of the law of appropriation, resulting in his discovery of the "missing" concept of "individual property." Circuit theory led to property theory, which in turn led to his original theory of civil society. He was thus able to make critical observations concerning the practical problems of the time from the perspectives of "civil society and the commune," "civil society and capitalism," and "civil society and socialism."

3.4 Gramsci and the Perspective of Hegemony and Institution

3.4.1 Civil Society and Hegemony in Gramsci

The late 1980s to the early 1990s correspond to the last decade of Hirata's life. In this period there was a great upheaval in the geopolitical structure of the postwar world, as seen on the one hand in civil revolutions in Eastern European countries and the collapse of the Soviet Union and on the other by the bursting of the bubble economy in Japan after it had become an economic power and by the signing of the Maastricht Treaty in 1992. Hirata began to make many comments on current events, and also, with respect to theory, to discuss both state and French régulation theory. What is important here is that he adopted anew the civil society theory of Antonio Gramsci (1891–1937); in so doing, his concept of civil society experienced a kind of transformation. While focusing on this point, I will now trace Hirata's development in his later years.

With the adoption of Gramsci's theory, Hirata's stance in questioning civil society changed. In the past he had placed an emphasis, under an approach that addressed "civil society and the commune" and "civil society and capitalism," on critiques that claimed that Japanese capitalism lacks civil society or that capitalist property lacks individual property. After adopting Gramsci's theory, however, the problems on which Hirata focused shifted to those of "civil society and the state." Of course, it is not the case that he had never dealt with this area before; on the contrary, one might say that the theme of "civil society and the state" had underpinned his thinking at least since the translation of *Misère de la philosophie* in his younger days, and that this theme had simply been revived by his encounter with Gramsci. In any case, Hirata in his later days discussed civil society in contrast with the state, rather than with the commune or capitalism, and with respect to its political aspect rather than its economic aspect as "bürgerliche Gesellschaft." Hirata himself explains this as follows:

> The more one sticks to contemporary Japan, I keenly believe, the more a common perspective across various generations is required.... Social relations in a given era cannot be thoroughly reduced to the economic relations of production ... it is contradictions, given the rhythmic movements by the former, that lead to a *transformational process in the dimension of the state*.... I once again came to confront a classical theme: civil society and the state. (Hirata 1993: 242–243)

Regarding civil society and the state, there are classically two well-known thinkers: Georg Wilhelm Friedrich Hegel, who argued for the "*Aufhebung* of civil society to the state," and Marx, who, reversing Hegel's argument, insisted on the "re-subsumption of the state to civil society." Hirata pays a lot of attention to Gramsci, who, inspired by Hegel and Marx, conceived a new theory of civil society during his time in prison in the interwar period. What is Gramsci's civil society theory? Hirata explains its essence as follows.

In Russia, where an actual socialist revolution took place, civil society was primordial and gelatinous and the state was all; in the West, on the other hand, civil society had already developed, and we see the sturdy structure of civil society when the state is shaken. Therefore, if one wants to realize a socialist revolution in Western Europe, one has no choice but to fight a "war of position" in the field of civil society, rather than attempting to seize the state through a "war of maneuver" as was the case in Russia. Gramsci located civil society between the basis (economic society) and the superstructure (state) and saw civil society as the main battlefield for emancipatory movements. In other words, civil society contains political and public elements as well as an ensemble of private interests (system of needs). Therefore, domination by the bourgeois state implies not only a compulsory domination by "political society" but also a process wherein the ruling classes gain the active agreement of the ruled through various private organizations in "civil society" such as schools, churches, and associations. The function of civil society is precisely to achieve agreement through the moral and intellectual leadership of the ruling classes or an apparatus of their hegemony. It is, therefore, decisively important for socialist movements to create a counter-hegemony in the field of civil society. Gramsci thus emphasized the position of civil society as the field upon which the battle for hegemony was waged and by extension the place where socialists must achieve popular agreement. Moreover, through the idea of this struggle for hegemony, he also actualized a Marxian viewpoint: "re-subsumption of the state to civil society" (Hirata 1993: 255–256).

Along with Hirata's shift toward Gramsci, the implications of his civil society began to transform from a notion concerning ordinary economic lives to one concerning political movements, from an expression of independent individuals to that of social individuals in solidarity, and from something to be realized and developed in Japan to a field of battle in advanced countries for hegemony. We also witness a diminishing of his former topics of inquiry regarding the differences between Western Europe and Japan with regard to civil society. This may have been a necessary change that originated from his new approach to civil society and the state.

3.4.2 Civil Society and Régulation

All of this having been said, however, how were the older Marxian civil society and this Gramscian civil society connected, and not connected, in Hirata himself? How were the "sticky communal relations lacking distinction between self and other" and "individual property" to be understood in Gramsci's civil society as the field of battle for hegemony? Hirata himself does not provide clear answers to these sorts of questions.

On the other hand, however, this adoption of Gramsci by Hirata can also be said to have cultivated a pioneering perspective. This can be seen in its having paved the way for – or at least contained perspectives that engaged with – the so-called new civil society theory that prospered after the events that occurred around 1990 such as the revolutions in Eastern Europe. It can also perhaps be said to have played the role of a bridge between postwar Japanese-type economic civil society theory and the type of civil society theory that emphasized the significance of "political" activities carried out through the "association" of people to various forms of intermediary groups. Gramsci cited places such as schools, churches, and various groups or associations as instances of civil society as the site of hegemonic dominance. Similarly, Habermas, a member of the Frankfurt school that has championed "new civil society" in recent years, also applies the name "Zivilgesellschaft" to various intermediary groups and associations such as cultural circles and academic societies – relationships of alliance based on free will – and pinned his hopes on them as a "third domain" in addition to "markets" and "the state" (Habermas 1990). Habermas emphasizes civil society as non-state/non-market, and while Hirata differs insofar as he also views "politics" involved in opposing the state as important, Gramsci/late-period Hirata can perhaps be said to have occupied a position surprisingly close to that of Habermas.

As it turned out, however, in his later years, Hirata shifted toward French régulation theory to an even greater extent than he drew closer to Habermas. As is well known, régulation theory, by exploring new concepts such as "regime of accumulation (or growth regime)" and "mode of régulation," was the first attempt to analyze the dynamics of advanced forms of capitalism in the postwar age as being manifestations of the "growth and crisis of Fordism." This approach has now become a political economy that presents real-time analyses of contemporary economies (e.g., the collapse of socialist economies, varieties of capitalism, developing economies, and the growth and breakdown of finance-led capitalism).

Hirata's interest in this theory lies not in its aspect of analyzing actual economic societies, but in its position in the history of economic thought, especially in the genealogy of the concept of régulation. His characteristic understanding of régulation theory is typified by statements such as "the concept of hegemony has prepared that of régulation" (Hirata 1993: 269) and "the régulationists found their basic concept in Gramsci" (Hirata 1988: 21). Of course, it is admitted by the French régulationists themselves (Lipietz 1985: 16) that the régulationist concept of "Fordism" has its origin in Gramsci (1971). Hirata, however, sought the origin of the concept of "régulation" in Gramsci's concept of hegemony. He therefore approached this new political economy that has risen in France since the 1970s in a very particular manner; he consistently remains a historian of economic thought, even when dealing with contemporary political economy.

From this point of view, Hirata argues as follows. According to Gramsci, civil society is a field where various classes and interest groups struggle against one another in search of their own hegemony, make compromises, and eventually arrive at social agreements. It is a field where domination is conducted through agreements and where the old regime of domination may be overthrown. The virtue of the régulation school, says Hirata, is found in the fact that it has emphasized the standpoint that various compromises in civil society are embodied in a series of *institutions*.

Here one can take the perspective of "institutional forms," or of various institutions in the domains of the wage-labor nexus, forms of competition, forms of money and finance, the state, and so on. The state is also considered "an institutionalized compromise." In a particular time and country, the ensemble of institutional forms constitutes particular norms, rules, and *habitus* – all of which, as a particular "mode of régulation," will support the economic structure of the capitalism found there. It is in this way of thinking the novelty and relevance of régulation theory, which goes beyond the traditional economics that have narrowly limited their field of view to analyzing markets, is to be found. In Hirata's words, "To the extent that hegemony is established fully through agreement in civil society, the apparatus of hegemony can be connected to the reality of the political economy only when it is comprehended in terms of institutional forms and modes of régulation as a social formation of agreement" (Hirata 1988: 20).

Thanks to régulation theory, today we understand that the institutional form of the wage-labor nexus, for example, cannot be reduced to simply the market economy – it requires social and political mediation. This may indeed be very close to what Hirata saw in Gramsci's concept of hegemony.

3.5 What Was Hirata's Thinking on Civil Society?

Having acquired his own perspective on the "circuit of productive capital and the structure of reproduction" from his study of Quesnay's *Tableau économique*, Hirata explored, through examinations of Marx's circuit theory beginning in the mid-1960s, a new approach to property theory. The latter led him, via an understanding of the reversion of the law of appropriation, to issues in the field of "civil society and capitalism" and also, via his mindfulness of Marx's words about the reestablishment of individual property, to the field of "civil society and socialism." When Japan's postwar capitalism was being established with an eye to achieving a high rate of economic growth, and when the many negative aspects of socialist countries were becoming clear, his civil society-centered Marxology caused a great sensation. During the collapse of socialist countries around 1990, Hirata adopted the thinking of Gramsci, thus shifting to the "civil society and the state" framework that places its emphasis on the struggle for hegemony on the battlefield of civil society.

We can see in the history of Hirata's own thought the predominance of his basic viewpoint: a critical understanding of economic society in terms of "circuit and reproduction" or "process and structure." Of course, this viewpoint sometimes experienced subtle shifts or changes in emphasis. Starting from the perspective of "process and structure" in his younger days, he developed his own thinking vis-à-vis civil society by making positive the standpoint of "process" or by drawing back that of "structure." This is reflected in his approach to régulation theory: his discussion of it leans more toward the concept of "mode of régulation" than toward that of the "regime of accumulation" or macroeconomic structure. Had it not been for his death he may have undertaken a full discussion of the regime of accumulation – another pivotal concept in régulation theory that can perhaps be said to correspond to his own concept of "structure."

Following Hirata's death, we have seen the rise of new theories pertaining to civil society, mainly triggered by the Eastern European civil revolutions and by the work of Habermas (1990). Where is Hirata's place in such contemporary research? One Japanese scholar asserts that in his later days Hirata became "a pioneer of the worldwide boom in civil society theory" (Yamaguchi 2004: 111). Alternatively, referencing the works of the Japanese Civil Society School, an American historian has argued that only during the postwar era did civil society "generate the analytical and moral force necessary to make it meaningful as more than a translated term" (Barshay 2004: 194). According to yet another authority, although the theoretical work of Hirata, as well as that of Yoshihiko Uchida, constituted "phase one of the contemporary renaissance of civil society," it was "short-lived" and "its influence was weak" (Keane 1998: 14). Pointing to the confusion that surrounds Hirata's notions of civil society, another Japanese scholar states that with Hirata, "the Civil Society School of Marxism has come to an end" (Uemura 2010: 260).

What sort of relationship exists between Hirata and Uchida as scholars of civil society? While on the one hand taking Uchida's perspective of metabolism (Stoffwechsel) as his foundation and developing this into first the perspective of the circuit of productive capital, then the theory of property, and finally the theory of individual property, in his later years Hirata adopted Gramsci's theory of civil society and shifted his focus to a political civil society theory. Both Hirata and Uchida undoubtedly sought the realization and maturation of "civil society," both in Japan and overseas, through addressing the issues of "civil society and capitalism" and "civil society and socialism." Ultimately Uchida worked his way down to the civil society that transcends narrow "modernity" and runs broadly and deeply through the foundations of human history and advocated the importance of becoming a nation in which each citizen engages in "academic inquiry" (see Chap. 2). In Hirata, on the other hand, while strengthening the understanding that economic civil society à la Marx was in reality inseparable from what is public/political, the focus becomes civil groups that engage in "politics." While remaining conscious of the idea of "from each person" in Uchida, Hirata seems to have wanted to add to this the notion that "each person" must first become allied or attached to various meso-level associations and develop himself or herself into a social individual.

Compared in this way, the differences between them are complementary; just as the theory of academic inquiry in Uchida was a theory of the formation of civil society as Uchida envisioned it, the theory of political civil society in late-period Hirata can perhaps be seen as one answer to the question of how middle-period Hirata's vision of a Marxian civil society is to be realized. While taking the idea of "each person" as the foundation, to bind the cooperation and division of labor of these individuals together in meso-level associations – this was perhaps the blueprint for the formation of civil society as Hirata envisioned it, i.e., a realization of Marxian civil society (the reestablishment of individual property) supplemented by and through a Gramscian civil society (the struggle for hegemony).

Ultimately, what is the essence of Hirata's theory? It seems appropriate to conclude that while some aspects of it are outdated, others indeed remain fresh. His approach focusing on "civil society and socialism" may attract less interest today among people who have witnessed the collapse of the socialist countries and experienced a resulting loss of faith in this model. In addition, the fact that civil society in Japan has progressed a little (though *only* a little) in tandem with the maturation of Japanese capitalism in the 21st century may have lessened the urgency of this issue in our consciousness, leading to fewer and fewer questions being asked about "civil society and the commune."

There are other aspects of his thinking, however, that remain groundbreaking even today. His framing of the questions pertaining to "civil society and capitalism" and "civil society and the state," for example, may perhaps give us some insights concerning the relationships between markets, the state, and civil society; the balancing of these three elements constitutes the main theme in the new theory of civil society. Furthermore, it is important to note here that his discussion of the "reestablishment of individual property," the very essence of his civil society thought, is one that must continue to be developed in any case, regardless of whether the politico-economic regimes found in the society in question can be characterized as capitalism or socialism, liberalism or social democracy, a finance-led regime or a welfare-led regime, or any other ways of organizing a socioeconomy.

References

Asai, Kazuhiro and Fumitaka Wakamori eds. (1983) *Hirata Kiyoaki Chosaku: Mokuroku to Kaidai* (*The Annotated Catalogue of Works of Kiyoaki Hirata*), Tokyo: Not for Sale.

Barshay, Andrew (2004) *The Social Sciences in Modern Japan: The Marxian* and *Modernist Traditions*, Berkeley, Los Angeles and London: University of California Press.

Gramsci, Antonio (1971) 'Americanism and Fordism,' in *Selections from the Prison Notebooks of Antonio Gramsci*, ed. and trans. by Q. Hoare and G. Nowell-Smith, New York: International Publishers. This article was first written in Italian in 1934.

Habermas, Jürgen (1990) *Strukturwandel der Öfentlichkeit: Untersuchungen zu einer Kategorie der bürgerlichen Gesellschaft*, mit einem Vorwort zur Neuauflage, Frankfurt am Main: Suhrkamp.

Hirata, Kiyoaki (1965) *Keizai Kgaku no Sōzō: Keizaihyō to Furansu Kakumei* (*Creation of Economic Science: Tableau économique and the French Revolution*), Tokyo: Iwanami Shoten Publishers.

——— (1966) 'Marukusu ni okeru Keizaigaku to Rekishi Ninshiki' (Political Economy and Philosophy of History in Marx), *Shisō* (*Thoughts*), 502, 503, 506 and 509; Also in Hirata (1971) .

——— (1969) *Shimin Shakai to Shakaishugi* (*Civil Society and Socialism*), Tokyo: Iwanami Shoten Publishers.

——— (1971) *Keizaigaku to Rekishi Ninshiki* (*Political Economy and Philosophy of History*), Tokyo: Iwanami Shoten Publishers.

——— (1977) 'Gendai Shakaishugi to "Shimin Shakai"' (Contemporary Socialism and the "Civil Society"), *Gendai no Riron* (*Theories Today*), 165.

——— (1978) 'Sur la notion de propriété individuelle chez Karl Marx,' *Keizai Kagaku* (*Economic Science*), Nagoya University, 25(4).

——— (1982) *Keizaigaku Hihan heno Hōhō Josetsu* (*Discourse on the Method of the Critique of Political Economy*), Tokyo: Iwanami Shoten Publishers.

——— (1988) 'Shakaiteki Seigyo Chōsei no Seiji Keizaigaku' (Political Economy of Social Régulation), *Shisō*(*Thoughts*), 771.

——— (1993) *Shimin Shakai to Regyurashion* (*Civil Society and the Régulation*), Tokyo: Iwanami Shoten Publishers.

Keane, John (1998) *Civil Society: Old Images, New Visions*, Stanford: Stanford University Press.

Lipietz, Alain (1985) *Mirages et miracles: Problèmes de l'industrialisation dans le tiers monde*, Paris: La Découverte.

Marx, Karl (1967) *Le Capital*, Tokyo: Far Eastern Book Sellers, Publishers. This is the first reprint of the first French edition published in Paris: Maurice Lachâtre et Cie, 1872–1875.

——— (1973) *Grundrisse: Introduction to the Critique of Political Economy*. Harmondsworth: Penguin Books. This is an English translation of *Grundrisse der Kritik der politischen Ökonomie (Rohentwurf) 1857–1858,* Berlin: Dietz Verlag, 1953.

——— (1996) *Capital*, vol. 1, in *Karl Marx-Friedrich Engels Collected Works*, vol. 35. New York: International Publishers. This reproduces the first English edition published in 1887, translated from the third German edition by S. Moore and E. Aveling.

Mizuta, Hiroshi (2006) 'The Japanese Concept of Civil Society and Marx's *bürgerliche Gesellschaft*,' in Hiroshi Uchida ed., *Marx for the 21st Century*, London and New York: Routledge.

Nozawa, Toshiharu (2008) '*Hirata Kiyoaki Chosaku: Mokuroku to Kaidai* heno Hoi to Sonogo no Tsuika' (Addition and Supplement to *The Annotated Catalogue of Works of Kiyoaki Hirata*), *Chiba Daigaku Keizai Kenkyū* (*Economic Journal of Chiba University*), 23 (2).

Souzou-no-kai ed. (1996) *Gakumon Bungei Kyōwakoku: Tsuitō Hirata Kiyoaki* (*Republic of Literature: In Memory of Kiyoaki Hirata*), Tokyo: Not for Sale.

Uchida, Yoshihiko (1967) *Nihon Shihonshugi no Shisō-zō* (*Intellectual Portrait of Japanese Capitalism*), Tokyo: Iwanami Shoten Publishers; in *Uchida Yoshihiko Chosaku-shū* (*Collected Works of Yoshihiko Uchida*: *CWYU*), 5, Tokyo: Iwanami Shoten Publishers.

Uemura, Kunihiko (2010) *Shimin Shakai toha Nani ka: Kihon Gainen no Keifu* (*What Is Civil Society?: Genealogy of Basic Concepts*), Tokyo: Heibonsha.

Yagi, Kiichirō ed. (1986) 'Hirata Kiyoaki Kyōju Chosaku Mokuroku' (Catalogue of Works of Professor Kiyoaki Hirata), *Keizai Ronsō* (*The Economic Review*), Kyoto University, 137(3).

Yamada, Moritarō (1934) *Nihon Shihonshugi Bunseki* (*Analysis of Japanese Capitalism*), Tokyo: Iwanami Shoten Publishers; Reprinted in 1977 in Iwanami Bunko.
Yamada, Toshio (1987) 'Les tendances du marxisme japonais contemporain', *Actuel Marx*, 2.
Yamaguchi, Yasushi (2004) *Shimin Shakai-ron: Rekishiteki Isan to Shin-tenkai* (*Theories of Civil Society: Historical Inheritance and New Developments*), Tokyo: Yūhikaku Publishing.

Part II
The Rise and Fall of Contemporary Japanese Capitalism

Chapter 4
The Introduction of Régulation Theory in Japan

4.1 The State of Political Economy in Japan in the 1980s

Régulation theory was introduced in Japan beginning mainly in the late 1980s and attracted the attention of no small number of economists and social scientists. This theory was first put forward in France in the mid-1970s, and after a lag of approximately 10 years it made its way to Japan, giving rise to distinctive analyses of the Japanese economy and leading to several joint international research projects focusing on comparative studies of Asian and European economies. Why was régulation theory embraced in 1980s Japan?

As we saw in Chap. 1, when the 1970s and 1980s arrived, the political economy that had dominated postwar Japan found itself at a major turning point, having lost its analytic power in the face of a new reality. While the 1950s and 1960s, in which developed capitalist nations realized rapid growth and high social welfare development, were referred to as "the golden age of capitalism," the 1970s saw the emergence of an economic crisis dubbed "stagflation." When it came to the socialist countries, not only had their repression of human rights symbolized by incidents in Hungary and Czechoslovakia been revealed, but beginning in the 1970s they too fell into a political and economic crisis even more severe than that experienced by capitalist nations. As for Japan, for the roughly 20 years referred to as its "period of rapid growth" it enjoyed one of the highest growth rates in the world, and even after the oil shock of 1973, its growth, supported by booming exports, remained relatively stable, to the point that it proudly proclaimed itself a "great economic power."

Was existing political economy able to provide appropriate perspectives and frameworks for analyzing both Japan and the world under these circumstances? To the extent that the theory of "state monopoly capitalism" was based on the "general crisis of capitalism" hypothesis that foresaw capitalism's destruction, from the start it lacked the capacity to analyze this new capitalist reality. Japanese Keynesians (particularly post-Keynesians) were sensitive to this new reality, providing key

T. Yamada, *Contemporary Capitalism and Civil Society*, Evolutionary Economics and Social Complexity Science 14,
https://doi.org/10.1007/978-981-13-0517-7_4

terms such as "corporate group," "price revolution," "multinational corporation," "era of mass consumption," and "era of technological revolutions" but were clearly inadequate when it came to positioning the whole of what was occurring in postwar capitalism within a broad historical context. From the 1980s onward, this school of thought increasingly lost its voice in the face of the "new classical macroeconomics" that was ascendant in America.

What about the theory of civil society that had been developed natively in Japan? Right in the middle of the period of rapid growth, Yoshihiko Uchida pointed to the view of capitalism in Marx's *Capital* and warned that it had been developed with a steady eye on its "surprisingly powerful vital force" (Uchida 1966: 5, 44). Regarding postwar Japanese capitalism, Uchida also said that in Japan the "powerful vital force" of capitalism did not discard the "premodern" but on the contrary swallowed it up as it developed and realized what might be called "super-modern" capitalism. "A super-modernity without modernity," "A melding of the pre-modern and the super-modern:" – These were the secrets of rapid growth and would later become the secrets of becoming a great economic power (Uchida, 1967: 336, 1981: 11). This argument provided a sharply critical view of Japanese capitalism, but unfortunately that was as far as its analysis went. Then during the 1980s, theories that on the contrary praised the Japanese model, beginning with the arguments presented in *Japan as Number One* (Vogel, 1979), became popular, and in the midst of this excitement the voice of the civil society approach was largely drowned out.

In this way, the civil society theory, contemporary capitalism theory, and Keynesian economics that had been vigorously debated in postwar Japan and produced commensurate results lost their former analytic power and influence in the midst of the zeitgeist of the 1980s. While continuing in the tradition of Marx and Keynes, there was a pressing need for new ideas, concepts, and methods to analyze capitalism's new realities. This was the state of political economy in Japan in the 1980s and the stage upon which French régulation theory made its entrance.

At first the introduction of this approach was centered on explanations and translations of foreign works, but by the 1990s analyses of the Japanese economy based on this theory began to be produced. At that point, however, the application of this theory to Japan required more than simply mechanically carving up the Japanese economy with concepts created in France. The concept of "Fordism" in place of "state monopoly capitalism" was truly revolutionary, but could Japanese capitalism really be understood using this concept? Japanese régulationists were immediately faced with these kinds of doubts and bemusement. They had no choice but to create new and original concepts and methods out of the existing elements of the theory that had been created in France. This will be discussed in the following chapters. In this chapter I will present the standard interpretations of "régulation theory" adopted by Japanese researchers, broken down into this theory's fundamental perspective and concepts, Fordism and the history of capitalism, and (as a slightly later development that did not begin until around 2000) the discussions of finance-led capitalism and capitalism's diversity.

4.2 The Fundamental Perspective and Basic Concepts of Régulation Theory

4.2.1 Fundamental Perspective: The Social Régulation of Capitalism

Régulation theory was born during the 1970s, a time of great upheaval. The oil shock of 1973 threw the economies and societies of developed nations into confusion, and they were then beset by "stagflation" in which stagnation/unemployment and inflation increased at the same time. Even before that, in 1971 President Nixon had declared a suspension of the convertibility of the dollar into gold, and along with this "Nixon shock" the Bretton Woods system (IMF system), the international framework that had supported the development of postwar capitalism, collapsed. The "golden age" of the 1950s and 1960s had clearly ended, and an era of crisis and confusion began.

Régulation theory was led by Michel Aglietta and Robert Boyer. At the time both were government economists involved in French economic planning and statistical analysis, but the economic prediction model on which they relied no longer applied to anything. What had happened to the postwar economy? What had the postwar economic development been in the first place? These were the questions from which their inquiry emerged.

The answers at which they themselves arrived developed into a theoretical awareness of the "growth and crisis of Fordism." The process leading up to that point required confronting or critically incorporating various social sciences. In doing so régulation theory worked out the distinctive perspective and concepts that would form the basis of its analysis of the crisis it was addressing. I will begin by going over this aspect of the theory's development (see Aglietta 1979; Boyer 1990a, 2015).

The rapid postwar economic growth in developed countries had been led by Keynesian economics, but the validity of this approach had clearly diminished in the face of the economic crises of the 1970s. Marxism, too, which ought to have been poised to display its competence in an era of crises, had already lost its capacity to analyze reality. What gained a stronger voice in their place was neoclassical economics. But its "equilibrium theory"-based market absolutism was completely unacceptable to the proponents of régulation theory.

The fundamental perspective of the young French régulationists was rooted in the following assumption. Far from naturally heading toward an "equilibrium," capitalism and market economies on the contrary are full of confrontations, conflicts, and contradictions between both groups and individuals. How had a capitalism so rife with contradictions nevertheless allowed for stability and growth over a significant period of time? This is the fundamental question for régulationists. The intuitive answer is that if their competing forces are steered in the right direction, capitalist societies are stably reproduced, but if they are not, they arrive at instability and crisis. In other words, if its various opposing forces are properly "régulated," then capitalism can secure stability and growth, but if not then it will fall into instability and crisis. The root of market economies should thus be seen not as "equilibrium" but rather "reproduction," and appropriate "régulation" is needed for the sake of this "reproduction." *Reproduction requires régulation.* Here "régulation" is not restricted merely to questions of government policy but is broadly and deeply rooted in the form of every type of "institution." And these institutions are not merely those created to increase "economic" efficiency but those strongly marked by the "political" factors of conflicts, alliances, and compromises between the various forces within society. That is why institutions and régulation vary historically and by nation. As a result, capitalism must be viewed not as an eternal and universal law but rather as something subject to spatial and temporal variation. In other words, capitalism must be understood in terms of its historical nature and diversity.

To rephrase this with capitalism as the focal point, unlike what occurred in traditional communities, capitalism is itself the revolutionary force that is constantly changing human society. Traditional communities may have been peaceful, but at the same time they were full of stagnation and outdated customs. In contrast, capitalism is constantly giving rise to change and reform but at the same time also gives rise to instability and disparity. Not only that, but capital itself always rushes ahead recklessly, and the result of its headlong forward motion is the destruction of society – its labor power, solidarity, and the natural environment. What must be kept firmly in view is the fact that while capital may be the force behind social reform, it does not possess a commensurate capacity to control or régulate its own rush forward. Capitalist markets do not have the ability to control and *régulate* themselves. What can régulate capitalism is only to be found on the side of "society," and it is only through social or institutional mediation that capitalism can be brought to heel. This is why Aglietta emphasizes that "capitalism is a force for change that does not possess within itself the principle of its own régulation; the régulating principle of capitalism is found in the coherence of social mediation" (Aglietta 1997: 437).

Reproduction must be régulated. We have just seen that this is the fundamental perspective of régulation theory. Taking this one step further, we now establish that *capitalism must be socially régulated.* It is when we analyze capitalism from this perspective that the true value of régulation theory emerges. It sharply opposes the neoclassical school that sees self-equilibrating and self-régulating forces in market economies. It breaks from traditional Marxism, which holds that the anarchistic nature of capitalism can only be overcome through its abolition. And it attempts to go beyond the narrow horizons of Keynesianism that relies exclusively on political policy to régulate capitalism.

4.2.2 Five Basic Concepts

This fundamental perspective is fleshed out with several basic concepts. At its inception the theory established five such concepts. Figure 4.1 shows each of these concepts and the relationships between them (cf. Yamada 1993).

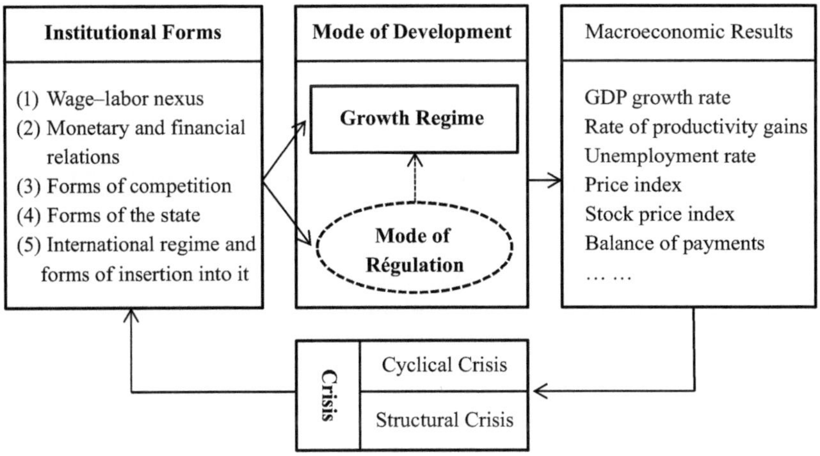

Fig. 4.1 Five basic concepts of régulation theory. (Source: Author)

The first concept is "*institutional forms*." Régulation theory is an institutional political economy that focuses on the role of various "institutions," but these roles vary greatly depending on the era and country in question. We should use the phrase "institutional forms" when we look at institutions from a perspective in which institutions can take various forms even when dealing with the same things. Economic society thus arises out of various forms of institutions; the institution referred to as the "market" is also a part of this, and the "market" is not the "economy" itself. If we set down the institutional domains of greatest economic importance, as in the figure, we have (1) the wage–labor nexus, (2) monetary and financial relations, (3) forms of competition, (4) forms of the state, and (5) the international regime and each nation's place in it.

These are all classifications by institutional domain, and within each domain there are countless specific institutions. The first domain, "the wage–labor nexus," includes all types of institutions involved in reproduction and the use of labor power, specifically forms of employment (institutions related to the state of various regular and irregular forms of employment), work (from labor laws to each company's work regulations and labor organization institutions), wage institutions (base pay, bonus, and various forms of benefit institutions, job-based pay, ability-based pay, performance-based pay, and so on), and institutions of advancement and promotion. Countless other examples can also be given, including all of the institutions related to consumption and public services. The relationship between labor and management is on the one hand a market relationship in which labor power is bought and sold; on the other hand, however, the fact that what is bought and sold is labor power (the people in question themselves) means that labor power commodities cannot be entirely left up to market mechanisms. After it is bought, labor power falls under the power and authority of the business operator, and this relationship of domination and subjugation gives rise to inherent conflicts. These conflicts cannot be régulated by market competition alone, and require nonmarket, institutional compromises and contrivances. It is also a domain that is intimately connected to "politics." The wage–labor nexus is the domain in which markets and power, or civil society and capitalism, directly intermingle. Régulation theory focuses on this characteristic of capitalism as much as possible and distinguishes the wage–labor nexus from markets in general for particular attention; the wage–labor nexus is "essential because it represents a particular kind of surplus appropriation" (Boyer 1990a: 37).

The second domain, "monetary and financial relations," includes not only monetary systems such as the gold standard or managed currency systems but also various institutions related to things like direct and indirect finance in the finance sector, corporate finance, consumer finance, bank finance, and even the stock market and central bank (interest rates). In the third domain, "forms of competition," the question of free competition versus oligopolies/monopolies is often examined, but here the various institutions they include, such as relationships between corporations, market structures, and formulas by which prices are determined, are viewed as the objects of inquiry. In the fourth domain, "forms of the state," the desirable state of government (an interventionist or noninterventionist state), tax and public finance institutions, and the scale and model of the welfare state (and at the same time its connection to the wage–labor nexus) are to be examined. Lastly, in the fifth domain, "the international regime and each nation's place in it," in addition to international institutions related to the international currency system (whether or not to have a fixed exchange rate), international trading system (various free trade and economic partnership agreements), and international flow of capital (foreign direct investment, foreign securities investment), the various institutions involved in how each country is incorporated into the international system (degree of openness to foreign capital, industrial specialization, the import/export structure of goods and services) are also to be considered.

Economic society is the overall body formed out of these institutions. The nature of institutional forms is connected to macroeconomic structure and performance. For example, the state of the labor organizing institutions in the wage–labor nexus within each company – and thus within each country – establishes the magnitude of productivity, and the state of wage institutions and consumer finance affect consumer demand. In short, the nature of institutional forms not only determines the magnitude of macroeconomic variables such as productivity, stock prices, wages, investment, consumption, demand, and employment but also affects the mutually determining and hierarchical relationships between these variables. For example, while under a certain institutional arrangement the determining relationship of "employment→wages" may be pronounced, under a different institutional arrangement, a strong relationship of "productivity→wages" may be found. The particular, stable macroeconomic relation that arises in a particular capitalist society is conceptualized as a "*growth regime*" (also called a "*regime of accumulation*"), and this is the second fundamental concept in régulation theory. A growth regime is the entire macroeconomic regularity in which capitalism lays out a route in a particular direction while absorbing its own contradictions.

These contradictions of capitalism are not absorbed automatically. Reproduction must be régulated, and capitalism must be socially régulated. In other words, *a growth regime must be appropriately régulated.* If there is anything that can guarantee appropriate régulation, it is only to be found within institutional forms. The institutions that arise in a given time and place, taken as a whole, both constrain the behavior of each individual and at the same time create predictions and expectations regarding the behavior of others, giving rise to fixed rules and norms within such societies. The nature of institutional forms not only gives rise to a particular macroeconomic configuration but also creates certain "rules of the game." If the rules of the game that are formed within a particular society are compatible with its growth regime they will stabilize its economic society, and if they are incompatible they will have a destabilizing effect. These rules of the game seen from the perspective of whether or not they guide or régulate a growth regime are called a "*mode of régulation.*" This is the third fundamental concept in régulation theory.

Institutional forms, or rather the human activities that underlie them when taken as a whole, result in a growth regime on the one hand and a mode of régulation on the other; the capitalism of a given country and era is a combination of a particular growth regime and a particular mode of régulation. The growth and stability of capitalism depends on the compatibility of these growth regimes and modes of régulation. A growth regime and mode of régulation taken together as a whole is referred to as a "*mode of development*," and this is the fourth fundamental concept in régulation theory. The changes in and differences between these modes of development are what shape capitalism's historical transformations and diversity in different countries.

Returning once again to Fig. 4.1, various items showing the macroeconomic performance of an economy, such as the rates of productivity gains and GDP growth, are given on the right edge of the figure. These are not concepts unique to régulation theory but economic statistics we see every day, and they are expressed using some kind of numeric value. From the perspective of régulation theory, these economic statistics stated in numerical values are significant as a summarized expression of the overall results of the economic activity carried out under a particular mode of development. Even though they are not distinctively régulation concepts, these economic statistical values are important indicators when it comes to determining the health of a particular capitalist economy.

The fifth and final concept in régulation theory is "*crisis*." While most economics ignores the "crisis" at the root of its theories, régulation theory positions it as one of its core, fundamental concepts. A "crisis" can have different sorts of content, so it is necessary to categorize its different types. First there are "cyclical crises" that correspond to the troughs in the Kitchin cycle (short-term fluctuations) and the Juglar cycle (medium-term fluctuations), but these are phases in which contradictions and disequilibria are removed from within the mode of régulation and can be described as proof that the mode of régulation is operating well. Second there are "structural crises" that correspond to the troughs in the Kondratiev cycle (long-term fluctuations). They signify a situation in which the stability and growth of capitalism can no longer be maintained by the growth regime and mode of development that have existed up until that point and in which structural reform on a large scale is required. This is seen in cases such as those in which contradictions reach a certain threshold within the repetition of cyclical crises and can no longer be responded to within the existing mode of régulation (and even the existing growth regime). These structural crises are the kind of crises régulation theory focuses on, and it is these crises that become the major driving factors behind capitalism's historical changes. The Long Depression at the end of the 19th century, the Great Depression of the 1930s, and the stagflation of the 1970s are well-known historical examples, and there is a significant chance that the "lost 20+ years" in Japan beginning in the 1990s and the 2008 financial crisis incited by the collapse of Lehman Brothers are both "structural crises" of this kind.

4.3 Fordism and Historical Transformations in Capitalism

As I stated at the start, régulation theory was born in the middle of an economic crisis in developed capitalist countries. Developed capitalism had flourished in the midst of the rapid growth and distributional fairness of what has been called its "golden age" following the WWII, but in the 1970s this came to a standstill. Régulation theory, which was launched by the need to examine the secret of this postwar growth and the eruption of its crisis, produced as the fruit of this inquiry an understanding of *the growth and crisis of Fordism*. In particular the term "Fordism," as a fresh and effective concept that had not existed in the past, widely took hold in place of older concepts. The fundamental perspective and concepts of régulation theory outlined in the previous section, too, had in fact been honed in this analysis of Fordism. These concepts and perspectives also prepared a point of view capable of looking back at earlier eras and developing a new understanding of the long-term history of capitalism before Fordism. After briefly looking back at the Fordism theory that served as the starting point for régulation theory, I will then trace the shape of the historical transformations in capitalism it engendered.

4.3.1 The Growth and Crisis of Fordism

Why was the unprecedentedly rapid growth in postwar developed capitalism possible? Put simply, it was because new institutions were formed in the countries of North America and Western Europe, and a new mode of régulation was being formed at the same time that these new institutions were leading to the emergence of a new growth regime. Moreover, the new mode of régulation was compatible with the new growth regime and able to guide it effectively. In greatly simplified terms, in the postwar period, a growth regime of "mass production – mass consumption" emerged, and if we take a brief look at the macroeconomic structure of this regime, we see the formation of the kind of connections seen in Fig. 4.2.

As seen in this figure, the driving force of the Fordist macroeconomy is found in high productivity gains in the manufacturing sector. The fruits of this productivity

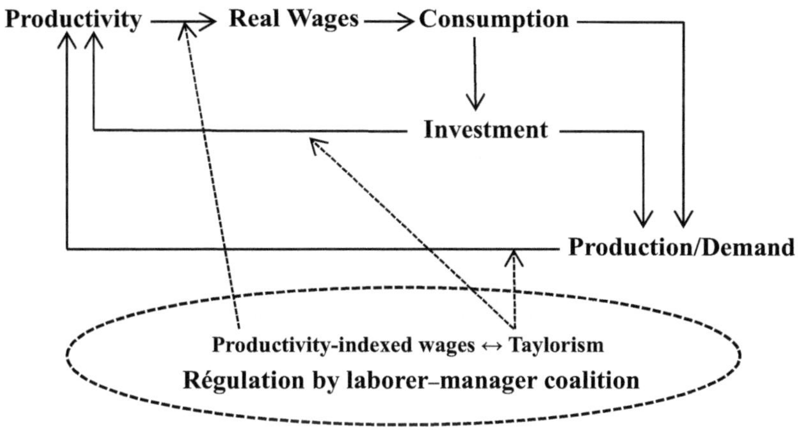

Fig. 4.2 Growth regime and mode of régulation in the Fordist mode of development. (Source: Author)

led to an increase in profits (this is omitted in the figure), but the important point that clearly differs in comparison to other eras is that these fruits were also distributed to workers as increased wages. Not only did nominal wages increase along with rising commodity prices, but real wages also increased even after accounting for these price increases. This increase in real wages stimulated individual consumption and led to spending not only on traditional consumer goods but also on durable goods such as appliances, houses, and cars, a change in workers' lifestyles, further concentration of the population in major cities, and the formation of a broad middle class. This increase in consumption caused an increase in investment. This investment (new machinery) not only contributed to increased productivity but also expanded demand (= production) corresponding to this consumption, or, in other words, grew the economy (putting aside for the moment trade and government activities). And as is indicated by the arrow from demand to productivity in the figure, the expansion of demand (the market) – in other words, economic growth – itself gives rise to increases in productivity. This is known as "economies of scale" and "increasing returns" in economics, and these phenomena are particularly apparent in this period. To sum up, a *productivity→wages→consumption→investment→demand→productivity* macroeconomic framework was constructed. According to Maddison (1991), between 1950 and 1973, the major OECD nations recorded average annual rates of 4.9% economic growth, 4.5% increases in productivity, and 3.8% increases in per capita GDP, all of which were unprecedented.

Phenomena such as high productivity gains and the simultaneous expansion of production of both consumer and production goods are emblematic of "intensive" growth regimes. The driving force behind the entire cycle is increasing productivity, but stated in terms of distribution and demand categories, it is a "wage and consumption-led type" of growth regime. Especially during this era of Fordism, particular attention is paid to the formation of the chain relationship between *productivity→wages* and *demand→productivity*. This is a new circuit that could not have existed in the 19th century British profit and investment-led type of growth regime (see Fig. 4.4 below). As a result, postwar Fordism created a "golden age of capitalism," supported by a relationship of cumulative causation between increasing productivity and economic growth, in which high increases in productivity gave rise to high demand formation (economic growth), and high economic growth gave rise to increased productivity.

What was the secret behind the longevity and stability of this growth regime? It was that a mode of régulation had been created alongside its new institutions. Labor unions were officially recognized, and wages and working conditions came to be decided through collective bargaining between labor and management. Even though it was not as if everything that had been determined by the labor market in the past had disappeared, it was the institution of collective bargaining that took the lead in shaping wages as a whole, and it was through this institution that "real wages indexed to productivity" were realized. Wages went from being low wages determined by competition to wages that rose along with productivity. In addition, minimum wage and social security institutions at both the national and local levels brought about equalization and a raising of the floor of income distribution. The institution of consumer loans was also put in place, which encouraged the purchasing of durable goods, and under stable international currency and trade institutions such as the IMF and GATT, each country individually implemented Keynesian policy interventions. Under these new institutions, workers accepted the "Taylorist simple labor" they had long rejected and worked to improve productivity. In other words, a compromise (rules of the game) between labor and management of "adoption of Taylorism in exchange for productivity-indexed wages" emerged in the wage–labor nexus. The adoption of Taylorism increased the efficiency of conveyer belt-type mass production and supported the circuit of "demand→productivity." The provision of productivity-indexed wages solidified the "productivity → wages" relationship. Both labor and management pushed stockholders to the "outside," so to speak, and formed a kind of labor and management alliance. Mediated by this "labor–management alliance-type" mode of régulation, a virtuous macroeconomic cycle of the wage and consumption-led type was stably realized. This was the secret of the rapid growth of the "Fordist-type" mode of development, and here capitalism experienced a major transformation from the "British-type" mode of development that had been predominant in the 19th century.

The growth regime of Fordism is often summarized as "mass production – mass consumption," and in that case the Fordist mode of development as a whole, including its mode of régulation, is as shown in Fig. 4.3. If it can be said that "Fordism" is a growth regime of "mass production – mass consumption" at the level of national economies, then what is critically important to understand is that it was guided and established by "Taylorism – productivity-indexed wages" rules of the game between labor and management.

This Fordism encountered a structural crisis in the 1970s. It was dubbed the "stagflation" crisis and represented a third major structural crisis following the Long Depression at the end of the 19th century and the Great Depression of the

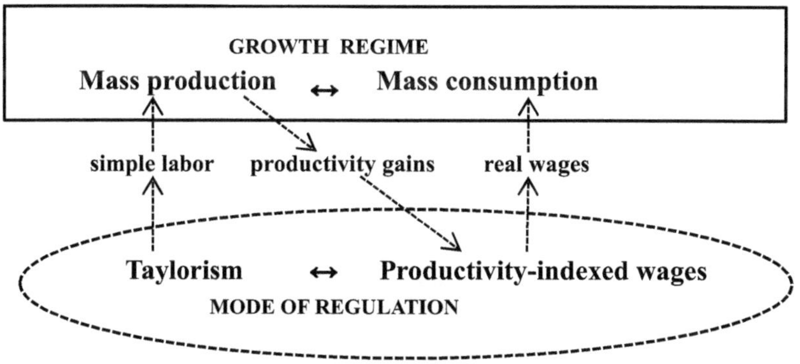

Fig. 4.3 Simplified schematization of the Fordist mode of development. (Source: Author)

1930s. The "Nixon shock" and "oil shock" were events that symbolized this crisis, but in the view of régulation theory it went beyond the dimension of currency and commodity prices and traced its origins deeper in the foundations of Fordism. Firstly, in its production/labor aspect, "mass production," the principle of efficient operation based on Taylorism, had reached its limit. Further simplification and fragmentation of work led to fatigue and resistance in workers. The general population that had become materially wealthy through the spread of mass manufacturing of single types of products began to seek more variety or personalized goods and services, and this was not a demand to which Fordist mass production techniques could respond. In short, the increasing-returns circuit of "demand→productivity" malfunctioned, and the mechanism that increased productivity ceased to operate. Secondly, in its distribution aspect, as a result of the rapid growth caused by the success of Fordism not only realizing quasi-full employment and strengthening upward pressure on wages but also, through the concentration of the population in major cities, destroying rural solidarity and community institutions (concerning childcare, education, medical treatment, nursing care, and old age), Fordist capitalism found itself facing an enormous social security burden (that also constituted wages in a broad sense) which could not be dealt with by wages tied to productivity (which had already been reduced). In other words, the "productivity→wage" index circuit had also become paralyzed.

In this way Fordism hit a wall in both its production and distribution aspects. The mode of régulation based on a "Taylorism versus productivity-indexed wages" compromise between labor and management broke down, and the growth regime cycle of "*productivity→wages→consumption→investment→demand→productivity*" was torn to pieces and collapsed. There were factors such as the oil shock that accelerated it, but this is where the deeper causes of Fordism's structural crisis were to be found. What must be born in mind is that when Fordism's endogenous metabolism hit a certain threshold it reached a crisis, and that it encountered this crisis as a result of its own "success." Capitalism is thus a phenomenon that is in constant transition and whose mode of development is also constantly being altered.

4.3.2 Historical Transformations in Capitalism

When the capitalism of postwar developed nations is understood in this way as the "growth and crisis of Fordism," a new way of looking at the history of capitalism up until this Fordism also emerges. In most cases, the development of capitalism since the 19th century has been understood with a focus on the state of competition in the form of a shift from free competition to monopoly capitalism. But when the history of capitalism is examined from the angles of institutional forms, modes of régulation, growth regimes, and crises pioneered by régulation theory, we are able to obtain a new understanding of history in terms of changes in modes of development. Let us lay this out here with a focus on capitalism in hegemonic countries.

The 19th century was an era during which Britain held sway over the globe. Having been the first country in the world to complete its industrial revolution, by establishing a competitive labor market with the abolition of the Speenhamland Law (1834) and a free trade system through the international gold standard and the abolition of the Corn Law (1846), it then positioned itself as the "world's factory" and the "world's bank." This is often referred to as the era of "Victorian prosperity." It is also the era in which capitalism established itself for the first time under its own power. The foundation of economic power lay in the factory system that revolved around mechanized large-scale industry, production centered on the production goods sector expanded, and corresponding increases in productivity were recorded. That said, however, in the dimension of labor, it was not as though the skill and autonomy of workers were dismantled in all aspects, and in the dimension of consumption wages were kept low through competitive low remuneration and there was no revolution in consumer lifestyles. Obviously development of the consumption goods sector was therefore left behind, and consumer demand did not occupy a prominent place in the macroeconomy. For the most part, economic growth depended more on quantitative expansion of the population and the scale of factories than on increases in productivity, and so-called "extensive" growth continued.

To rephrase all of this in terms of the concept of régulation, this era constitutes an "extensive growth regime," and if we diagram its growth in a bit more detail, we get something like Fig. 4.4 (see Boyer 2015: 76). If we exclude foreign trade for the sake of simplification, the driving macroeconomic force is found in investment (premised on corporate profits), and a virtuous economic cycle is realized on the basis of a macroeconomic circular relationship of "*profit→investment→productivity→production (=demand)→employment→wages→profit*." Focusing on its driving force, this can be characterized as a "profit and investment-led" growth regime. The issue is the mode of régulation that undergirds this growth regime. A competitive wage–labor nexus that leads mainly to starvation wages, free competition between corporations, and a noninterventionist form of the state régulate this growth regime. Polanyi describes this era and refers to it as a "self-regulating market" (Polanyi 2001), and these were indeed the "rules of the game" for this period. In short, a "market competition-type" mode of régulation centered on labor power as a commodity guided a "profit and investment-led type" growth regime. Taken as a whole,

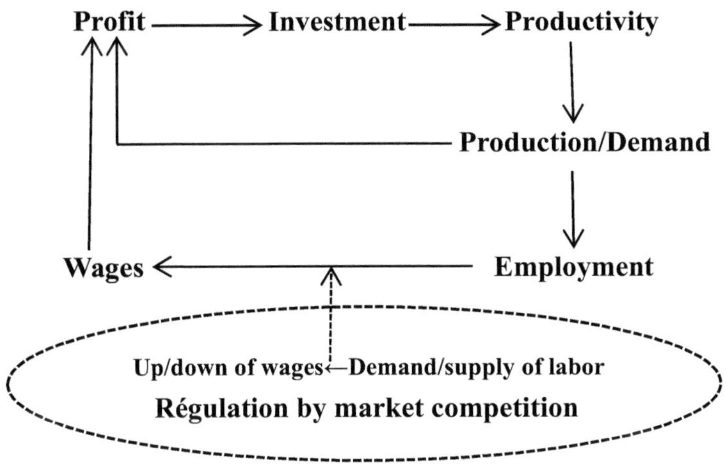

Fig. 4.4 Growth regime and mode of régulation in the British mode of development. (Source: Author, based largely on Boyer (2015: 76))

let us call this the "British-type" mode of development. This was the capitalism Marx observed. And what is generally referred to as the "Long Depression" (1873–1896) was the structural crisis of this British-type mode of development.

In the midst of this structural crisis, signs of a new mode of development that would break free of it emerged not in Britain but in the new country of America. America did not achieve genuine hegemony until the second half of the 20th century, but economically America's era had already begun in its first half; the beginning of the 20th century saw the emergence of the "scientific management" of Frederic W. Taylor and the conveyer belt-type mass production techniques of Henry Ford. These were a revolution in technology and management that sought to surpass the old British factory system that had become a factor impeding productivity. They involved a move from dependence on skill to the dismantling of skill (Taylorism), from an autonomous rhythm of work to simple operations and piece rate wages, from the production of production goods to automobiles, a consumption good, and from low wages to high wages (in the case of Ford's company). Then, following the First World War, in America the 1920s ushered in a temporary era of frenetic growth in both consumption and finance called the "roaring twenties."

During this period, however, Ford's policy of high wages was by no means spread throughout the entire country, and most of the general population was still bound by low competitive wages as they had been in the past. Whether one cites increases in productivity or the parallel development of the production of production goods and consumption goods, the growth regime had a strongly "intensive" coloring, but when it came to its mode of régulation it was still governed by the "market competition-type" régulation of the 19th century, and since the resulting low wages could not form sufficient purchasing power, mass production did not lead to mass consumption. Eventually this contradiction exploded as the "Great

Depression" of the 1930s. This was proof that a market competition-type mode of régulation was not suited to an intensive growth regime and constituted a second structural crisis following the Long Depression at the end of the 19th century. In the midst of this crisis, the search began for new institutional forms, such as the policies of the New Deal and Keynesian economics, until eventually WWII (1939–1945) broke out.

This period of the first half of the 20th century can also be described as "an intensive growth regime without mass consumption." But while it included a period of temporary prosperity, this era marked by violent panic and two global conflicts must be seen as not having been blessed with a firm and distinctive growth regime, as the term "growth regime" assumes a regime with a certain degree of durability and stability. In this sense, the first half of the 20th century can be positioned as a "long transition period" between the British-type mode of development and the Fordist-type mode of development. Capitalism was mediated during this "long transition period," and its mode of development was greatly transformed from the 19th century to the Fordism of the second half of the 20th century. This is the picture of the history of capitalism that emerges when we make full use of the various concepts of régulation theory.

4.4 Finance-Led Economies and the Diversity of Capitalism

In the previous two sections, I have looked at the main content of régulation theory in its founding period and its introduction to Japan from the second half of the 1980s to the first half of the 1990s. With this as my starting point, in the following chapters I will examine what kind of analyses of the Japanese economy were developed by Japanese régulationists. In what remains of this chapter I will jump ahead and lay out how régulation theory in France developed following this period (see also Petit 2005). From the second half of the 1990s to the present day in the 21st century, régulation theory has been developed in truly diverse ways in various countries around the world. Here I present a greatly simplified overview of this development focusing on only two points, the debate over the "finance-led mode of development" and the "diversity of capitalism."

4.4.1 The Finance-Led Mode of Development

From the 1970s onward, a search for new institutions to replace the Fordism that had encountered a crisis was pursued in various countries. Needing to break through the bottleneck of domestic demand, countries looked for a way forward through demand for exports, and economic globalization proceeded at a rapid pace. Amidst Japan and other Asian countries expanding exports to America, and Europe changing course toward European market integration that would secure its own markets, only the United States of America was bemoaning an industrial collapse – this was the global economic backdrop in the 1970s and 1980s. Then, in the 1990s, the American economy staged a powerful recovery. This rejuvenated America was not an industrial America but a financial (and information technology) America. The America of Detroit had become the America of Wall Street. What had occurred in this country?

Institutional forms changed completely. Most saliently workers were banished from corporations, and management and stockholders developed a closer bond. The alliances between management and labor that had existed in the past were destroyed, and cooperation between management and stockholders was strengthened. Activist stockholders became powerful within institutional investors (pension funds, insurance companies, investment trusts, hedge funds, and so on). These stockholders demanded high financial returns from companies, and the pressure to adopt management that prioritized stock prices (stockholder sovereignty) increased. These stockholders not only applied pressure but also came up with institutional apparatuses such as stock options to make high stock prices advantageous to managers themselves, and here a compromise between managers and financiers emerged regarding high stock prices. This power of finance, as an institutional apparatus positioned above all other institutions, came to occupy the highest position in the institutional hierarchy.

In other words, the institutional domain of the wage–labor nexus that had played the most prominent role in the bygone Fordist era had now become a subordinate institution dominated by monetary and financial relations (and bearing in mind international finance, at the same time by the international regime). This wage–labor nexus that had become subordinate to finance expanded flexible and unstable employment, caused wages to stagnate, and, when it came to social security, was content to retrench welfare through "workfare" policies. To make up for decreased income and income instability, workers' dependence on finance was again strengthened, whether in the form of consumer loans or investment in stocks for the purposes of capital gains. In terms of the forms of the state, deregulation and privatization were promoted in the name of "small government," the dependence of the state on the financial markets was strengthened because of a need to cover budget deficits, and these financial markets then leveled demands for austerity policies. It goes without saying that this transformation of institutional forms was deeply connected to the ideology of "neoliberalism."

These new institutions created a new macroeconomic configuration as shown in Fig. 4.5 (Aglietta 1998; Boyer 2000; Yamada 2008). The economy's driving force lies in increases in asset prices (stock prices, home prices, and so on). Stated in stronger terms, it is an asset bubble. The driving force is no longer to be found in industrial productivity but has shifted to the financial variable of asset prices. And these asset prices are connected to financial returns. This causes a rise in the financial income of institutional investors and households, particularly those of the wealthy class, and consumption expands through this asset effect. Since high stock prices make it easier for corporations to raise funds, this stimulates investment. In Fig. 4.5 other demand elements are abstracted, so this consumption and investment

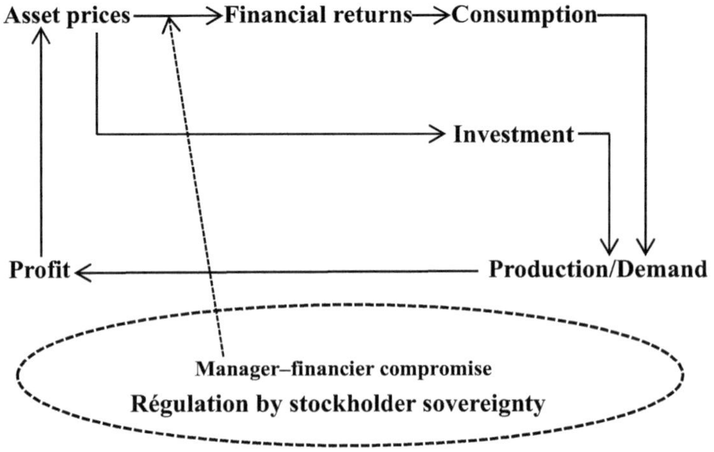

Fig. 4.5 Growth regime and mode of régulation in the finance-led mode of development. (Source: Author)

comprise the total demand, and in short the economy grows. This economic growth increases corporate profits, and these increased profits give rise to the expectation of even greater profits which further increases the price of these corporations' stock. To sum up, an *asset prices→financial returns→consumption→investment→demand →profit→asset prices* cycle led by financial variables, in other words, a "finance-led" growth regime, was formed in the United States in the 1990s.

What played a pivotal role in supporting this growth regime was the institutional apparatus that connected the increase in asset prices to the increase in financial returns just described. Financial returns include not only income gains and capital gains belonging to stockholders but also the stock options managers can expect to obtain, and here a symbiotic compromise between managers and stockholders arises that régulates the new growth regime. This is a "stockholder sovereignty" mode of régulation. It was in the United States from the 1990s onward that a mode of development that can be called "finance-led," based on this kind of finance-led growth regime and stockholder sovereignty mode of régulation, took shape. At the end of the 20th century, history had clearly turned the page on the era of Fordism, and the hegemonic country's capitalism had embarked on the path of a new mode of development.

With the possible exception of Britain, however, this new mode of development did not spread to any countries other than America. While in this sense it was not a universal phenomenon, its international impact was large, and countries around the world were forced to deal with the pressure of financial liberalization. And with its aspects that engendered bubbles, this mode of development was extremely unstable. In fact, as was shown by the 2008 Lehman shock and ensuing global panic after 15 years of growth under the "new economy," it seems to have reached its period of structural crisis, referred to in this instance as a "global financial crisis" (Boyer 2011).

4.4.2 The Diversity of Capitalism

This chapter has examined the history of changes in modes of development with a focus on hegemonic countries, but world history is not driven only by hegemons. Even among the so-called developed nations, not all of these countries are necessarily the same as America and Britain, nor do they necessarily converge on the Anglo–American model. While at first régulation theory presented a view of "national varieties of Fordism," eventually research on individual countries made it clear that Fordism was not so universal, leading to the creation of a "bifurcation of national trajectories" hypothesis that addressed the global structure after Fordism (Boyer 1990b). Various approaches were put forward, but none of them went beyond a typical pattern centered around the wage–labor nexus. A genuine theory of the diversity of capitalism from the régulation school did not arrive until Amable (2003).

Amable's argument is built on a critical continuation of the varieties of capitalism (VOC) approach. Prominent VOC text Hall and Soskice (2001) strikingly asserts the existence of the German model (referred to as "coordinated market economies (CMEs)," examples of which were also considered to include Northern European countries and Japan) in contrast to the American model (referred to as "liberal market economies (LMEs)," examples of which also included various Anglo–Saxon nations). These two types of capitalism differed in their institutional structures, and these differences are manifested in differences in their capacity for innovation and industrial comparative advantages. What Amable valued in this approach was its taking the American liberal market model as a kind of standard for comparisons of capitalism and that it furthermore criticized the view of global convergence on this model. Amable's criticism of VOC, on the other hand, lay in its forcing Northern European nations and Japan into the German model and treating major Western European countries like France and Italy that did not belong to either model as constituting exceptional types.

Eschewing comparison settings biased toward a particular country or institution, Amable then conducted a comparison of the 21 OECD nations encompassing numerous institutions stretching across 5 institutional domains (product markets, labor markets, finance, welfare, and education). In addition to qualitative/theoretical analysis, layers of quantitative techniques (factor analysis and cluster analysis) were added, and ultimately "five capitalisms" were distinguished. These were the market-based model (America, Britain, Canada, Australia), the Asian model (Japan, South Korea), the Continental European model (Germany, France, Austria, the Netherlands, etc.), the social democratic model (Northern Europe), and the Mediterranean model (Italy, Spain, Greece, Portugal). Amable plots the resulting measurements on a graph with "market" and "welfare" axes as shown in Fig. 4.6.

Looking at this figure, the following points become clear. (1) The similarities between the countries characterized as LMEs ("market-based" in Amable) in the VOC approach are high, and they are clearly distinguished from other models. In this sense, the market-based model is the starting point for comparisons of different forms of capitalism. (2) When it comes to CMEs, on the other hand, there are strong

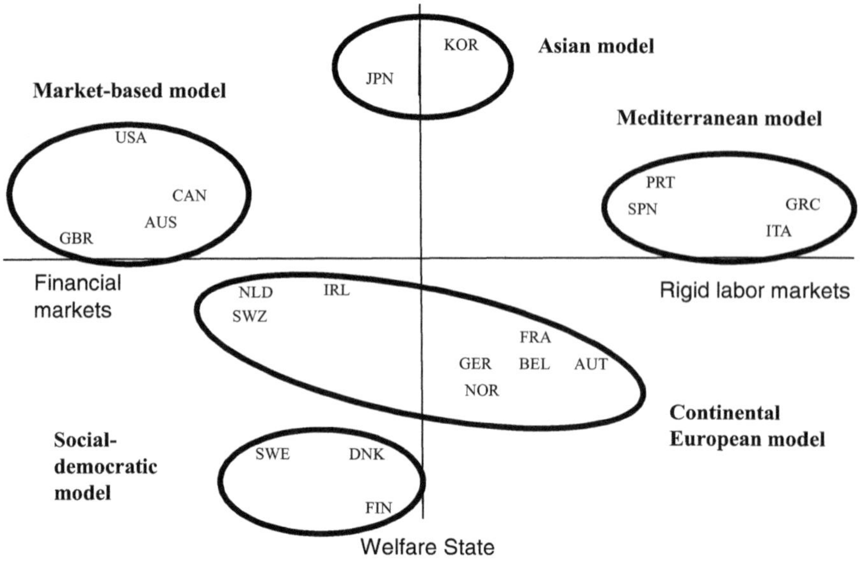

Fig. 4.6 Typology of capitalism for the main OECD countries. (Source: Amable (2003: 176) slightly modified by the author)

differences between countries that make it difficult to gather them together as a single model, and they must be divided into Continental European model, social democratic model, and Asian model economies. (3) In the sense of the degree of market liberalization, the polar opposite of the American model is not the Asian, social democratic, or Continental European model, but the Mediterranean model. We should therefore be cautious in representing the comparison of capitalist models as the comparison of Germany and America, Japan and America, or Northern Europe and America. (4) Germany and France are grouped together in the Continental European model, thereby critically overcoming the deficiencies regarding France in the VOC approach. (5) Italy is also classified as belonging to the Mediterranean model, overcoming one of the difficulties of the VOC model.

In addition, regarding the hypothesis of convergence on the American model, when we compare the position of the various countries on the axes shown above at the end of the 1980s and the end of the 1990s, not so much change is seen. In other words, convergence on the American model is not observed, so this view can be rejected; the development of capitalism continues to be diverse in the midst of globalization.

4.5 Conclusion

In this chapter I have attempted to present the theory and view of history of French régulation theory as generally understood by people in Japan after it was introduced here in the 1980s (I also included a follow-up on the latest discourse from the 1990s onward in the previous section). Among the various aspects of this theory, in Japan the strongest impression was made by its view of Fordism.

Through its concept of Fordism, this régulation theory that analyzed postwar developed economies achieved quite astounding success. But this astounding success at the same time sowed the seeds of confusion. Postwar Japanese economic growth could not be fit so easily into the framework of "Fordism," and presumably could not be completely explained by it. Faced with this enigma, Japanese régulationists were inevitably forced to look for revisions of the original theory's concepts and methods. In Boyer's words, "it [régulation theory] has not ceased to rework its concepts, its methods, and to extend its scope of application" (Boyer 2015), and its analysis in Japan was no exception. The first results of Japanese analysis emerging from this confusion were the hypotheses of "companyist régulation" and "hierarchical market-firm nexus." The former, as we will see in the next chapter, shifts the focus variable from a Fordist "wage" compromise to a different "employment" compromise, and the latter is an attempt to grasp the complex whole composed out of the supplementary nature of different institutions and their hierarchical systems.

When Japan is analyzed with concepts created in the West, what falls outside of these concepts has generally been treated as "old-fashioned," "delayed," or "distorted." But when this approach is taken, the analysis will inevitably miss the mark. The structural complexity possessed by Japanese society and the Japanese economy is discarded. This was also the problem identified by Japanese civil society theory in the past; the complex nature of Japanese society that cannot be summarized with the equation "capitalism = modernization" must be included in our field of view. This will be covered in detail in the next chapter, but Japan's social and economic structure cannot be understood without a keen awareness of the complex relationship between this nation's society and economy, and here there is a strong connection to issues concerning civil society in Japan. Looking at the current state of affairs in which the spread of "omnipotent market" prescriptions and the convergence on the American model view have had real, negative consequences, it is clearly very important to keep this in mind.

References

Aglietta, Michel (1979) *A Theory of Capitalist Regulation: The US Experience*, London: NLB. Translated from the French: *Régulation et crises du capitalisme: L'expérience des Etats-Unis*, Paris: Calmann-Lévy, 1976.

——— (1997) *Régulation et crises du capitalisme*, Nouvelle édition revue et corrigée, augmentée d'une postface inédite, Paris: Odile Jacob.

——— (1998) 'Le capitalisme de demain,' *Notes de la Fondation Saint-Simon*, 101.

Amable, Bruno (2003) *The Diversity of Modern Capitalism*, Oxford: Oxford University Press.

Boyer, Robert (1990a) *The Regulation School: A Critical Introduction*, New York: Columbia University Press. Translated from the French: *La théorie de la régulation: Une analyse critique*, Paris: La Découverte, 1986.

——— (1990b) 'The Capital Labour Relations in OECD Countries,' *CEPREMAP*, 9020.

——— (2000) 'Is a Finance-led Growth Regime a Viable Alternative to Fordism?: A Preliminary Analysis,' *Economy and Society*, 29(1).

——— (2011) *Les financiers détruiront-ils le capitalisme?*, Paris: Economica.
——— (2015) *Economie politique des capitalismes: Théorie de la régulation et des crises*, Paris: La Découverte.
Hall, Peter and David Soskice eds. (2001) *Varieties of Capitalism: The Institutional Foundations of Comparative Advantages*, Oxford: Oxford University Press.
Maddison, Angus (1991) *Dynamic Forces in Capitalist Development: A Long-run Comparative View*, Oxford and New York: Oxford University Press.
Petit, Pascal (2005) *Croissance et richesse des nations*, Paris: La Découverte.
Polanyi, Karl (2001) *The Great Transformation: The Political and Economic Origins of Our Times*, Boston: Beacon Press; First published in 1944.
Uchida, Yoshihiko (1966) *Shihonron no Sekai* (*The World of* Capital), Tokyo: Iwanami Shoten Publishers; in *Uchida Yoshihiko Chosakushū* (*Collected Works of Yoshihiko Uchida*: *CWYU*) 4, Tokyo, Iwanami Shoten Publishers,
——— (1967) *Nihon Shihonshugi no Shisō-zō* (*Intellectual Portrait of Japanese Capitalism*), Tokyo: Iwanami Shoten Publishers; in *CWYU* 5.
——— (1981) *Sakuhin toshite no Shakai Kagaku* (*Social Science as a Popular Work*), Tokyo: Iwanami Shoten Publishers; in *CWYU* 8.
Vogel, Ezra F. (1979) *Japan as No.1: Lessons for America*, Cambridge and London: Harvard University Press.
Yamada, Toshio (1993) *Regyurashion Riron: Keizaigaku no Saisei* (*Régulation Theory: Renaissance of Political Economy*), Tokyo: Kōdansha.
——— (2008) *Samazamana Shihonshugi: Hikaku Shihonshugi Bunseki* (*Various Capitalisms: A Comparative Analysis of Capitalism*), Tokyo: Fujiwara Shoten Publishers.

Chapter 5
Postwar Japanese Capitalism and Companyist Régulation

5.1 Companyist Régulation

During the long global recession of the 1970s and 1980s, Japan's high productivity growth rate enabled it to launch a huge export offensive and become an economic superpower. Yet after going from a period of high growth (the 1950s and 1960s) to a period of real economic power (1970s and 1980s), Japan underwent drastic change during the so-called lost decades beginning in the 1990s. During the past 30 years, Japanese capitalism has experienced a humiliating reversal of fortunes from industrial winner to economic failure. It is no exaggeration to say that Japanese capitalism stands poised at one of the most important crossroads in its history.

If we define the term "postwar era" as referring mainly to the period from the 1950s to the 1990s, what has been the nature of Japanese capitalism in the postwar era, especially in the period following the first oil shock? And how is it changing today? Régulation theory and its advocates have sought to identify the Japanese system's "mode of development" and then to explain the nature of the "crisis" it has encountered and the transformations it has been undergoing. To achieve this goal, it is necessary, as we saw in the previous chapter, to identify the major "institutional forms" that regulate the mode of development, determine the nature of the overarching "mode of régulation" that they create, and ultimately identify the "growth regime" or "regime of accumulation" that they generate. This should allow us to identify the nature of the crisis that has been afflicting Japan since the 1990s and determine the means by which it might be resolved.

Having posited this basic framework and methodology, the main purpose of this chapter is to present a hypothesis regarding the mode of régulation which has guided the postwar Japanese mode of development. The mode of régulation posited by régulation theory includes five major institutional forms: the wage–labor nexus, monetary and financial relations, forms of competition or intercompany relations, forms of the state, and the international regime (see Chap. 4). Here, the focus is the

T. Yamada, *Contemporary Capitalism and Civil Society*, Evolutionary Economics and Social Complexity Science 14,
https://doi.org/10.1007/978-981-13-0517-7_5

wage–labor nexus and monetary and financial relations (with some reference to intercompany relations). Labor and finance are key factors in the mode of régulation; furthermore, they lie at the heart of the Japanese economy and are thus crucial to achieving a full understanding of the long-lasting crisis.

In presenting this chapter's basic thesis, the postwar Japanese mode of régulation can be described as "companyist régulation" or a "companyist compromise." The two pillars of the companyist compromise are a labor–management compromise (or a labor–capital compromise) predicated on employment security and a financial compromise predicated on management security, and it is constructed through the complementarity that arises between them. The impressive initial success and subsequent failure of Japanese capitalism from the 1970s to the 1990s and beyond can be explained in terms of the compatibility and the incompatibility of these two accords. The key to dissecting and examining the Japanese economy is this *companyism*.

It is commonly claimed that you cannot understand prewar Japan without looking at farming villages and you cannot understand postwar Japan without looking at companies. The poverty of villages is often considered to have been an essential part of the foundation of the imperialism and militarism of the prewar era. Similarly, the prosperity of companies might be regarded as the secret of the rapid growth and rise to economic superpower status of postwar Japan and of its peculiar company-centered social composition as well. So much so that the distinctive organizational group of the company holds the key to understanding postwar Japan. Whether its influence is judged in terms of the macroeconomy or institutional forms, neither the market nor the state nor civil society, unions, regions, or even the family exercises a more decisive influence than the company. Companyism and the meanings embodied within this term must be considered at the outset (Baba 1997).

5.2 The Labor–Management Compromise at the Level of the Company

5.2.1 Unlimited Duties in Exchange for Employment Security

The companyist accord rests on two pillars, the labor–management compromise and the financial compromise, and is built on the isomorphic and complementary structural relationship that exists between them. The two major resources of companies being human and financial, their most important functions are labor management and financial management. While the main aim of this chapter is to analyze the interactions and distinctive institutions of these two principal components, we will look first at labor and the formation of the postwar labor–management compromise, and in particular at the regular male workers in large companies who typify it (and who are often regarded as constituting the primary stratum of the labor market). In reality, of course, this stratum cannot be taken to represent the entire Japanese wage–labor nexus because it exists in a close and complementary relationship with the secondary labor market stratum, but a discussion of this relationship is beyond the scope of this chapter. The broader system including the dual labor market and subcontracting system is addressed, for example, by the "hierarchical market–firm nexus" (HMFN) hypothesis proposed in close cooperation with our companyism hypothesis (Ebizuka et al. 1997; Isogai et al. 2000). Here we will therefore focus only on regular male workers at large firms. This is not merely because they constituted some 20–30% of the total workforce, but because their accord with management served as the dominant model of social values in postwar Japan.

What is the fundamental basis of the labor–management compromise? The usual answer to this question is "employment" or "continuous employment." A large body of research has emphasized this point. For example, Nitta (1995) has stated, "One of the most important issues of the postwar labor movement has been preventing dismissals." Accordingly, "Since dismissals were bad, an unspoken agreement that they should be avoided was established between labor and management." As a result, this agreement became a sort of social principle or norm. The protection and stabilization of employment became the core principle of postwar industrial relations in Japan.

This was in strong contrast to the United States, where, as Aoki observes, "the American union is more concerned with wage issues than job security issues" (1988: 92). The Fordism-oriented American industrial relations compromise has emphasized wages rather than employment security. To extend this point a bit further, the emphasis on wages means that it might indeed be categorized as a compromise: *the acceptance of Taylorism by workers* in exchange for *the provision of productivity-indexed wages by managers*.

In contrast, the major point of contention in Japan was the establishment of a compromise emphasizing jobs and job security. In brief, managers extended strong employment guarantees to workers, while workers acceded to the "unlimited duties" demanded by management (see Table 5.1).

"Unlimited duties" mean "it is strongly expected that the members of a given organization will exercise responsibilities and duties whose limits are not specified, and whose natures are difficult to foresee" (Iwata 1977). The conditions and hours of work to be performed by employees are not clearly specified in their contracts with their organization.

Both the nature and degree of employees' everyday duties, and of their future tasks as well, are thus highly amorphous and subject to constant change. Major

Table 5.1 Comparison of the US and Japanese labor–management compromises

	On	Labor	↔	Management
United States (Fordism)	Wages	Acceptance of Taylorism		Provision of wages indexed to productivity
	Employment	Limits on the nature and duration of duties		Flexible dismissal
Japan (Companyism)	Employment	Acceptance of unlimited duties		Provision of employment security

Source: Author

companies guarantee the employment of their regular male workers in return for the acceptance of these unlimited duties. Since some dismissals and so-called involuntary early retirement do occur, it would be more precise to state that there is no absolute guarantee of job security, but rather an unspoken commitment by management to exert itself to avoid dismissals. That being said, the following discussion uses the term "job or employment security" as a convenient description of Japanese practice. As noted above, we may characterize Japan's wage–labor nexus in terms of the following concessions: *the acceptance of unlimited duties by workers* in exchange for *the provision of employment security by managers*.

5.2.2 Japanese and American Compromises Compared

In the American Fordist system, labor demanded wages indexed to productivity as compensation for its acceptance of monotonous, Taylorist labor, whereas workers in Japan gained job security in compensation for their concessions to management in accepting unlimited duties. Moreover, this is not simply job security, but the continuous protection of employment carried out within the context of a unified company structure. This means that it is a companyist form of job security. Thus the distinctive feature of the Japanese compromise is that it is fundamentally based on employment rather than wages.

If the main emphasis in the labor–management compromise is placed on employment, then we can see that this is not, of course, an element in the American Fordist system. Managers in the United States are guaranteed the freedom to dismiss workers. Of course, contemporary economic systems have institutionalized legal protections for workers, so that even American managers no longer enjoy unlimited power to fire. Instead, certain rules (such as those based on seniority) have been enacted. In general, however, compared to Japan, there has been a social consensus supporting the use of dismissals as an employment adjustment measure. It is within the limitations of this consensus that managers possess the "freedom" to fire.

American workers commit themselves to their firms only partially or functionally; in short, they ensure that there are "limited duties" (limits on the nature and duration of their duties). In order to enforce these limits, unions exercise checks on management or job control. Thus, if the American compromise is primarily about the nature of employment, then the trade-off of the acceptance of Taylorism for guarantees of the freedom to fire (the reverse side of the Fordist wage-centered compromise) may be bundled into a set with the trade-off of guarantees of limited duty for guarantees of the freedom to fire. In employment terms, Japan's job security guarantee can be seen as a complete inversion of the American compromise, because it involves establishing a trade-off of the acceptance of unlimited duties against the provision of job security. The central foundation of the postwar Japanese labor–management accord is this "employment compromise."

If we reevaluate these labor–management compromises in the United States and Japan from the perspective of "flexibility," we can make the following observations.

The institutionalization of "unlimited duties and job security" (in Japan) promotes flexibility in reassigning tasks and job content (internal and functional flexibility), but job security means restrictions are placed on flexibility in deciding the number of workers (external and quantitative flexibility). In contrast, "limits on jobs and freedom of dismissal" (in the United States) mean that quantitative flexibility is guaranteed. In short, there is a mixture of flexibility and rigidity in either system. But unlike the "flexible job content – rigid employee numbers" (for regular male employees of large firms) found in Japan, the United States features "rigid job content – flexible employee numbers." In general, companies must assure themselves some means of adjusting flexibly to external environmental changes such as technological innovation or economic shifts, but the means of adjustment differ between the two countries. Miyamoto (1998) identified institutional differences in corporate governance between management-dominated companies (in Japan) and shareholder-dominated companies (in the United States) as the basis for the differences between "rigid employment adjustment and flexible job definition" (in Japan) and "flexible employment adjustment and rigid job definition" (in the United States).

5.3 Background of the Employment Compromise in Japan

5.3.1 American and Japanese Workers Under Capitalism

Why does the Japanese labor–management compromise center on employment rather than wages? Questions about how Japanese workers perceived industrial relations and how they tried to resolve their problems are easier to answer if we compare them with workers in the West (see Kurita 1994). The West is diverse, however, and this chapter focuses primarily on American Fordism. Europe is considered through this "stylized fact" only to the extent that its institutions are congruent with those of the United States.

The basic problem is that while on the one hand contemporary society as a whole extols the freedom and equality of people in civil society, on the other hand it seeks to establish the domination of authority in capitalist society. Inside a company, this means that while workers demand equality in their relations with management, in reality they must accept a subordinate position. In this regard, the problem faced by workers in both Japan and the West is essentially the same. The difference is in the attempted means of resolving it. Here there is a conspicuous contrast.

In the West, workers acknowledge and accept their subordinate status and then deal with it by compartmentalizing and limiting the internal tasks of the company into functional roles. Workers limit the maximum scope of their own duties within companies, contractualize them, and then submit only to orders pertaining to duties lying within the scope of these contracts. They seek to establish themselves as nothing other than the subject of contracts. In this manner, on the basis of concepts of freedom, equality, and ownership, workers fully ensure their equal status with those (managers) who purchase labor power as a commodity from those (workers) who are selling it. Labor power is organized as a commodity product, and its purchasing conditions are established through contracts with management. After it has been purchased, workers prevent the arbitrary use of this labor power through job control unionism. The resolution to the problem of internal company submission is achieved through the equality of the market and by the use of union restrictions. In other words, workers must accept a subordinate status, but by using contractual relationships or by "clarifying" (limiting) contractual obligations, this submission is compensated and limits are placed on the domination of capital.

Japanese workers also acknowledge their inferior status, but they conceive of it on an individual-by-individual basis in limited terms as something that is temporary and transitory. Social and market relations are confirmed outside of the company, so submission is not something spatially limited to within the firm; rather, in Japan's case, it is a temporary stage in one's personal history or career path. The problem of submission is to be resolved, so to speak, by the passage of time.

However, there is an essential condition for the acceptance and understanding of this temporary submission: one's status as a worker must be fully acknowledged (Saguchi 1991). Further, both labor force and management must maintain the understanding that all workers in a single company are "producers" as well as "workers" and are therefore homogeneous and equal. Japanese workers are not divided within their companies but united on the basis of human relationships. They have not dealt with the reality of submission (authority relations) by checking them from the outside, but have attenuated them (where there are differences in rank) by using parent-child, family, and peer relations to foster the perception of homogeneity. The abolition of status differentials between blue and white-collar workers and the formation of company unions after the war strengthened this perception.

Whereas contractual relations in the West are premised on differences among workers and managers, Japanese workers have sought "trust" relations based upon the homogeneity of all company members. Whereas Western workers have held capitalist domination in check by relying on human rights granted by civil society, Japanese workers attenuated it by appealing to norms of community/family relationships.

But Japanese workers did not stop at obtaining "equality" in this fashion. The belief that subordinate status is temporary naturally gives rise to an eruption of energy from the worker that should in the future elevate him to a higher status: the competition for promotion. Ultimately, this is a pursuit of equality that enables workers to achieve (or approach) managerial status. Stated the other way around, there is not the sort of class-based difference between workers and managers seen in the West; in Japan, we can think of the differences as being instead among the workers themselves (Hanada 1997). Labor–management relations can be regarded not as a discontinuation of class, but as a continuous stairway on which an individual's status is determined by differences across time. In comparison with the Western practices of ensuring equality through spatial limits to subordination (in workplaces) and market (class) restrictions, equality is promoted through time-based (subjective) limits to subordination and (individual) efforts to escape subordination.

5.3.2 *Employment Compromise and Company Growth Compromise*

Let us next consider the issue of employment. The major premise of the Japanese approach to managing subordination and equality is that workers will affiliate continuously with a single company, building long-term relations with it. Needless to say, this long-term affiliation to a company constitutes job security itself. Only if employment is continued in the same company does the hope of escaping a present status of subordination present itself. Of course, even if a person pursues his (or, occasionally, her) career in just one company, in reality the number that can successfully escape subordination through promotion is small. However, in a Japanese firm, all employees can, at least at the beginning of their careers, see the superficial and exoteric opening of the possibility of promotion. Even if these possibilities with which they are presented are merely lip service or illusion, it is the continuation of employment that is of greatest importance to workers.

The path to equality for Western workers lies in compartmentalizing and limiting the reality of being employed. In contrast, the path chosen by Japanese workers is to maintain and indeed maximize their status of being employed; what they have striven to limit is the reality of losing one's job. The Japanese pursue equality within employment. This is the dominant vision of employment for Japanese workers. Differently stated, Western workers have bargained within the framework of *accepting subordination* in exchange for *job control*, while Japanese workers have, figuratively speaking, bargained within the framework of *accepting subordination* in exchange for *job loss control* (see Table 5.2).

In other words, Japanese do not seek to restrict the contents of duties – of jobs – but rather to reduce the possibility of job loss. In contrast to Western workers, who have refused the extension of labor content beyond what is contractually stipulated but have in a sense accepted the risk of job loss, Japanese workers have refused job loss as a violation of their settlement with management, but have accepted the extension or alteration of the content of their labor.

From another point of view, regarding the dominant-subordinate personal relations of employment relationships, Western workers have attempted to protect themselves by "sectioning (clarifying) relationships" or through "contractual relationships," while Japanese workers have, in contrast, tried to protect themselves by forming "personal (long-term) relationships" and "relationships of trust." As I will explain in the following section, long-term and trust-based relationships are not distinctive features of employment relations alone but also of institutional structures

Table 5.2 What US and Japanese workers got at the price of their subordination to management

	Acceptance of	↔	Gain of
American workers	Subordination to management		Job control (= limited duties)
Japanese workers	Subordination to management		"Job loss control" (= employment security)

Source: Author

such as intercompany relations and company–bank relations. Grasping this phenomenon is essential to understanding the Japanese mode of régulation in the postwar era.

Needless to say, the employment transaction is not expressly stipulated in writing but exists in the form of unspoken agreements between labor and management. As a result, management is sometimes able to assert its power advantage, but even in these cases, managers in large companies still see fit to establish the employment compromise, even if only in formal terms. Such practices indicate that the employment compromise embedded in the structure of Japanese companies constitutes the fundamental compromise in Japan. It is because of this fundamental compromise that Japanese workers hurl themselves into meritocratic competition within firms, while on the outside they apply themselves with equal fervor to winning the battle for market share for the firms to which they are affiliated. The labor–management compromise in postwar Japan was a structure of *employment compromise–meritocratic compromise–company growth compromise* centered within companies.

5.4 Financial Compromise and Management Security

5.4.1 The Main Bank System and Cross-Shareholding

The above sections have examined companyist régulation through a focus on labor. As stated at the beginning of the chapter, human and financial resources are a company's most important assets, and this section will examine companyist régulation in terms of finance. Financial relations are not limited to the provision and procurement of capital, but include corporate governance and control of companies. In short, finance and governance are different aspects of the same structure.

Unlike in the United States, the prevalent form of capital procurement in postwar Japan has been indirect finance, notably bank loans. Although the importance of banks in Japan has declined, indirect finance has continued to play a much more important role than in the United States. Whereas the American and British forms of governance rely heavily on stock markets and market forces operating on company ownership, the bank loan-centered structure of finance in Japan has produced the "contingent governance" of monitoring by main banks (Aoki 1994). Furthermore, the company groups built around main banks have, through their shareholders, helped to support Japanese-style corporate governance. Corporate governance of major firms is implemented through both company–bank relations and intercompany relations, and this system corresponds to a main bank-based corporate financial structure. This finance–governance structure can be regarded as the result of the particular transactions and compromises accompanying Japan's company–bank relations and of mutual relations between companies within company groups.

One aspect of company–bank relations is that companies generally receive more financing from their main banks than is actually needed and therefore pay excess interest costs. This means that they extend special treatment to the banks in the conducting of financial transactions. In return, main banks not only provide information to company clients but also extend emergency assistance to troubled companies. By bearing the burden of high interest costs, companies receive valuable information and financing from main banks, as well as special assistance in case of distress. In short, Japanese companies overpay interest to main banks, but what they demand – and receive – in exchange is "management security" in the form of "continuous security" from the banks.

Management security, however, does not necessarily mean personal security for managers, and in fact their retirement and replacement are sometimes necessary. As the terms "long-term company security" and "management security" indicate, what is protected is the identity of the firm as a legal entity encompassing much more than its individual managers. It is only when this company identity is protected that it becomes possible to establish among employees a sense of membership in and identity with the firm.

In any case, the give-and-take financial relationship between firms and banks in the postwar era can be termed the Japanese financial compromise. We can formulate this compromise between companies and banks as *preferential treatment for banks* in exchange for *securing companies' continued existence.*

High-interest payments and other forms of preferential treatment extended to main banks can be regarded as premiums paid by companies to protect themselves from management risks. In general, it is well known that the capital procurement system simultaneously acts as a corporate governance system, but the most distinctive feature of the postwar Japanese financial structure is that it has also served as an insurance system to protect the long-term survival of companies. The company–bank relationships of postwar Japan underlay not only finance and governance relations but insurance relations as well.

These insurance relations were not based upon company–bank relationships alone. Intercompany relations in the form of cross-shareholding (within company groups) performed management security and insurance functions. Cross-shareholding developed as a means of preventing hostile takeovers of companies and promoting stable shareholding, so we can conjecture that the close company relations thus obtained have served as a means of strengthening management security. In reality, companies that are members of company groups earn lower returns than those that are not, proving that stability is more important to them (Nakatani 1984). Thus the formation of company groups has the effect of serving as a type of insurance as well as risk sharing. We can describe the individual company–company group compromise with the following formula: *preferential treatment for members of company groups* in exchange for *security of company management.*

Through this company relationship as well as the company–bank relationship, or rather the main bank-centered company group, postwar Japan's capital procurement/corporate governance system has simultaneously played the role of management security system. The unique nature of the Japanese financial system becomes more apparent when compared to the American financial system. In the United States, there is a division of labor among the distinct institutions that exercise monitoring and rule-making functions before, during, and after investment. These institutions are investment banks and venture capital (before investment), credit rating agencies and capital markets (during the course of investment), and hostile takeovers (after investment). These institutions are, of course, engaged solely in financial or investment transactions, or in related monitoring, and not in taking charge of management security or risk insurance for companies.

5.4.2 Implications of Japan's Financial Structure

The fact that the Japanese financial–corporate governance structure also provided a structure for ensuring the long-term survival of companies (management security) as described above has three important implications.

First, this financial compromise as a form of management insurance has a complementary relationship with the labor–management compromise underlying job security. Naturally, a crucial prerequisite for the realization of a job security compromise is that there should be continuity – stable continuity – of management. Stable shareholding serves as the "collateral" for stable employment, so the financial compromise underpins the employment compromise. In this regard, many studies have already indicated the complementarity of Japanese industrial relations (especially long-term employment), intercompany relations (cross-shareholding), and company–main bank relations (Aoki 1988; Sheard 1994; Aoki and Patrick 1994; Uemura et al. 1998).

Second, the distinctive feature of the postwar Japanese system has been the strong, long-term relationships between labor and management, among companies, and between companies and their banks. This feature stands out against American practice. The strong, long-term relations of the principals can be ascertained from the institutionalization of long-term employment in industrial relations, from *keiretsu* transactions and cross-shareholding in company groups, and from the long-term capital procurement, corporate governance, and management security supported by the main bank system. In this sense, there is a homologous relationship between the sectors. It is because the three forms interacted so closely that the postwar Japanese system functioned so well. Relationships of trust and cooperation were formed among principals in the Japanese system through their long-term relations, and these relations served at the same time as insurance and security networks, enabling the economy as a whole to achieve high efficiency. Of course, a virtuous cycle did not always materialize, nor could all causation be purely positive. The problem with close relations is that they can generate exclusivity as well as distrust toward and disinterest in outsiders, and they all too often have given rise to nontransparent and unfair practices.

Third, the postwar Japanese system was based on the foundations of the homologous and complementary relationship between labor and finance. The heart of the system is ultimately the security accorded to both employees and managers and thus the priority given to the perpetuation and growth of the firm. Once again, we may call these compromises that governed postwar Japanese capitalism "the companyist compromise" or "companyist régulation." Companyist régulation derives its distinctiveness from the strong, long-term nature of employment and financial (and transactional) relationships. Whereas the American model was a "spot and contract model" stressing the pursuit of efficiency through short-term, fluid, and open relations, companyist régulation was a "long-term trust model" emphasizing the pursuit of efficiency through long-term, fixed, and closed relations.

5.5 Investment-Led Followed by Export-Led Growth Regimes

How has companyist régulation, in the configuration outlined above, intervened in and guided the postwar Japanese growth regime? If we do not clarify this point, neither the mode of régulation nor the regime of growth or accumulation can be fully explained. Did some feature of companyist régulation lead postwar Japanese capitalism into a growth system, just as the "acceptance of Taylorism for productivity-indexed wages" in the postwar American labor–management compromise stimulated mass production and mass consumption, creating a Fordist mode of régulation? This has been a crucial question that Japanese régulationists have been tackling in their research. Figure 5.1 shows a somewhat synthetic view of the connection between growth regimes and modes of régulation in Japan during the 1950s–1980s.

There is nearly complete accord among researchers that there was a shift in the growth regime from being profit (investment)-led during the high-growth era to being export-led in the post-oil shock era (Uemura 1992, 2000). Tohyama (1990)

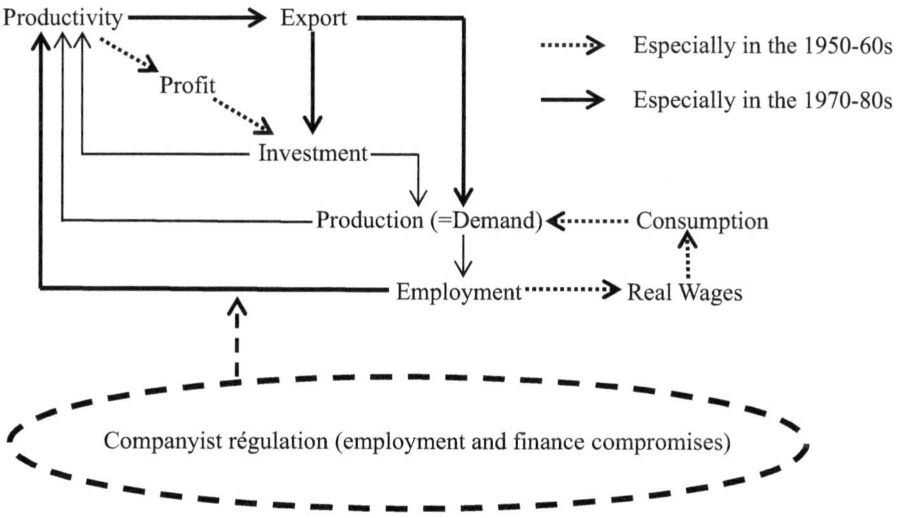

Fig. 5.1 Growth regime and mode of régulation in postwar Japan. (Source: Author)

described the profit-led growth pattern of the high-growth era as a distinctive macroeconomic cycle of "productivity → profits → investment," while Uni (1998) characterized the export-led pattern of the post-oil shock era as "productivity → exports → investment." At the same time, Uni noted the existence of an "export → production → employment" chain. What was viewed as a typical export-led growth pattern in the early 1980s resulted in some of the productivity gains being lost to foreign competitors, but increasing exports still brought rises in productivity and in employment and thereby proved effective in keeping the unemployment rate low.

Furthermore, as suggested by a large body of research, and in contrast to a typical Fordist case, postwar Japan's real wage formation does not seem to have been indexed to productivity. This was true of both the high-growth era and the post-oil shock era. In this way, the high-growth era, through the mechanism of the competitive wage formation of the "production → employment" type, enacted an "employment → real wages → individual consumption → production/demand" cycle (Boyer 1990b), but this demand regime declined beginning in the 1970s.

A productivity regime was then in operation until the 1980s, featuring the effects of investment (investment → productivity), Kaldorian effects on the economy of scale (production/demand → productivity), and the effects of innovation. In addition, the productivity effect of employment security (employment → productivity) was a uniquely Japanese phenomenon (Isogai and Uemura 1996). Nevertheless, it has been repeatedly pointed out by Hirano (1996) that Japan cannot be analyzed through the wage variable alone; employment must also be examined.

While considering the above, one point to be reiterated here is that, at least until the 1980s, a circuit existed in which management security served as collateral for employment security, and employment security in turn was linked to a productivity-raising effect. This gave rise to a causal chain of *management security–employment security–productivity*. However, some qualifications must be made. First, the circuit principally applied to core workers, that is, to regular male workers in large companies. Second, employment security did not lead directly to higher productivity, but rather the implicit employment security contract acted as an effective incentive mechanism in promoting practices such as meritocratic competition and skill formation that themselves bolstered productivity. Third, while the "employment → productivity" chain was functioning during the high-growth era, its importance was dramatically heightened following the oil shock.

The institutions of companyist régulation thus linked employment and productivity. All of the large firm-based institutions were constructed around fixed, long-term relationships. These institutions included the subcontracting system, *keiretsu* transactions, cross-shareholding, company groups (a "form of competition," to use the régulationist concept), indirect financial institutions, the main bank system (monetary and financial relations), the convoy system of administration (a form of the state), and, finally, so-called long-term employment, seniority-based wages, company unions, and meritocracy (the wage–labor nexus). It was through these relationships that collateralized management security and job security ultimately stimulated increases in productivity. The companyist régulation institutions thus gave rise to a superb productivity regime.

However, these institutions of companyist régulation failed to stimulate the development of an adequate demand regime circuit, particularly with regard to consumption. From the mid-1970s onward, in fact, they functioned to hold real wages to relatively low levels. When productivity gains are accompanied by tight wage restraint, industry relies more heavily on exports, causing economic growth to become export-led. The export-led nature of the Japanese economy became especially pronounced during the early 1980s when the strong dollar made Japanese exports to the United States even cheaper (Uni 1998). As a result, Japan was often labeled an "export giant – lifestyle midget." This export-led Japanese economy continued until the beginning of the 21st century, when China took the place of Japan and Japanese firms drastically bolstered their overseas production.

As described above, companyist régulation and investment-led and export-led growth regimes clearly guided Japanese capitalism from the high-growth era through the stable growth era that followed the oil shock. Consequently, Japan ascended to the status of an economic superpower in the 1980s, and from the end of that decade through the beginning of the 1990s enjoyed a nearly unparalleled economic boom. As we now know, of course, the boom was caused by the distortions of the "bubble economy." As a result of the collapse of the bubble and subsequent policy-making failures, Japanese capitalism suffered severe financial instability and entered a long-lasting recession or even depression accompanied by deflation. The period since the 1990s may well be considered one of structural crisis for Japanese capitalism. But what does this crisis mean for companyist régulation?

5.6 Companyism and Civil Society

5.6.1 Companyism in Crisis

To begin with, what is clear about the crisis that began in the 1990s is that the financial component of the previous mode of régulation collapsed into paralysis (Nabeshima 1997, 2000). The share of bank loans in corporate capital procurement declined substantially, as did the influence of main banks in corporate governance. On the other hand, however, the immaturity of the capital market meant that it was not ready to exercise monitoring functions in place of main banks. Moreover, the banks themselves, threatened by the intensifying competition brought by financial liberalization and globalization, pursued risky investments, an unfortunate course which the convoy system of financial administration could no longer prevent. In the new context of the 1980s and 1990s, companies, banks, and the established system of corporate governance were all paralyzed. From the end of the 1980s, corporate governance became a virtual empty shell, and the financial system consequently became unable to perform its "insurance" functions in support of corporate management or company continuity. The company–bank relationship collapsed. The term "governance depression" applied by the Economic Planning Agency to the 1990s recession was well chosen (Keizai Kikakuchō 1998: 205). Since then the companyist financial system has found itself in a deep crisis.

But what about labor? There is little chance that the labor–management compromise can survive in its previous form now that the financial compromise underpinning management security is in jeopardy, but it would also be premature to conclude that long-term employment is quickly collapsing. To be sure, there is increasing diversification and fluidity of employment (Miyamoto 1998), but while the sphere of long-term employment is contracting, regular male employees in large companies continue to be the core of the labor–management compromise. While the financial compromise is vulnerable to globalization, the labor–management compromise, although it has been altered, displays relatively stronger path dependence. Its restructuring has therefore been proceeding at a gradual pace, notwithstanding its serious consequences in the long run.

What, then, is the condition of companyist régulation? Returning to the perception of régulation theory, when even one of the core institutions becomes inappropriate, the established adjustment mechanisms prove unable to resolve an economic crisis, inevitably leading to a crisis of the system of régulation (Boyer 1990a: 52–52). In the domestic and international environment since the 1990s, companyism certainly has done nothing to prevent crises. Moreover, since the bubble burst companyism has lost its capacity to promote systemic adjustment. Companyism defined a Japanese mode of régulation which guided the nation through a cycle of *companyism–exports–strong yen–companyism*, on a trajectory toward becoming an economic superpower. In the end, however, it has entered a vicious cycle of *companyism–the bubble and its collapse–the collapse of the financial system–crisis of companyist régulation*. Are we now experiencing a new era of post-companyism?

5.6.2 Company-Centered Society and Civil Society

As I stated at the start of this chapter, just as prewar Japan cannot be understood without looking at farming villages, postwar Japan cannot be understood without looking at companies. This is the extent to which the "company" is the key to understanding postwar Japan.

Postwar Japanese capitalism went from recovery to rapid growth, then from the oil shock to a rush to become an economic superpower, and then from the collapse of the bubble to a prolonged period of stagnation. So what supported this economic development, at least until the 1980s? At the end of the 20th century, it was stridently argued that the answer was the "Japan Inc." created through the skillful guidance of the Ministry of International Trade and Industry and a diligent work ethic inspired by Confucian morality. Looking back from the vantage point of the present, the most persuasive view turns out to have been the "company-centered society" approach. This was a view that tried to explain Japan's economic "success," at least until the 1980s, in terms of the unique nature of Japanese companies and the unique nature of the Japanese society that was centered on them.

In postwar Japan, in exchange for shareholders being banished to the "outside" of Japanese companies, workers were subsumed and integrated into them. This is symbolized by the fact that the Japanese word "*shain*," which had originally meant "shareholder," came to refer to the employees of a company instead. Having thus been incorporated into the company, workers were given equality of opportunity, granted authority commensurate with their responsibility, and could expect to be promoted in accordance with their ability and the results they achieved. Responding to this state of affairs, workers saw value in working hard and "autonomously" applied themselves to their jobs, fierce meritocratic competition developed between coworkers, and employees identified the growth and expansion of their company with their own happiness. Of course, the strata that could not be assimilated in this way were skillfully excluded, but this was the kind of structure and mentality that could be seen in common among male regular employees of large Japanese companies. And Japanese society as a whole, both institutionally and ideologically, was constructed in a manner that centered or converged on these companies. In other words, postwar Japan was neither market-centered nor state-centered, nor was it based on a civil society foundation. It was instead a society constructed around large corporations – a "company-centered society."

This company-centered society was inseparable from the widespread emergence of a unique new tribe called "company people." Company people were different from workers in the original sense of the term and can be described as workers who have been endowed with a spirit of capital, i.e., self-valorizing value. In the past, Marx had referred to capitalists as the "personification of capital," but what emerged in postwar Japan were workers who "personified capital." And while Marx said that workers were "machines for the production of surplus value" and capitalists "machines for the transformation of surplus value into capital (accumulation)," what we see in the company-centered society of postwar Japan are workers who embody both roles. Japan's emergence as an "economic superpower" was a product of the "success" of this company-centered society.

With the crisis of companyism, however, this company-centered society also reached an impasse. Signs of this include the problem of *karōshi* (death by overwork), the low birth rate–aging population, condemnation of "black companies" (companies that abuse or overwork their employees), young men and women refusing to become company people, and the long-term stagnation and increased inequality in the Japanese socio-economy following the collapse of the bubble. The Japanese government, too, has had no choice but to take up the tasks of creating a "society in which women are active" and enacting "reforms in the way work is done." Both of these initiatives are presumably premised on doubts and misgivings about living one's life as the personification of capital (a company).

What is unfolding in Japan today is a reexamination of the relationship between companies and individuals. This is in fact primarily a reexamination of interpersonal relationships within companies. In the past, the standards for the behavior of company people were determined directly by the views of their "superiors" and ultimately by the logic of their company. This logic was internalized by company people through intracompany competition. Moreover, this was not competition that broke down the status system within the company, but rather a struggle in which individuals competed to climb to a higher level within the existing hierarchy. The greater the disparity in status, the fiercer the competition became. And in practice, this disparity in status is indeed so great that someone at the bottom, a "loser" in this competition, is not thought of or treated as a human being.

This being the case, in order to be an "ordinary person," individuals must see through their company's eyes and transform themselves into its personification. Companyism goes beyond a simple mode of régulation and requires this vision of humanity. Here the view of an "impartial spectator" or "objective third party" – in other words, the view of a genuine "ordinary person" – that transcends the company is not cultivated. And when such perspectives do emerge, they are eradicated. This schema is by no means limited to for-profit companies, but can be seen in all organizations including universities. In any case, the overall result of this "ordinary person" competition was a "great economic nation." But this inevitably came as part of a set with becoming a "minor lifestyle nation" and "minor human rights nation."

Comparing Japan and the West at the beginning of the 20th century, Hajime Kawakami (1911) claimed that "in Europe, God created human rights, and afterwards man created the rights of the state. Conversely in Japan, God first created the rights of the state, and then the state created human rights" (see Chap. 1). Adopting these terms, we might say that in postwar Japan "God created the rights of the company, and then the company created human rights," and in this country, "human rights" were positioned below both the "rights of the state" and the "rights of the company." But in the 21st century, Japan is at last beginning to relativize the "divine" corporation and company-centered society. We are now once again, or indeed perhaps for the first time, standing at a point from which we must set out on the basis of "human rights." We must allow an "impartial observer" to dwell inside us. By doing so, we must transform ourselves from "company people" into *homo economicus* in the truest sense of the word – not the people reduced to "creatures of self-interest" described by orthodox economics, but rather human beings who embody justice and the law. "Civil society" is an extension of this. Now that cracks have begun to appear in companyism and a company-centered society, once again "civil society" must presumably emerge as an eternal subject of inquiry.

References

Aoki, Masahiko (1988) *Information, Incentives, and Bargaining in the Japanese Economy*, Cambridge: Cambridge University Press.

——— (1994) 'The Contingent Governance of Teams: Analysis of Institutional Complementarity,' *International Economic Review*, 35.

Aoki, Masahiko and Hugh Patrick eds. (1994) *The Japanese Main Bank System: Its Relevance for Developing and Transforming Economies*, New York: Oxford University Press.

Baba, Hiroji (1997) 'Japanese Companyism and the End of Cold War,' in Junji Banno ed. *The Political Economy of Japanese Society, vol.1: The State or the Market?*, Oxford: Oxford University Press.

Boyer, Robert (1990a) *The Regulation School: A Critical Introduction*, New York: Columbia University Press.

——— (1990b) *Nyūmon Regyurashion* (*Introduction to the Régulation*), Tokyo: Fujiwara Shoten Publishers.

Boyer, Robert and Toshio Yamada eds. (2000) *Japanese Capitalism in Crisis: A Regulationist Interpretation*, London and New York: Routledge.

Ebizuka, Akira, Hiroyasu Uemura and Akinori Isogai (1997) 'L'hypothèse de "la relation hiérarchisée marché-firme" et l'économie japonaise d'après-guerre,' *L'Année de la régulation*, 1, Paris: La Découverte.

Hanada, Masanori (1997) 'Syndicalisme japonais et gestion des conflits sociaux,' in J.-M. Bouissou éd., *L'envers du consensus*, Paris: Presses de Sciences Politiques.

Hirano, Yasuro (1996) *Nihonteki Seido to Keizai Seichō* (*Japanese Institutions and Economic Growth*), Tokyo: Fujiwara Shoten Publishers.

Isogai, Akinori and Hiroyasu Uemura (1996) '"Seido no Keizaigaku" to Kahei – Rōdō no Dainamikusu' ("The Economics of Institutions" and the Dynamics of Money and Labor), *Keizaigaku Kenkyū* (*Journal of Political Economy*), Kyūshū University, 63(2).

Isogai, Akinori, Akira Ebizuka and Hiroyasu Uemura (2000) 'The Hierarchical Market-Firm Nexus as Japanese Mode of Régaltion,' in Boyer and Yamada (2000).

Iwata, Ryūshi (1977) *Nihonteki Keiei no Hensei Genri* (*The Organizational Principles of Japanese Management*), Tokyo: Bunshindo.

Kawakami, Hajime (1911) 'Nihon Dokutoku no Kokkashugi' (An Etatism Peculiar to Japan), *Chūō Kōron* (*Central Public Opinion*), March; in *Kawakami Hajime Zenshū* (*Complete Works of Hajime Kawakami*), 6, Tokyo: Iwanami Shoten Publishers, 1982.

Keizai Kikakuchō (Economic Planning Agency, Government of Japan) (1998) *Keizai Hakusho* (*White Paper on the Japanese Economy*), Tokyo: Ōkurashō Insatsukyoku.

Kurita, Ken (1994) *Nihon no Rōdō Shakai* (*The Society of Labor in Japan*), Tokyo: University of Tokyo Press.

Miyamoto, Mitsuharu (1998) 'Nihon-gata Koyō Shisutemu ni Towareteiru Mono: Kokusai Hikaku no Kanten kara' (The Japanese-style Employment System in Question: From a Point of View of International Comparison), in Ken'ichi Tominaga and Mitsuharu Miyamoto eds., *Mobiritii Shakai heno Tenbō* (*Towards a Mobility Society*), Tokyo: Keiō Gijuku University Press.

Nabeshima, Naoki (1997) 'La transformation du système financier et la crise contemporaine: Le mode de régulation financière dans le capitalisme japonais,' *Revue d'économie financière*, 43.

——— (2000) 'The Financial Mode of *Régulation* in Japan and its Demise,' in Boyer and Yamada (2000).

Nakatani, Iwao (1984) 'The Economic Role of Financial Corporate Grouping,' in Masahiko Aoki ed, *The Economic Analysis of the Japanese Firm*, Amsterdam: North Holland.

Nitta, Michio (1995) 'Rōshi Kankei no Hen'yō to "Futatsu no Moderu"' (Transformation of Industrial Relations and the "Two Models"), in Jurō Hashimoto ed., *20 Seiki Shihonshugi* (*The 20th Century Capitalism*), vol.1, Tokyo: The University of Tokyo Press.

Saguchi, Kazurō (1991) *Nihon ni okeru Sangyō Minshushugi no Zentei* (*Preconditions of Industrial Democracy in Japan*), Tokyo: University of Tokyo Press.

Sheard, Paul (1994) 'Interlocking Shareholdings and Corporate Governance,' in Aoki and Dore (1994).

Tohyama, Hironori (1990) 'Kōdo Seichō-ki ni okeru Chinrōdō Keitai: Regyurashion Apurōchi no Shiten kara' (Wage-Labor Forms in the High-growth Period: From a Viewpoint of the *Regulation* Approach), *Keizaigaku Zasshi* (*Journal of Economics*), Osaka City University, 91(4).

Uemura, Hiroyasu (1992) 'Growth and Distribution in the Postwar Regime of Accumulation: A Theory and Realities in the Japanese Economy,' *Monde en développement*, 79/80.

——— (2000) 'Growth, Distribution and Structural Change in the Postwar Japanese Economy,' in Boyer and Yamada (2000).

Uemura, Hiroyasu, Akinori Isogai and Akira Ebizuka (1998) *Shakai-keizai Sisutemu no Seido Bunseki: Marukusu to Keinzu wo Koete* (*The Institutional Analysis of Socio-economic Systems: Beyond Marx and Keynes*), Nagoya: Nagoya University Press.
Uni, Hiroyuki (1998) *Kōzō Henka to Shihon Chikuseki* (*Structural Change and Capital Accumulation*), Tokyo: Yūhikaku Publishing.

Chapter 6
The Collapse of Companyism and Today's Post-companyist Transformation

6.1 Introduction: New Economic Environments and Multinationalization of Japanese Companies

The 20-year period centered on the year 2000 seems to have been a major turning point for both the world and Japanese economies. It is evident, however, that these two economies have not always been on the same page. While Japan suffered from a long period of stagnation after the bursting of the "bubble economy," the world economy surged into a phase of globalization that was driven in particular by the finance-led growth of the United States and the so-called export-led industrialization of China. The trend toward globalization still prevails, albeit having experienced setbacks in the form of the economic crisis that hit the world economy after the autumn of 2008 and the recent rise of nationalist or rightist movements in the United States and Europe.

Today, in the second decade of the 21st century, the Japanese economy is experiencing greater changes and faces various problems. In this chapter, I will explain these developments from the perspective of contemporary changes in the companyist mode of régulation. Before doing so, however, I will very briefly point out some new circumstances in the economic environment that forms the background of these changes in the Japanese economy.

First, we can point to "globalization" itself. In Asia, following the lead of the newly industrialized economies (NIEs) and the Association of Southeast Asian Nations (ASEAN) countries, China and India initiated their industrialization efforts and are experiencing high economic growth. In the fields of trade and investments, Japan is very dependent on Asian countries. This implies the emergence of multinational enterprises and intense international competition. It also increases the urgency of solving the environmental problems that will further intensify because of the increased industrialization and higher energy demand.

Second, the current wave of globalization is being led largely by the United States, and as a result financial liberalization is being imposed on all countries.

T. Yamada, *Contemporary Capitalism and Civil Society*, Evolutionary Economics and Social Complexity Science 14,
https://doi.org/10.1007/978-981-13-0517-7_6

Consequently, the influence of the financial sector and stock market is strong in all countries, and companies cannot neglect them in their management practices. Japan is no exception to the influence of "financialization" or "finance-led capitalism." The negative consequences of this phenomenon are manifested in many ways: an increasing number and proportion of non-regular workers, low wages, increasing unemployment, retrenchment of welfare, uneasiness among the general population about being able to maintain their lifestyles, a society with increasing inequality, and so on. Financialization has resulted in a social crisis. At the same time, however, Japan has accumulated, although this was initially less well known, massive foreign financial assets, and the surplus in its balance of income (mainly its return on foreign investment) is higher than the surplus in its trade balance. In this regard, it can be said that Japan is a major financial power.

Third, we are seeing "the rise of the tertiary sector." In Japan, there is a dire need to improve the medical and social services sectors, given the fact that Japanese society is the most rapidly aging society in the world. Furthermore, if in the future Japan faces a severe shortage of labor because of its declining population, it will have to increase its investments in education and training in order to promote technological innovation and facilitate the establishment of a knowledge-based economy. The shift from a goods-centered to a service-centered economy is an evolution Japan must inevitably undergo.

Globalization, including the economic integration of East Asia, financialization, under which labor is subordinated, and the shift to a service economy with active social services and educational sectors have thus formed the background against which the recent changes have occurred. Having established these three factors that are currently transforming the Japanese economy, this chapter focuses on what has become of companyist régulation from the analytical angle of globalization, and in particular from that of the multinationalization of Japanese companies.

In fact, over the last 20–30 years, major Japanese companies have actively developed their overseas business sectors, especially in Asian countries, and have thus become multinational firms. As is well known, this has played an important role in establishing an international division of labor in the East Asian region. But what impact has this multinationalization had on the Japanese economy and its mode of régulation? In short, what kind of relationship can we find between the multinationalization of Japanese firms and the structural transformations occurring within the Japanese economy? This chapter approaches this question while bearing in mind our concept of "companyist régulation."

6.2 The Breakdown of Companyist Régulation

6.2.1 Companyist Régulation Revisited

As shown in Chap. 5, "companyism" is a concept that characterizes the mode of régulation that supported Japan's postwar economic growth. This mode of régulation is propped up by two main pillars: a labor–management compromise on employment security and a company–bank compromise on management security (security of a company's continued survival). In short, companyism rests on both an employment compromise and a finance compromise. Let me begin with a very brief summary of the main points discussed in the previous chapter.

The employment compromise, the first pillar of companyism, contrasts markedly with what is seen in the United States. In the case of postwar American Fordism, a wage compromise formulated as *the acceptance of Taylorism (strictly delimited work) by workers* in exchange for *the provision of productivity-indexed wages by management* drove a growth regime typically seen as "mass production–mass consumption." In contrast, what drove Japan's postwar growth was an employment compromise defined as *the acceptance of unlimited duties by workers* in exchange for *the provision of employment security by management.* In return for workers' devotion and loyalty to their company in the form of accepting unlimited duties, Japanese workers, especially regular male employees employed by large companies, mostly preferred employment security to wage hikes; more precisely, they wanted a guarantee of continued employment at the company at which they were currently employed. After a trial-and-error period, this demand from workers was accepted by management, and so-called lifetime employment and seniority-based wages became the "rules of the game" in Japan, or the social norms established between management and workers.

To bring about a robust realization of a wage–labor nexus (*rapport salarial* in French) that centers on employment security, it is essential to secure the continued existence of the company, i.e., management security. In postwar Japan, where an indirect finance system prevailed, in times of managerial hardship a company would seek to obtain various relief measures (e.g., additional financing, favorable interest rates, and the assistance of executives dispatched from banks) in order to survive. In exchange for the ability to receive relief measures should the need arise, a company would fix a particular bank as its preferential business partner and shareholder. This finance compromise, the second pillar of companyism, leads to corporate governance by a main bank, and in this way company survival is secured. This is the so-called main bank system. The main bank system thus represents a core compromise between a company and a bank for the purpose of the management security of the former. This company–bank compromise, together with cross-shareholding and convoy systems, has helped ensure the stability and survival of Japanese companies.

Employment security in the wage–labor nexus and management security in finance and intercompany relations – two elements that form an institutional complementarity – became the kernel of companyist régulation. This mode of régulation resulted in high levels of productivity among core workers who engaged in meritocratic competition within the context of employment security, and each company aimed to maximize sales or market share. Companyist régulation thus supported an investment and export-led growth regime in postwar Japan, which in turn led to high economic growth in Japan and its status as a global "economic power."

6.2.2 *The Collapse of Management Security: The Marketization of Finance*

By establishing finance in an advantageous position over labor, however, the globalization that originated in the United States in the 1980s has placed immense pressure on the Japanese economy through financial liberalization. In the stagnant Japan of the 1990s, various economic policies aimed at financial deregulation and marketization were implemented, thereby definitively altering the financial structure of Japanese companies. This change also resulted in the breakdown of the conventional company–bank nexus, intercompany nexus, and bank–government nexus that together constituted an important pillar of companyist régulation. In other words, this change resulted in the collapse of the management security system of Japanese companies. Let us now examine this in greater detail.

As is well known, one can point to the following facts as the distinctive features of corporate finance in postwar Japan (Itoh 1995; Nabeshima 2000): (1) The ratio of external funds to internal funds is large. (2) The borrowing ratio is large, and the proportion of securities in external funds is small. (3) Nevertheless, over time the ratio of internal funds has increased. (4) Since the 1980s, while large companies have increased their ratio of internal funds and decreased their borrowing ratio (the separation or estrangement of large companies from banks), small and medium-sized companies still have a financial structure centered on borrowings from banks.

With regard to large companies' separation from banks, the ratio of borrowing to total assets in the case of large and medium-sized companies (companies with a capital base of more than a hundred million yen) has fallen sharply in the 2000s after a slow decline before and during the 1990s (Naikakufu 2008: 137). These facts clearly signify that, particularly for large enterprises, corporate finance has changed from indirect (borrowing from banks) to direct finance (stocks and bonds) and that corporate finance is now mainly market-based.

At the same time, the structure of stock holdings has changed drastically since the 1990s. The share of stock held by financial institutions (city banks, regional banks, and so on) has fallen sharply since the second half of the 1990s. The amount of stock held by nonfinancial incorporated enterprises has also decreased. The decrease in the amount of stock held by banks can be attributed to the following causes: (1) pressures to sell stocks because of sluggish stock prices that lead to depreciated asset values, (2) the Bank for International Settlements (BIS) banking regulation that requires an equity ratio of more than 8%, and (3) the introduction of current value-based accounting. Furthermore, it is foreign individuals and entities, particularly foreign institutional investors, that have overwhelmingly raised their share of stock holdings; the ratio of stocks held by foreign investors in value terms has increased drastically from less than 5% in 1990 to more than 25% in the mid-2000s. These factors suggest a loosening of the bond between companies and banks, and therefore a decline in the function of corporate governance being performed by main banks. Large companies no longer consider the bank as a source of financing, and banks have also lost their desire and ability to monitor and come to the rescue of large companies. Here we can confirm a breakdown of the main bank system.

The ratio of stock cross-holdings among enterprises has also dropped since the 1990s, falling from 18% in value base in 1991 to 8% in 2003. We can refer to financial institutions and nonfinancial enterprises as "stable stockholders" and observe that the percentage of stable holdings in value base has dropped from 45% in 1991 to 24% in 2003 (Nissei Kiso Kenkyūjo 2003). As the foreign stockholders whose numbers are consistently increasing are, in general, short-term holders who expect only high stock prices and high yields, Japanese enterprises are experiencing increasing pressure to give serious thought to short-term profits and stockholders' interests and at the same time are no longer financially and managerially stable. The protective banking policies of the government, i.e., the so-called convoy system, have also been abandoned. The system of bank-guaranteed security of firm management that was an important part of companyist régulation is thus no longer in effect.

6.2.3 *Non-regularization of Employees and Survival of Limited Employment Security*

Finance, which has come to occupy a dominant position in the new environment of globalization, has begun radically to change labor. In short, the abovementioned marketization of finance has forced the conventional wage–labor nexus to undergo a radical transformation. How did the collapse of management security affect employment security within the companyist régulation that included complementarity between management security and employment security?

The greatest changes in the wage–labor nexus in the last 20 years have been the non-regularization of employees and the discontinuation or suspension of wage increases. With regard to the non-regularization of workers, both the number and proportion of regular workers have declined continuously since 1997, while those of precarious non-regular workers have increased rapidly. In fact, while only one fifth of employees were non-regular workers in the first half of the 1990s, this figure had increased to one third by the year 2005 and to almost 40% by the year 2016 (Sōmushō 2005, 2016). In this regard, we can say that there has been a change in both industrial structure (the role of the service industry, in which the proportion of non-regular workers has always been high, is increasing) and employment strategy (all industries, including the manufacturing industry, are increasing the number and proportion of non-regular workers in their ranks).

Moreover, while in the 1990s the increase of non-regular workers was observed mainly in small and medium-sized companies, in the 2000s the same was mainly seen in large companies. And among non-regular workers, although there has been no increase in the proportion of part-time workers with short working hours, the proportion of dispatched workers (workers not hired by a company directly but dispatched by a "temp agency" or similar service) with regular working hours has increased (Naikakufu 2006: Figure 3-1-3). This fact signifies that regular workers are now being replaced by non-regular workers even in the large companies that are at the center of the Japanese economy (Uni 2009: Ch. 4). In addition, it has been observed that once a company had increased the proportion of non-regular workers in its ranks, it did not hire regular workers even during the recovery phase of 2002–2007 (Naikakufu 2007: 176). This suggests a clear structural change in company behavior and labor institutions in Japan. In short, today the non-regularization of employees has become one of the characteristics of the wage–labor nexus in Japan. Just as we referred to the main change in the financial sector as the "marketization of fund raising," this non-regularization of employees can accurately be referred to as "marketization of labor procurement."

Another great transformation of the wage–labor nexus in the last 20 years has been the discontinuation of wage increases. It is easy to see why the non-regularization of employees and the discontinuation of wage increases occur simultaneously, because the primary reason that firms hire non-regular workers is to reduce wage costs. Moreover, in Japan the traditional seniority-based wage system has in many cases been transformed into a performance-based wage system, and it is clear that firms have introduced performance-based systems not only to improve performance incentives but also to curb personnel expenditures.

This development was particularly obvious in the 2000s. During recovery phases before 1999, increases in ordinary profits had been accompanied by increases in wages. Beginning with the recovery of 1999, however, increases in corporate profits have not seen a corresponding increase in wages. And following the recovery of 2002, wages even began to decrease in spite of the fact that corporate profits had increased drastically. As a result, the proportional relationship between labor productivity and real wages that had characterized the Japanese economy before 1990 (not to speak of the Fordist era in the Unites States) has completely disappeared (Fig. 6.1). Since 1990, Japan has been transformed into an economy with quasi-zero wage increases regardless of whether or not there is an increase in productivity.

We can give several reasons to explain why this transformation occurred. First, Japanese companies began to adopt a new distributive policy favorable to stockholders because of the increasing pressure they found themselves under as a result of the marketization of corporate finance. Second, faced with the collapse of the management security offered by the main bank system, companies reduced wage costs and added savings to their retained earnings or internal reserves in order to safeguard themselves against fierce international competition as well as to maintain relative autonomy of management from stockholders. Third, during the long-lasting stagnation beginning in the 1990s, workers once again began to prefer employment stability to wage hikes.

We have thus established the non-regularization of employees and discontinuity of wage increases as elements that have greatly transformed the conventional wage–labor nexus. What needs to be examined is how these facts have changed the employment security of regular male workers in large companies that has formed the core element of the companyist wage–labor nexus. According to some studies, Japanese enterprises, particularly large enterprises, have in the past retained their

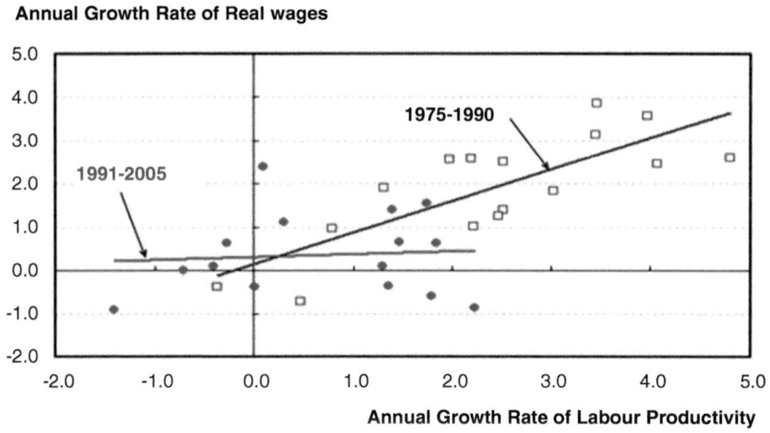

Fig. 6.1 Elasticity of real wages to labor productivity 1975–2005. (Source: Naikakufu 2007)

core employees for a long period of time and intend to continue this going forward. In short, Japanese companies intend to retain their core workers for as long as possible. For example, when we refer to the length of service by generation for manufacturing and construction industries where the ratio of regular workers is relatively high, it has hardly changed between 1997 and 2007; the trend of retaining regular workers for a long period of time has in principle continued (Naikakufu 2008: 138).

During the past 25 years, the proportion of regular workers has decreased so sharply that they now constitute only 60% of the labor force. Particularly in large companies, the proportion of non-regular workers has increased markedly in recent years. Regular workers in large enterprises have therefore been carefully segregated and reduced accordingly. Nevertheless, companies still seek long-term retention of the remaining regular workers and have expressed their willingness to continue this in the future. We refer to this as the "persistence of limited employment security."

6.2.4 *The Dysfunction of Companyist Régulation*

With regard to the employment situation, we have confirmed a parallel, or rather complementary, evolution of apparently contradictory phenomena: the non-regularization of employees and persistence of limited employment security. As a result of marketization of corporate finance and the collapse of management security centered around the main bank system (finance compromise), we observed, in the field of employment, the non-regularization of employees and the limited provision of employment security. Japanese enterprises have nevertheless retained the intention to preserve employment security for their remaining core workers. The wage–labor nexus in Japan has thus maintained the conventional source of productivity gains as the preservation of limited employment security in spite of having experienced great changes in its employment and wage systems. Or, in the words of a Japanese government White Paper, Japanese companies today aim at "maintaining the long-term employment of regular employees by altering their wage system into a performance-based one and by making use of non-regular workers like part-time and dispatched workers" (Kōsei Rōdō Shō 2008: 51).

In short, with regard to companyist régulation, the institutionalized corporate finance system (main bank system) has been marketized (direct finance system), and company-guaranteed employment (employment compromise) has been reduced and marketized. In other words, what we see today is employment security without management security provided by a main bank and decreasing numbers of workers with employment security accompanied by increasing numbers of non-regular workers without employment security. Companyist régulation now continues on a perilous flight path with only one of its engines working; simply put, companyist régulation is now very much dysfunctional.

This dysfunction can be broken down into the following aspects: (1) poor conditions faced by non-regular workers and increasing inequality, (2) defective welfare and social security systems faced with the repercussions of an aging society, and (3) a vicious circle of uneasiness over lifestyle security and inactive domestic demand (confounded by this vicious circle, the Japanese government has begun, very recently, to demand wage hikes from managers' associations).

6.3 The Multinationalization of Japanese Companies

6.3.1 The Development and Characteristics of the East Asian Production Network

In the previous section, we traced the course of events by which, triggered by the globalization and financialization of the world economy, Japanese companyist régulation has fallen into a crisis. But an era of crisis is also an era of searching for new approaches. The leading approach attempted by Japanese companies in this situation has been multinationalization. This multinationalization was a consequence of the decline of companyist régulation as well as an important factor accelerating this decline. The result of this acceleration is that today the Japanese economy has entered a state that can be accurately called "post-companyism." Although this does not yet signify the establishment of a new mode of régulation or new growth regime, Japanese capitalism is now entering a new phase that is obviously different from the era of companyist régulation. In this section, I describe the actual conditions of the multinationalization and overseas deployment of Japanese firms that constitute one of the driving forces behind this post-companyist transformation of the Japanese economy.

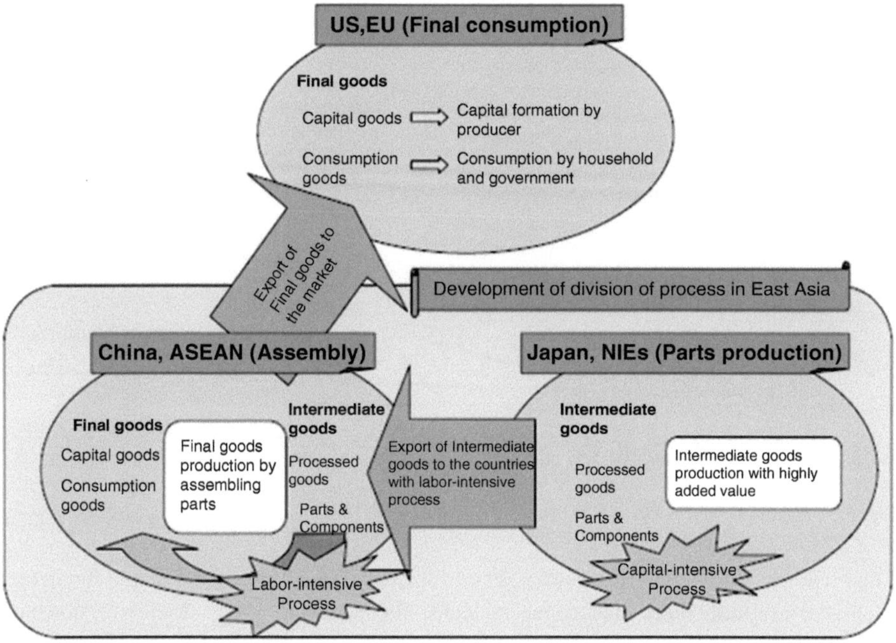

Fig. 6.2 Triangular global trade structure. (Source: METI 2005)

The global trade structure from the 1990s until the early 2010s can be roughly envisioned as a triangle with the following poles: the United States and Europe, China and the ASEAN (Association of Southeast Asian Nations), and Japan and the NIEs (newly industrializing economies), as shown in Fig. 6.2. This triangular structure has gradually taken shape since the 1990s around the machinery industry (transportation equipment, general machinery, electrical machinery, etc.) in which East Asia has comparative advantages. The position and role of each pole are as follows:

1. Japan and the NIEs produce intermediate goods (parts, components, and processed goods) in a capital-intensive process and export them to China and ASEAN.
2. China and ASEAN assemble the imported intermediate goods into final goods (consumption goods and capital goods) in a labor-intensive manner before exporting them to the United States and Europe (it should be noted that in recent years, China has strengthened its industrial abilities and can no longer be characterized as either a simple importer of intermediate goods or a simple exporter of final goods).
3. The United States and Europe consume the imported final goods.
4. In short, a global trade structure has become established containing the following roles: parts production (Japan and the NIEs), assembly production (China and ASEAN), and final consumption (the United States and Europe).

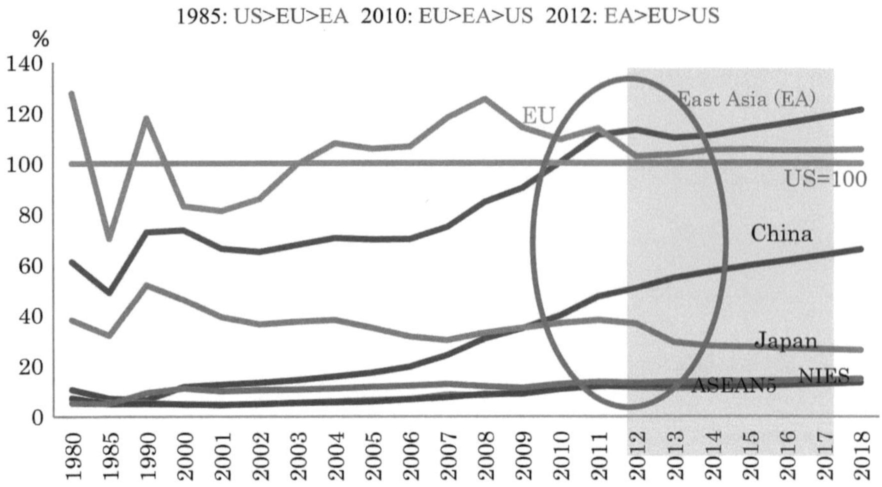

Fig. 6.3 Nominal GDP ratio against the United States (=100). (Source: Hirakawa 2014)

The position of East Asia in the world economy has been rapidly enhanced by virtue of this triangular trade structure. In 1985, the nominal gross domestic product (GDP) of East Asia was about one half of that of the United States; by 2010, however, the GDP of East Asia had surpassed that of the United States, and it has now surpassed even that of the EU (European Union) as shown in Fig. 6.3.

While goods exported from East Asia to other regions have been mainly final goods, intra-regional trade within East Asia has to a large extent consisted of intermediate goods. This constitutes the most salient trade-related feature of the East Asian zone, as is clearly evident when we compare intra-regional trade goods in this zone with those of other international economic zones such as those comprising the EU and the NAFTA (North American Free Trade Agreement) nations as seen in Fig. 6.4.

Looking at Fig. 6.4, although in all three economic regions (East Asia, NAFTA, and EU) the proportion of trade in processed products is the highest, East Asia shows two distinctive characteristics. First, this region shows a high proportion of parts and components trade that has undergone rapid growth (about 30% in 2010). Second, East Asia's proportion of consumption goods trade is not only low but has also declined drastically (about 10% in 2010). In contrast, in the case of both NAFTA and EU members, the proportion of parts and components trade has been low and dropping (below 20% in 2010), and the relatively high proportion of consumption goods trade has been stable (over 20% in NAFTA nations and 30% in the EU).

The high proportion of intra-regional trade in intermediate goods suggests the high weight of *intraindustrial trade* rather than interindustrial trade. The presence of both exports and imports within the same industry indicates the existence of a division of process in which intra-regional countries take charge of different processes in order to produce final goods. In short, in East Asia an international network of process division has been established that centers on the machinery industry.

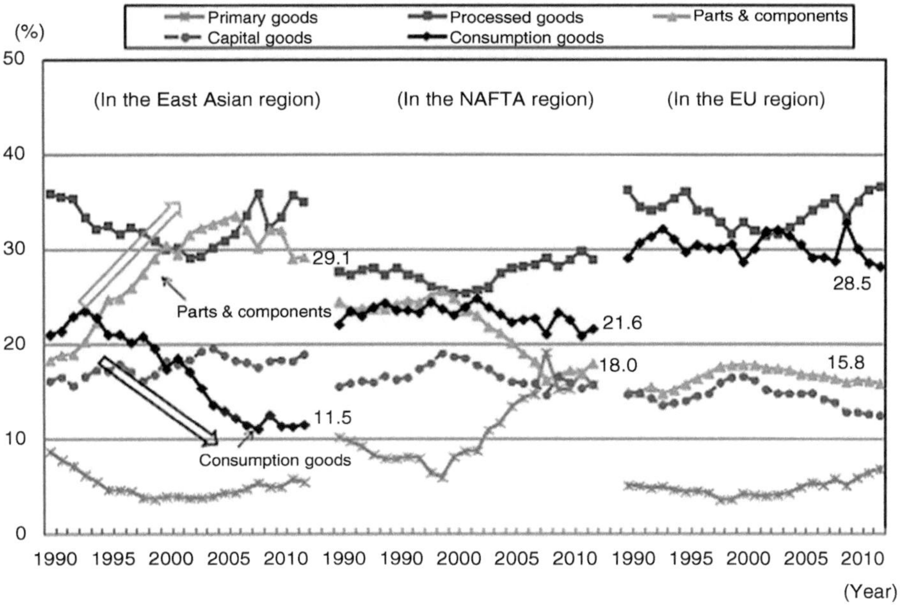

Fig. 6.4 Trends in the value of intra-regional trade. (Source: METI 2014)

By tightening this production network or supply chain, de facto economic integration has developed in East Asia, leading to the formation of a large cross-border production base.

6.3.2 *Business Activities of Japanese Companies in East Asia*

Foreign direct investment (FDI) by Japanese companies, especially manufacturers, has played an important role in the development of this international division of production processes. Although companies from the United States, Europe, South Korea, and Taiwan have also established overseas affiliates in East Asia, the presence of Japan-affiliated companies is much stronger.

In the late 1980s – that is, in a period of rapid yen appreciation following the Plaza Accord of 1985 – Japanese companies embarked for the first time on large-scale FDI. Japan's FDI position thereby grew to 30 trillion in 2000 and 70 trillion yen in 2011 (METI 2013: Figure III-3-3-10). Although at first FDI was principally concentrated in North America and was mainly undertaken by nonmanufacturing industries, manufacturers then started to actively establish overseas affiliates, mostly in East Asia. From the 1990s to 2012 there was a general trend toward the appreciation of the yen, albeit with volatile ups and downs in the exchange rate. In this context, Japan has increased the weight of its investment in Asia, both in general and in the manufacturing industry in particular.

In the manufacturing industry, the number of Japanese overseas affiliates in Asia has tripled, going from fewer than 2000 (about one half of all Japanese FDI) in 1990 to more than 6000 (more than 70% of FDI) in 2010 (METI 2012: Figure 2-2-2-1). The number of Japanese overseas affiliates in Asia and the percentage of total FDI this investment represents have increased almost without pause and with little correlation to exchange-rate fluctuations. This means that in terms of Japanese manufacturers' incentives for overseas development, market factors that project potentially greater demand within newly emerging Asian markets have become more important than cost factors, including wage hikes or yen appreciation.

As a result, total overseas production by Japanese manufacturers had already exceeded that of export by 1998, and since then, the gap has continued to widen. In 2012, the overseas production rate among manufacturers was 20% for all domestic companies and 35% for those developing their business overseas (METI 2014: Figure II-3-2-32). The overseas production rate of the transportation machinery sector in particular was 40%. Following the Lehman Brothers shock of 2008, Japanese companies' investments in plants and equipment have continuously increased abroad, but domestic investment has stagnated (Fig. 6.5). This stagnation in domestic investment is a very serious problem, and Japan is the only major capitalist country in which it has occurred. This may be a sign of the decoupling of Japanese firms from the Japanese economy as well as a sign of an emerging post-companyist environment.

What has been the state of Japanese manufacturing affiliates' business activities in Asia? In terms of sales, although there was a considerable decline on account of the Lehman Brothers shock, figures have steadily increased from the 2000s to the 2010s, growing from 20 trillion yen in 2000 to 50 trillion in 2012. The ratio of local sales has also grown, from 50% in 2000 to 60% in 2011 (Fig. 6.6). The increase in

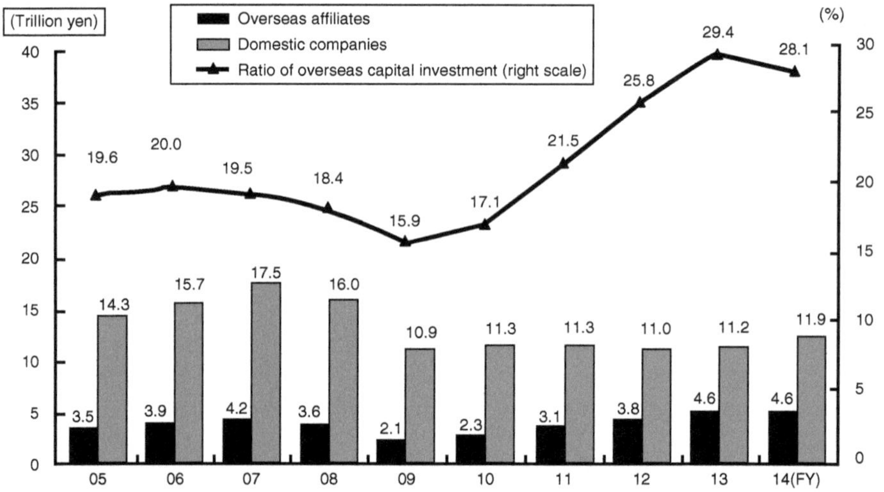

Fig. 6.5 Trends in capital investment in overseas affiliates and domestic companies (manufacturing industries). (Source: METI 2015)

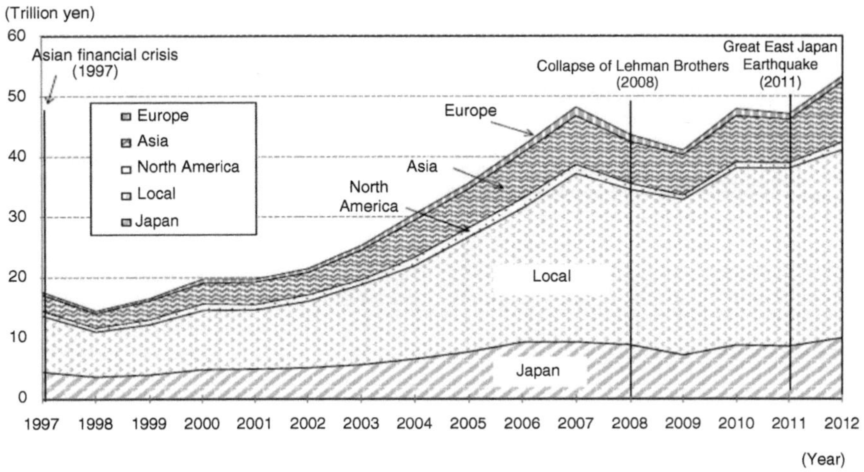

Fig. 6.6 Sales trends of overseas affiliates of Japanese manufacturers in Asia. (Source: METI 2014)

the local sales ratio confirms that in recent years Japanese firms have placed more importance on market incentives than cost factors.

In line with the increase in production and sales, procurement has also increased, from 15 trillion yen in 2002 to 35 trillion in 2010. The ratio of local procurement has increased as well, rising from 40% in 2000 to 60% in 2010. On the other hand, total procurement from Japan (i.e., exports from Japan to overseas affiliates) has stagnated since the Lehman Brothers shock, although prior to that event it had been increasing (METI 2014: Figure II-3-2-17). The share of procurement from Japan by overseas affiliates of Japanese manufacturers also decreased, from 40% in 1990–1996 to less than 30% in 2012.

6.3.3 *Japan's Reduced Export Competitiveness and Enhanced Returns from FDI*

As evidenced by the reduced share of procurement in Japan by Japanese overseas affiliates, the Japanese economy seems to have experienced a decline in its export-related competitiveness. Special attention must be paid to the fact that, despite positive expectations of increasing exports and economic growth since the phase of yen depreciation that began in 2012, Japan is still seeing export stagnation and a declining trend in export surplus, often experiencing trade deficits. As Japan's main export items are general machinery, electrical machinery, and motor vehicles (which together account for about 60% of all exports), it is useful to examine changes in export competitiveness while focusing on these three categories of export items.

Table 6.1 Japan's share of major export items among global exports

				Share of global exports (%)		
Rank	Items	Share (%)		1995	2000	2011
1	General machinery	21.9	57.3	15.2	11.5	8.5
2	Motor vehicles	18.9		18.0	16.1	11.9
3	Electrical machinery	16.5		17.2	12.8	6.5
–	Others	42.7				
–	Total export amount	100.0		9.5	7.8	4.9

Source: METI (2013)

For example, when we measure Japan's export competitiveness in terms of Japan's share of major export items among global exports, we see that Japan's total export share has declined by about 50%, from 9.5% in 1995 to 4.9% in 2011 (Table 6.1). Concerning the three main export items mentioned above, we can see a decline in the share of each – from 15.2 to 8.5% in general machinery, from 18.0 to 11.9% in motor vehicles, and, most strikingly, from 17.2 to 6.5% in electrical machinery.

Japan's trade surplus has rapidly contracted in line with reduced export competitiveness, and there have even been many trade deficits recorded in recent years (Fig. 6.7). On the other hand, the balance of primary income, which is made up of returns from direct and securities investments abroad, shows a steady and growing surplus, thus constituting the main factor behind the surplus in the current account balance. The trade deficit in services, on the other hand, is gradually declining due to the increasing number of tourists who are visiting Japan. As a result of all of these factors, Japan has for a long time managed to maintain a surplus in its current account balance. According to the stage theory of international account development, Japan seems to be shifting from an "immature creditor nation" that earns its income from trade to a "mature creditor nation" that earns its income from overseas investments. In any case, the old Japan that had built up an export-led growth regime under the companyist mode of régulation no longer exists. In this sense, too, Japan is now in the midst of a post-companyist transformation. For the moment, however, the nature of this post-companyism in a positive or active sense remains unclear.

6.4 The Post-companyist Transformation of the Japanese Economy

So far we have examined how conventional companyist régulation fell into dysfunction through the globalization and financialization of the socioeconomic environment, as well as through the multinationalization of Japanese companies represented by large exporting manufacturers. The multinationalization of Japanese companies was realized by accumulating internal reserves within these firms at their workers'

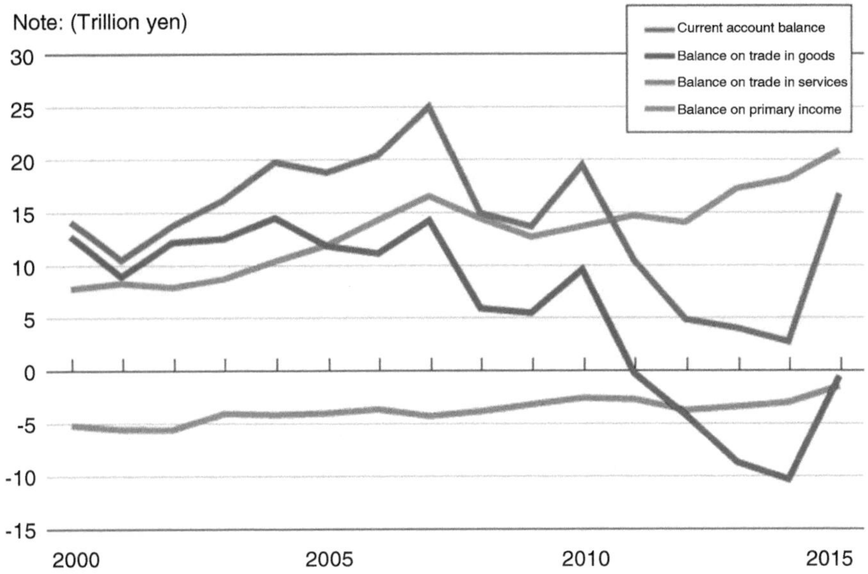

Fig. 6.7 Evolution of Japan's current account balance with its components 2000–2015. (Source: http://www.nippon.com/ja/features/h00135/)

expense, through such means as the non-regularization of employment and discontinuation of wage increases. This multinationalization contributed to economic growth in East Asia but reduced the export competitiveness of the Japanese economy. This has led to new problems in contemporary Japan that can be described as "post-companyist syndrome": a decoupling of multinational firms from the Japanese economy, a gap between multinational and national companies, stagnation in domestic demand both in terms of consumption and investment, and an inability to adapt to an aging society and declining population that requires medical and social services and high quality education and training services.

We refer to the actual situation in Japan today as "post-companyism," a situation in which companyism is paralyzed and in flux. This "post-companyism," however, does not refer to a new mode of régulation that has supplanted companyism but simply to a state of transition within contemporary Japan.

The post-companyist transformation process is marked not by rapid changes or a particular tipping point but by a series of gradual institutional changes (Thelen 2004). In today's Japan, in other words, while on the one hand some elements of companyism – such as employment security for regular workers in large enterprises, albeit to a reduced extent – have survived by virtue of the effect of path dependence, on the other hand we can also see the expansion of new post-companyist elements such as, among others, the breakdown of the main bank system, an increase in shareholder pressure, an increase of non-regular workers, and increased FDI gains.

Table 6.2 Companyism and post-companyism in Japan

	Companyism	Post-companyism
(1) Period	1960s–1980s	Definitively since the 2000s
(2) Superior institution	Wage–labor nexus	Financial and international relations
(3) Labor–management compromise	Employment security vs. acceptance of unlimited duties	Higher profitability vs. employment security for limited regular workers on the basis of their company's survival
(4) Management–finance compromise	Management–main bank compromise underpinning companies' survival	Management–shareholder compromise on more dividends (and higher stock prices) vs. management autonomy
(5) Principal business objectives	Sales amount (market share, growth of the company)	Profitability (return on assets, value of the company)
(6) Response to foreign markets and its consequences	Export to the United States	FDI in East Asia
	Surplus in balance on goods	Rapidly declining surplus and/or deficit in balance on goods
		Surplus in balance on income
(7) Effects on growth regime	Supports the investment and export-led growth regime	Does not lead to a new growth regime
(8) Effects on income distribution	Synchronizes wage hikes through initiatives such as the "spring offensive"	Leads to the bifurcation of wages between multinationals and nationals

Source: Author

To understand the post-companyist transformation more precisely, we can compare it directly with companyist régulation as it existed in the past (Table 6.2). As is shown in the Table, (1) post-companyism has been clearly evident since the beginning of the 21st century, and (2) financial and international relations have taken a dominant institutional domain position, supplanting the wage–labor nexus that has fallen into a subordinate position in the institutional hierarchy. (3) This has resulted in an increase in the number and proportion of non-regular and precarious workers, given the reduced number and portion of employees covered by employment security, and the imposition on workers of sacrifices such as declines in wages and labor's share. (4) Behind these transformations in the wage–labor nexus, there has also been a collapse in the management security system that had been supported by the main banks and cross-shareholding, and this has led to increased stock market pressures on companies. The management class has responded to shareholder pressure by providing greater dividends (and by achieving higher stock prices) and has increased their companies' own internal reserves in order to maintain relative autonomy from shareholders. In short, companies have realized increases in both dividends and internal reserves at the expense of workers.

When it comes to their principal business objectives, (5) Japanese companies have come to attach importance to profitability (e.g., return on assets) rather than to sales amounts (e.g., market share) to ensure their survival by virtue of their own actions without relying on external assistance. They have come to pursue company value rather than company growth. A narrow compromise concerning profitability may be established between shareholders, managers, and only a few workers, while the vast majority of employees are excluded. (6) Given the contraction of Japan's domestic market due to long-term deflation and an increase in emerging markets in East Asia, Japan's principal firms – which hold ample internal reserves – have embarked on full-scale FDI in Asia. Consequently, while the Japanese economy is experiencing a large surplus in terms of balance on income, following a rapid decline in its trade surplus it has recently begun to face concerns about serious trade deficits. (7) We can no longer call the Japanese economy an "export-led growth regime." A new paradigm for the Japanese economy that can supplant the previous regime remains to be seen. (8) Under this post-companyist state of affairs, the bifurcation of wages between multinationals and nationals has widened, leading to greater inequality in income distribution.

To reconstruct the Japanese economy will require not company-centered decision-making but an extensive development of associative activities synchronized with political will. It will need "political will" on the parts of both the central and local governments and "associative activities" not from above but from below. "Associations from below" is nothing other than a "civil society," the development of which will thus entail a "civil society-based régulation."

References

Hirakawa, Hitoshi (2014) 'Kōzō Tenkan no Sekai Keizai to Higashi Ajia Chiiki no Seidoka: ASEAN ni Chūmoku site' (Structural Transformation of the World Economy and Institutionalization of the East Asian Region: With Special Reference to the ASEAN), in Hiroyasu Uemura et al. eds., *Tenkanki no Ajia Shihonshugi* (*Asian Capitalisms in Transition*), Tokyo: Fujiwara Shoten Publishers.

Itoh, Osamu (1995) *Nihongata Kin'yu no Rekishiteki Kōzō* (*Historical Structure of the Japanese Type of Finance*), Tokyo: Tokyo Daigaku Shuppankai (The University of Tokyo Press).

Keizai Sangyō Shō (Ministry of Economy, Trade and Industry) (2014) *Dai 43-kai Kaigai Jigyō Katsudō Kihon Chōsa* (*The 43rd Basic Survey of Overseas Business Activities*). http://www.meti.go.jp/statistics/tyo/kaigaizi/result-2.html. http://www.meti.go.jp/english/statistics/tyo/kaigaizi/pdf/h2c406je.pdf

Kōsei Rōdō Shō (Ministry of Health, Labor and Welfare) (2008) *Kōsei Rōdō Hakusho 2008* (*Annual Report on Health, Labor and Welfare 2008*), Tokyo: Gyōsei.

METI (Ministry of Economy, Trade and Industry) (2005, 2012, 2013, 2014) *White Paper on International Economy and Trade*, each year. http://www.meti.go.jp/english/report/index_whitepaper.html#trade

——— (2015) *Summary of the 45th Basic Survey on Overseas Business Activities (conducted in July 2015)*. http://www.meti.go.jp/english/statistics/tyo/kaigaizi/

Nabeshima, Naoki (2000) 'The Financial Mode of *Régulation* in Japan and its Demise,' in Robert Boyer and Toshio Yamada eds., *Japanese Capitalism in Crisis: A Regulationist Interpretation*, London: Routledge.

Naikakufu (Cabinet Office, Government of Japan) (2006) *Keizai Zaisei Hakusho 2006* (*Annual Report on the Japanese Economy and Public Finance 2006*). http://www5.cao.go.jp/zenbun/wp-e/wp-je06/06-0000.html

——— (2007) *Keizai Zaisei Hakusho 2007* (*Annual Report on the Japanese Economy and Public Finance 2007*), Tokyo: Jiji-Gahō-sha.

——— (2008) *Keizai Zaisei Hakusho 2008* (*Annual Report on the Japanese Economy and Public Finance 2008*), Tokyo: Jiji-Gahō-sha.

Nissei Kiso Kenkyūjo (NLI Research Institute) (2003) *Kabushiki Mochiai Jōkyō Chōsa 2003* (*Survey on Cross Shareholding 2003*). http://www.nli-research.co.jp/files/topics/36431_ext_18_0.pdf?site=nli

Sōmushō (Ministry of Internal Affairs and Communications) (various years) *Rōdōryoku Chōsa* (*Labor Force Survey*). http://www.soumu.go.jp

Thelen, Kathleen (2004) *How Institutions Evolve: The Political Economy of Skills in Germany, Britain, the United States, and Japan*, Cambridge: Cambridge University Press.

Uni, Hiroyuki (2009) *Seido to Chōsei no Keizaigaku* (*Political Economy of Institutions and Régulation*), Kyoto: Nakanishiya Shuppan.

Chapter 7
Analyses of Japanese Capitalism Based on the Régulation Approach: An Overview of 30 Years of Research

The study of postwar Japanese capitalism based on the régulation approach started in about 1990. We have therefore been studying this subject for nearly 30 years. During this time, we have concentrated successively on four main topics of research: (1) Was Japan's high economic growth in the 1950s and 1960s Fordist? (2) How was Japan as an economic power in the 1970s and 1980s régulated and coordinated? (3) In which type of crisis has Japan been suffering during the long stagnation after 1990? (4) What position or role has Japanese capitalism assumed in Asia in recent years? The first topic was debated mainly in the first half of the 1990s, the second in the second half of the 1990s, the third in the 2000s, and the fourth in the 2010s. Although in the first part of these studies we of course could not perform real-time analyses and there was a time lag between the current developments in the Japanese economy and our main subject of research, scholars applying the régulation theory to the Japanese economy have arrived at some common findings concerning postwar Japanese capitalism. Here I give a retrospective overview of our analyses of Japanese capitalism.

7.1 Was the High Growth in the Japanese Economy in the 1950s and 1960s Fordist?

When it was first introduced, régulation theory explained, based on the analyses of American and French economies, the durable high economic growth seen in the postwar advanced capitalist countries with the notion of "Fordism." Here Fordism means the growth regime of "mass production–mass consumption" sustained by the mode of régulation (or capital–labor compromise) of "real wages indexed to productivity in exchange for Taylorist labor" (see Chap. 4). The concept of Fordism became very popular as a characterization of advanced postwar capitalism. This naturally raised in Japan the question of whether postwar Japanese capitalism,

T. Yamada, *Contemporary Capitalism and Civil Society*, Evolutionary Economics and Social Complexity Science 14,
https://doi.org/10.1007/978-981-13-0517-7_7

which recorded the highest growth in the world during this period, was Fordist. Some debates on Fordism occurred in the early 1990s, just after the introduction of régulation theory to Japan.

To begin with, Itoh (1988) proposed that Japan in the era of high growth could be categorized as a "Fordist regime of accumulation" because, notwithstanding the absence of a real wage hike indexed to productivity gains, there had been wage augmentation through the "spring offensive" (*shuntō*), the augmentation of farmers' incomes, and the economic growth led by domestic demand caused mainly by strong investment in plants and equipment. Boyer (1990) also characterized, albeit intuitively and without detailed analysis, the postwar Japanese economy as "hybrid Fordism." Using the word "hybrid," he saw in Japan an amalgam of Fordist mass production and non-Fordist social relations (the absence of a contractual wage system, welfare state, and so on.)

More refined Fordist theses were proposed by Uni and Hirano. Uni (1991, 1992) confirmed on the one hand the absence of the capital–labor compromise of "Taylorism in exchange for productivity-indexed wages" in postwar Japan, and on the other hand the mechanization of the consumer goods sector and the augmentation of real wages, at least during the years 1962–1973. He thus verified the existence of a "Fordist loop" and the "homogenization of consumption" at the level of the accumulation regime, ultimately defining Japan in this period as "Fordism without the Fordist capital-labor compromise." Hirano (1993, 1996) argues that the concept of Fordism and its formulation by Boyer (1988) must be understood in the medium–long term. And he found in postwar Japan consumption-led growth in the medium–long term, in spite of the existence of investment-led growth in the short term. In this way he concluded that "the postwar Japanese economy, although its *high speed* growth was caused by investment in plants and equipment, took the path of consumption-led growth *in the long run*" (emphasis Hirano's).

These were, in a manner of speaking, Fordist views on high-growth Japan. Uni and Hirano, placing their focus on accumulation regimes or growth regimes rather than on modes of régulation and conceiving of "Fordism" mainly in line with Boyer's (1988) model, argued for a Fordist Japan on the basis of the very existence of consumption-led growth. Tohyama (1990a, b), on the other hand, took a non-Fordist view. According to him, in the high-growth era we saw productivity sharing that was profitable to the capital side, and therefore the growth regime was led by investment not by consumption. As for the mode of régulation and especially for the wage–labor nexus, he emphasized the extensive continued existence of rural economies in the high-growth era. This meant the widespread survival of "noncapitalist environments" that had the effect of restraining wage increases and the development of social security. Tohyama thus concluded that Japan in this period was not a "pure Fordist regime." For more on the "Fordist Debate," see also Inoue and Yamada (2002).

The opposition between Fordist and non-Fordist views may, in reality, be quite superficial; both views confirm the absence of the typical Fordist capital–labor compromise and the presence of an investment-led growth regime of some sort, so there is not such a great distance between them. The only point on which they differ is whether or not there was a consumption-led growth regime operating in Japan during this period.

Here it became necessary to reexamine the concept of "Fordism" itself. In the beginning, French régulationists were inclined, based on their findings of consumption or wage-led loops in the American and French economies, to define this kind of loop as Fordist. However, the accumulation of economic analyses on many other countries, including Japan, has prompted a new question: How can one explain the investment or profit-led growth in this context? In this respect, Uemura, after categorizing profit-led and wage-led growth patterns (Uemura 1990, 1992), clearly contrasted the postwar Japanese macroeconomic characteristics with "typical" Fordism as shown in Table 7.1 (Uemura 1998). This provided a productive basis for later debate. Empirical studies started with the question of whether Japanese high economic growth was Fordist, and this line of inquiry led to an investigation of the theoretical question of the definition of Fordism. Asking "What is Fordism?" was, in effect, the first step in a reflection on the concept of Fordism, or, in other words, the de-standardization of Fordism among régulationists. In fact, the French régulationists themselves later came to acknowledge that the "diffusion of the genuine Fordist model" was not necessarily realized in every instance of advanced capitalism (Boyer 2004b: 54).

Table 7.1 Growth patterns of the postwar Japanese economy and the "Fordist" model

		Postwar Japan	
Macroeconomic indices	Fordism	Period of high economic growth	Period of a new trajectory
Cumulative causation	Output ⇔ Productivity	Output ⇔ Productivity	
Growth pattern	Wage (consumption)-led	Profit (investment)-led	Export-led (particularly before 1986)
Relationship between the investment goods and consumption goods sectors	Simultaneous development of the two sectors	Quasi-simultaneous development; More development in the investment goods sector in the prosperity phase	
Productivity growth	Rapid growth in the consumption goods sector	Growth in both sectors	More rapid growth in the investment goods sector
Relationship between productivity and wages	Real wage increase = productivity gains; Explicit and implicit indexation	Real wage increase < productivity gains; No indexation	Product wage increase = productivity gains; Constant profit sharing; No explicit indexation
Fluctuations	Small and stable	Large	Small
Production and consumption	Mass production – mass consumption	Mass production – mass consumption	Mass production with product differentiation

Source: Uemura (1998)

7.2 How Was Japan as an Economic Power in the 1970s and 1980s Régulated?

7.2.1 *Japanese Capitalism in the 1970s and 1980s*

In this period after the first oil shock, the Japanese economy experienced, in spite of the end of high speed growth, the highest economic performance of any of the advanced countries, and the "Japanese model," described in popular books such as Ezra Vogel's *Japan as Number One* (1979), was admired all over the world. The Japanese themselves also gradually came to recognize their country as an "economic power." In this Japan as an "economic power," what kind of growth regime was established, and by what kind of mode of régulation was this regime guided? These were the new questions to which we turned our attention.

The period in question was, to use the terms of the régulation approach, that of the "crisis of Fordism." By the middle of the 1990s, French régulationists had shifted their main focus from "Fordism" to the "bifurcation of national trajectories," naming the Japanese trajectory "Toyotism" or "meso-corporatism." In Japan in the second half of the 1990s, instead of debating the question of whether Japan was Fordist, we were more inclined to focus our attention on specifying Japan's unique trajectory or developmental model. What was unique to Japan? How unique was Japan?

In the second half of the 1990s, we started to organize some study groups for the analysis of Japanese capitalism and also some seminars and international conferences centered around French régulationists who often visited Japan. These initiatives served to clarify the characteristics of the Japanese model, and their main results are collected in Boyer and Yamada (2000). This period also saw the publication of many books concerning the régulationist interpretation of Japanese capitalism, including Yamada (1994), Hirano (1996), Inoue (1996), Uni (1998), and Shimizu (1999). Next we will examine these régulationist analyses of the Japanese economy during the 1970s and 1980s, looking firstly at its growth regimes and secondly at its mode of régulation.

7.2.2 *Export-Led Growth and Successive Structural Changes*

It is almost universally understood among Japanese régulationists that the growth regime of the Japanese economy from the second half of the 1970s to the first half of the 1980s, that is, from the oil shocks to the Plaza Accord, was characterized by an "export-led" pattern. On this point Uni's (1995, 1998) analyses are persuasive. During this period, he says, the Japanese economy recorded relatively high economic performance through export-led growth. This growth pattern was supported by high productivity gains in the export goods sector, the suppression of wage hikes, and the depreciation of the yen. This meant that the results of productivity gains were not returned to the Japanese people but leaked out and were distributed globally among foreign parties who bought Japanese products.

But it also meant that the Japanese economy was compensated with some positive consequences: creation of (export) demand, creation of employment, and productivity growth as a result of the effects of dynamic increasing returns. Contrary to many Western countries that suffered from sluggish demand, mass unemployment, and stagnation in productivity gains during this period, Japanese high economic performance was based on these positive effects that were brought about by this export-led growth pattern. Japan therefore experienced relatively high economic growth with a large trade account surplus. But this entailed, on the other hand, a big trade deficit in its counterpart countries, particularly the United States. This kind of international imbalance could not last forever, so this export-led growth lacked viability over the long term. According to Uni, this pattern of growth could not be an alternative to Fordism and could only serve to enable transitory growth in the post-Fordist era.

Uemura also presented similar analyses. After defining the growth pattern of this period as "export-led" early on (Uemura 1992), Uemura (2000) then found, through his additional econometric analyses, that investment was explained more by export than by profit. The Japanese growth regime had shifted, he said, from a profit–investment-led pattern in the high-growth period to an export-led pattern in the 1980s, passing through a turning point in the middle of the 1970s. The strength of his argument resides in his methodology that, by establishing the concepts of wage-led, profit-led, and export-led growth regimes, grasps the evolution and structural changes of Japanese capitalism in terms of the transformations of its growth regime. In the context of Japanese academic analysis, his methodology pointed the way toward overcoming the conventional points of view on the postwar Japanese economy that had fallen into a rigid scheme of stage theory (the theory of state monopoly capitalism described in Chap. 1) or into a mere description of history.

Uni has also developed a similar theory of "successive structural changes." As mentioned above, Uni (1992, 1995) had observed the consumption-led growth in Japan in the 1960s and the export-led growth in the 1980s. That being the case, under what kinds of growth patterns has the overall postwar Japanese economy, including that of the 1950s and 1970s, developed so rapidly? This question is all the more important because Japan was a country that experienced exceptionally high and durable economic growth for about 40 years until 1990. Uni (1998, 1999, 2000) answered this question by proposing his theory of successive structural changes.

Uni pays special attention to the relative prices or productivity of durable goods compared with those of other commodities. By the phrase "durable goods" he implies, in addition to "goods that are used as fixed capital," durable consumption goods like "automobiles and household electric appliances," and also "residential construction that is usually included in investment." The most outstanding characteristics of postwar Japan in contrast to other countries consist in a continuous fall in the prices of durable goods and a continuous increase in productivity when it came to their manufacture. A drop in prices brings an increase in demand. The proportion of durable goods demand to total final demand did in fact rise continuously (Uni 2000: Table 3.3), and postwar Japan experienced successive structural changes in final demand.

To clarify the mechanism of these structural changes, Uni established the concept of "demand structure parameter" that expresses the ratio of the total durable goods demand to profit income. This parameter comprises three elements: (*a*) the percentage of investment expenditure in profit income (investment factor), (*b*) the percentage of durable goods in total consumption expenditure (consumption factor), and (*c*) the ratio of the exports of durable goods to domestic investment (export factor). Given that the final demand is in general composed of investment, consumption, and export, the demand structure parameter is composed of the respective ratio of durable goods in each demand factor. Precisely speaking, Uni also takes account of one additional element, (*d*) the ratio of wage income to profit income (income distribution factor).

Since factors of investment, consumption, and export, which compose the final demand, are exposed to great fluctuations caused by many economic conditions, an increase in the demand structure parameter is not necessarily guaranteed. In Japan, however, this parameter has continuously risen (Uni 2000: Table 3.4). The secret of the continuous increase of this parameter resides in the fact that one demand factor after another has increased in postwar Japan, and in this way the increase of this parameter has been sustained without pause. In other words, we saw in succession (*a*) an investment-led structural change in the 1950s, (*b*) a consumption-led change in the 1960s, (*d*) a change in income distribution in the first half of the 1970s, (*c*) an export-led structural change from the second half of the 1970s to the first half of the 1980s, and ($a + b$) the "bubble-led" transformation in the second half of the 1980s (Table 7.2). Postwar Japan has thus maintained relatively high economic growth through successive changes in the leading factor in its final demand, and in fact has realized high growth in productivity in durable goods sufficient to sustain the growth of demand. In short, postwar Japan has undergone successive structural changes in its demand regime as well as in its productivity regime, and it has been this very succession of structural changes that has provided the dynamism of its capital accumulation.

In contrast to the case of the United States, in Japan there indeed existed a strong correlation between output growth and productivity growth. This meant, especially in the growing sectors of its economy, a powerful operation of what is known as "Verdoorn's law": a cumulative virtuous causal relationship between economic growth and productivity gains. Through the Verdoorn effect, the successive changes in the leading demand factor have thus realized high economic growth. Why and how? Uni finds the answer to these questions in an institutional factor: employment guarantees. According to him, employment security in Japan has promoted not only productivity growth in sectors of high demand growth but also the accumulation of

Table 7.2 Changes in Japanese growth

1950–1960	"Investment-led" structural change
1960–1970	"Consumption-led" structural change
1970–1975	Change in income distribution
1975–1985	"Export-led" structural change
1985–1990	"Bubble-led" structural change

Source: Uni (2000)

labor's skills and knowledge, which in general correspond to length of service. Having arrived at this topic, we have already gone beyond the question of growth regime and reached that of the mode of régulation: How was the Japanese economy in the 1970s and 1980s guided and régulated?

7.2.3 Companyist Régulation and the Hierarchical Market–Firm Nexus

Regarding the mode of régulation that led Japan to become an economic power, two important hypotheses were proposed at the end of the 20th century: companyist régulation and the hierarchical market–firm nexus. Having paid early attention (Yamada 1992) to the distinctive organization of postwar Japanese society, which has been firmly centered around the company, Yamada (2000) proposed the concept of "companyist régulation" as a postwar Japanese capital–labor compromise or mode of régulation.

As was stated in detail in Chap. 5, while in American Fordism the wage compromise between the acceptance of Taylorism (limited jobs) and the provision of wages indexed to productivity led the growth regime of mass production and mass consumption, in postwar Japan it was on the contrary the compromise between the acceptance of unlimited duties and the provision of employment security that led Japan to its high economic growth and status as a major exporting power. In other words, the Japanese capital–labor compromise was centered precisely around the issue of employment. It was not wage hikes but employment security in the same company that postwar Japanese workers demanded most in exchange for their devotion to the company (see Table 5.1). After some years of trial and error, their demand was accepted by managers, and before long "lifetime employment" became part of the "rules of the game" or a social norm between capital and labor. In reality the employment guarantee was primarily applied to and enjoyed by regular male workers in large companies, but its status as an ideal or norm of justice was for the most part shared by the nation as a whole.

Corresponding to this kind of wage–labor nexus (employment compromise) specific to postwar Japan, other systems such as intercompany relations (business groups or *keiretsu*), company–bank relations (the main bank system), bank–government relations (the convoy system), and so on were instituted so that companies and banks could endure and survive. Both employment security within a company and the security of the survival of the company itself, being an isomorphic and complementary relationship, resulted in the formation of the postwar Japanese mode of régulation: companyist régulation. Employment security in a time of recession might trigger "labor hoarding" in general and thus have a negative effect on productivity. In post-oil shock Japan, however, the companyist employment security system seems to have been transformed into a factor of productivity enhancement. That is, under the system of employment security, Japanese workers, particularly the regular male workers in large firms, supported the productivity regime through subscribing to its incentive mechanism, developing their skills, and engaging in meritocratic competition. Companyist régulation, having been instituted in increments since the high-growth era, flourished in the 1970s and 1980s while guiding and coordinating export-led growth (see Fig. 5.1) but now finds itself in a precarious position in the context of the enduring post-bubble stagnation of the Japanese economy and the multinationalization of Japanese firms.

The word "companyism" itself has come to be used to characterize the postwar Japanese mode of régulation or compromise, as illustrated by the use of phrases such as "companyist compromise" (Boyer and Juillard 2000), "companyist régulation" (Hanada and Hirano 2000; Tohyama 2002), and "companyist mode of régulation" (Boyer 2004a). So this hypothesis of companyist régulation has been generally accepted. It has its limitations, however, insofar as its perspective is restricted to large firms and their core workers. Such a hypothesis is of course appropriate as long as the core worker group in large firms constitutes the foundation of the Japanese economy. Along with this group of workers, however, the Japanese economy is also characterized by the existence of other groups of companies and workers – medium and small companies, subcontractors, female workers, and non-regular workers. In other words, there are various other strata of peripheral firms and workers that help define the characteristics of the Japanese economy. How then was the Japanese economy as a whole coordinated and régulated?

This question was answered by a second hypothesis, that of a "hierarchical market–firm nexus" (HMFN). After having first been proposed in the early 1990s (Uemura and Ebizuka 1994), it was gradually modified and enlarged before finally reaching a finished state around the end of that decade (Ebizuka et al. 1997; Isogai et al. 2000). In these texts the authors argue as follows.

Concerning the analytical apparatus of the "market–firm nexus" (MFN), they raise important doubts about the fact that the arguments of French régulationists and the Japanese companyist hypothesis are too single-mindedly focused on the wage–labor nexus. According to them, it is impossible to understand the Japanese mode of régulation without introducing not only the wage–labor nexus concerning large companies but also the labor market and intercompany relations that are inseparably linked to the wage–labor nexus. In other words, to analyze postwar Japan it is necessary to synthesize at least company organization, labor market, and interfirm relations. The synthesis incorporating these three factors is called MFN.

From this point of view, postwar Japan is characterized by its "hierarchical" organization: the rank hierarchy in company organization, the segmented structure of the labor market, and the subcontractor system in intercompany relations (Fig. 7.1). The hierarchy in firm organization functions as an incentive mechanism both in the labor market, as a system penalizing employees for leaving their company prematurely (or pressuring them to remain at their present company), and in intercompany relations, as a wage disparity structure (lower wages and unstable employment for subcontractors). The employment security and high productivity of core workers that are highlighted by the hypothesis of companyist régulation were in effect supported by this HMFN, and it is impossible to define the Japanese mode of régulation without it.

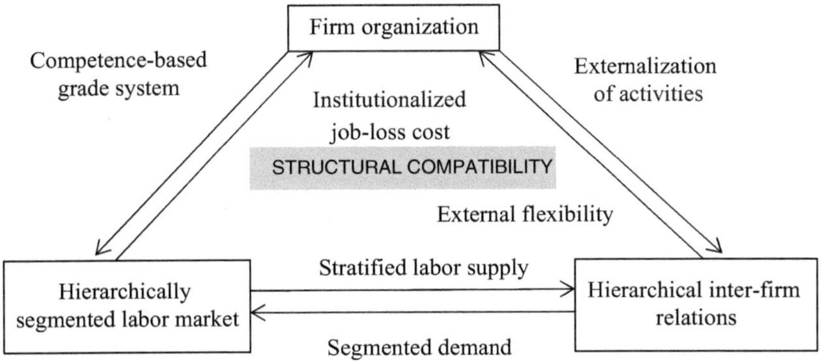

Fig. 7.1 The Hierarchical market–firm nexus hypothesis (Source: Isogai et al. 2000)

They also point out that a high incentive to work hard for regular workers in large firms cannot be properly explained without, in addition to the existence of rank hierarchy in large firms, the existence of a segmented structure in the labor market that means a mid-career job change from a large company to a medium or small company implies a considerable cut in one's lifetime income. The high degree of flexibility regarding the work they are willing to perform that Japanese workers have shown must be explained not only by the internal flexibility of regular male workers in large companies but also by the external flexibility that is forced on the peripheral workers and inseparably combined with it. Japanese HMFN, having initially formed in the high-growth era, was established and matured over the course of the 1970s and 1980s and has been restructured in the long economic stagnation since the 1990s.

The concept of HMFN has illuminated, given a demand regime led by export and investment, the nature of the institutional structure that led the productivity regime in Japan. As such it must be considered highly successful. In short, according to the proponents of this view, the sources of productivity (or incentives and flexibility) in Japan during this period are to be found not in a particular institution but in an institutional nexus ranging from company organization to labor market structure and intercompany relations. This constituted a major contribution to the idea of "institutional complementarity" (or in the authors' words "structural compatibility") developed in recent institutional economics. The concept of HMFN is also important from this point of view. But at the same time it has its own problems. First, the HMFN must include in its nexus the domains of finance and innovation; second, it must include in its perspective its relationship not only with the productivity regime but with the demand regime as well.

Besides these two hypotheses, we had in the years 1996–2000 several studies on each institutional form that constitutes the mode of régulation. Shimizu (1999) investigated work and production at Toyota, and Tohyama (2000) examined the retreat of wage coordination or increase of wage differentials between industrial sectors and between companies at the time, as well as the related transformation of the financial system. Hanada and Hirano (2000), by paying attention to the role of "industrial welfare" as a specific feature of the Japanese welfare system, suggested the possibility of the reproduction system of the labor force centered around companies becoming a drawback in the coming aging society. Nabeshima (1997, 2000), focusing on the financial system that had been ignored by Japanese régulationists, defined the institutional complementarity of the postwar Japanese financial mode of régulation as a triangle of (1) the low interest rate policy and "convoy system" (financial regulatory system), (2) the bank-based structure (corporate finance), and (3) the main bank system (corporate governance). He thus ultimately described its collapse in terms of the development of international finance and the massive issue of national bonds since 1970s. Inoue (1996, 2000), illuminating the international regime that had also been often neglected, re-situated Japanese capitalism in a new context of East Asian countries that were gaining in influence and experiencing instability at the end of the 20th century.

We have just examined the régulationist analyses of Japan in the period during which it became an economic power – the 1970s and 1980s. These analyses suggest several new perspectives not only on Japanese capitalism but also on the theoretical and methodological viewpoints of French régulation theory. First, there can be medium or short-term changes in growth regimes. As shown by successive alternations of the investment-led, consumption-led, and export-led regimes of growth in Japan over the 40 years following the war, the transformation of growth regimes does not necessarily take place at an interval corresponding to that of Kondratieff's long waves – such as that from the 19th century's extensive regime to the 20th century's intensive regime – but can also occur over a shorter interval, as was demonstrated by postwar Japan. Second, there can be a transformation of growth regimes without a transformation of modes of régulation. In Japan between the 1950s and 1980s, we identified on the one hand a change of growth regime from investment-led and/or consumption-led to export-led, but on the other hand we could not identify any changes in the régulation mode over the same period. We found instead an ongoing process of perfection of the same régulation principle – that of companyist régulation or the HMFN. We can therefore add these insights obtained from the analyses of Japanese capitalism to the arsenal of régulation theory.

7.3 In Which Type of Crisis Has Japan Found Itself During Its Long Stagnation Since the 1990s?

7.3.1 Japan and the Transformation of World Capitalism

As capitalism proceeded into the second half of the 1990s, it became clear that it was under such a great and worldwide transformation that contemporary capitalism had become fundamentally different from the capitalism of the past. During these years and those that followed, we saw the collapse of socialism and then its transition to a market economy, the rise and sway of East Asia including China, European integration and the birth of a common European currency, the revival of the

American economy, and the Long Depression of the Japanese economy. Political and military events such as the Gulf War, 9/11 Attacks, the Iraq War, and so on have also had an impact. As for the United States, it has been revived by the innovation of information technology and the financialization of its economy. Japan has on the contrary suffered through the "lost decades" after the burst of its bubble economy. In correspondence with the revival of the American economy, the propaganda of neoliberalism or market fundamentalism has grown louder, powerfully transforming the entire world under the mantra of "globalization." The years since the 1990s mark a great turning point in the history of capitalism, comparable to World War II and the oil shocks.

A "great turning point" is also an apt description in the case of the Japanese economy. Japan, after having risen to its status as an "economic power" through an export-led growth regime and companyist régulation and/or the HMFN, fell into a long period of stagnation beginning in the 1990s. Although in the intervening years there have been some phases of weak recovery, on the whole it has truly been an era of depression. To use the terminology of régulation theory, this should be considered a "crisis," and more precisely a "structural crisis" or "major crisis."

The development of this crisis can be summarized as follows. To begin with, overaccumulation under the bubble economy triggered a turn toward depression. This depression was then intensified by several political failures, such as the government's policy of rejecting the disposition of bad debt and the increasing of the consumption tax, leading ultimately to a contraction of credit and deflation. For several years around 2000, Japan thus fell into a so-called deflationary spiral through a vicious circle of worsening profitability (companies), nonperforming loans (banks), uneasiness about the future (households), and worsening public finances (government). It is impossible to view the Japanese economy as having started to take strides toward growth with a new mode of development.

In what kind of crisis has Japan been mired when viewed from the perspective of régulation theory? If it is a structural crisis, what type of structural crisis? Boyer (2004a) summarizes the factors behind this crisis in Table 7.3. According to him, the origins of the crisis can be usefully categorized in a matrix composed of a temporal axis of short, medium, and long-term factors and an economic axis of real, monetary, and institutional factors. Our intuition that the Japanese economy is in a structural crisis will ultimately cause us to focus our attention on the "long-term" and "institutional" factors. In other words, our question is mainly posed around changes in the growth regime and mode of régulation during this crisis.

7.3.2 Incoherence of the Mode of Régulation

The earliest analysis of the crisis of the Japanese economy was presented by Boyer and Juillard (2000). Though their articles were only published right at the end of the 20th century, their ideas had already been presented at conferences as early as 1995. They compared the Japanese depression in the 1990s with developments in other

Table 7.3 A simple typology of interpretations of the origin of the crisis in Japan

Time horizon	Factors		
	Real	Monetary	Institutional
Short term	Insufficiency of demand; Errors in fiscal and budgetary policies	Errors by the Bank of Japan in the management of interest rates	Excessive confidence in the effectiveness of the previous policies
Medium term	Lack of new products promoting growth; Negative impacts of uncertainty	Inability to resolve the crisis of nonperforming loans	Tensions in the institutional architecture designed for a period of "catch-up"
Long term	Drying up of the postwar growth regime	Dramatic ineffectiveness of the banking and financial system	Irrelevance of the mode of régulation in the current international and domestic context

Source: Boyer (2004a)

countries during the same period and with preceding depressions in Japan. By comparing macroeconomic variables like GDP, productivity, employment, and wages, they pointed out distinctive developments concerning these variables in the recent depression. In the end they provisionally characterized this depression as a crisis of the whole mode of régulation rather than one primarily caused by the archaism of the wage–labor nexus.

According to Boyer and Juillard, the existing mode of régulation of the Japanese economy had obviously fallen into a crisis. When it came to the wage–labor nexus, however, the postwar Japanese status quo had not been overturned but indeed had largely survived at least into the 1990s. In other words, while on the one hand new forms of (international) finance had indeed been pushed forward by the pressure of globalization since the 1980s, on the other hand the inertia of the companyist wage–labor nexus continued to carry it forward, thus resulting in a "diverging evolution between the wage–labor nexus and other institutional forms" (Boyer and Juillard 2000). In short, the wage–labor nexus (and forms of the state) lost its compatibility with the forms of finance (and forms of competition), and the institutional forms thus became incoherent with each other, particularly the wage–labor nexus and (international) finance. The internal incoherence of institutional forms implies a dysfunction of the mode of régulation. Boyer and Juillard thus provided for the first time an analytical key to understanding the structural crisis of the Japanese economy.

As they point out, since the 1980s the pressure of global finance has led the Japanese economy to experience a great institutional change in this domain – the liberalization, marketization, and internationalization of finance in its economy. But as for the wage–labor nexus, although there had been many indications of institutional changes (e.g., the collapse of lifetime employment, the increase of non-regular workers, and the introduction of performance-based wages), in their view, changes to this nexus on the microeconomic level were not yet reflected in the macroeconomic statistics, at least in the middle of the 1990s. (Today, in the 2010s, we may of course be in another phase of this crisis. Institutional changes that originated from the domain of finance, such as the revival of stockholder sovereignty, have now reached the wage–labor nexus in the form of increased external flexibility of labor – non-regular workers now account for almost 40% of all workers. This may be a sign of a breakdown or transformation of the existing capital–labor compromise.)

Nevertheless, however strong the inertia of the companyist wage–labor nexus may have been, it is clear that the companyist mode of régulation as a whole was internally dysfunctional. Or rather, the more coherent companyist wage relations were, the severer their incoherence with market-led finance became. This resulted in the long duration of the crisis. The incompetence of the Japanese government and its policies, as well as the people's distrust of them, prolonged the crisis still further. As mentioned above, Boyer's analyses, including one published a bit later (Boyer 2004a), detected in this way the profound origins of the long stagnation or structural crisis of the Japanese economy in the lapse of complementarity between institutional forms, especially between labor and finance, or, in other words, in the incoherence of the mode of régulation.

7.3.3 *Negative Structural Change*

While Boyer approached the crisis from the angle of the mode of régulation, Uni (2002, 2003) mainly approached it from that of the growth regime. As shown above, Uni had proposed a theory of successive structural changes to explain the durable high economic growth of postwar Japan. How to then explain the long crisis after the 1990s from the same point of view? As he notes, not only Japan but also Sweden and Norway experienced the bursting of a bubble economy at the beginning of the 1990s. Contrary to the early recovery from recession in the Nordic countries, Japan fell into a long period of stagnation (Table 7.4). What lies behind these contrasting evolutions? Posing this question, Uni provides an analysis of structural change in the 1990s and the following period.

According to Uni, employment in the manufacturing industry tends to increase when there is a big structural change, that is, a powerful specialization toward the high-growth sectors within this industry. When we examine statistics regarding this relationship, we can observe the following facts about the Japanese economy. In the manufacturing industry from the 1960s to the 1980s, the differences in the growth rate of both output and productivity between growing and declining sectors were remarkably large. This fact indicates a rapid structural change and also a shift toward greater employment in the manufacturing industry. In the 1990s, on the other hand, both output and productivity grew very little even in the growing sectors of this industry. The differences between growing and declining sectors became slight, and the number of people employed in the manufacturing industry declined. Japan before 1990 indeed experienced, as is shown above, a high rate of economic growth even without a mechanism that promotes supply-side structural changes, thanks to successive structural changes on the demand side – first investment, then consumption, and finally export. But after 1990, the driving force of demand-side

Table 7.4 Comparison of the economic performance of manufacturing industries

	Japan	Sweden	Norway
Growth rate of employment	−1.6	−2.5	−0.5
Growth rate of output	−0.9	3.1	3.4
Growth rate of productivity	0.8	5.7	3.9

Source: Uni (2003)
Note: Average rate for the 10 years after the bursting of the "bubble economies" in these countries (Japan: 1991–2001, Sweden: 1990–2000, Norway: 1988–1998)

structural changes had stalled. In fact, the export-led regime had no durability. Investment demand could not be expected to arise from companies that were suffering from overcapacity and bad debt. Augmentation of consumption by households was hardly desirable from the viewpoint of future lifestyle and environment problems. So in the end, there was no alternative to the promotion of structural changes on the supply side.

Uni concludes by asserting the necessity of a new mechanism that transfers productive elements (particularly employment) from declining to growing sectors. He identifies its ideal model in the Swedish "solidaristic wage system" and "active labor market policy." These measures, by nationally equalizing wages, would lead to a disproportionate profit share among companies and industries and so promote the flow of capital from low productivity to high productivity sectors as well as increased labor turnover through active vocational training. In Japan, on the contrary, low productivity sectors have paid low wages. This has enabled low productivity sectors to secure as much profit share as high productivity sectors, and therefore the former have survived longer than would otherwise have been the case. In the end, Japan, both at the time these analyses were conducted and since, has thus found itself in a situation in which its economy, in addition to having exhausted all of the conventional stimuli from the demand side, allows for hardly any supply-side structural changes, a fact that has made it difficult to get out of the crisis.

Uni then developed his theory of the "stall of structural change" further into one of "negative structural change" (Uni 2007a, b). Negative structural change means a relatively high rate of growth in the demand for commodities accompanied by low productivity growth. According to Uni, while the necessary condition for macroeconomic growth is a positive structural change, in other words, a relatively high rate of growth in the demand for commodities accompanied by high productivity growth, the Japanese economy in the 1990s was transformed into one undergoing negative structural change, contrary to the US economy in the same period. More precisely, based on his model that expands on Kaldor's theory of cumulative causation and Boyer's model (Boyer 1988), he finds that in Japan in the 1990s the demand for investment goods, which recorded relatively high productivity gains, declined, while that for consumption goods, which recorded relatively low productivity gains, conversely increased. The necessary condition for growth was thus not satisfied in the Japanese economy in the 1990s.

The Japanese growth regime has thus been paralyzed by an exhaustion of mechanisms for promoting not only demand-side but also supply-side structural changes. And behind the dysfunction of the growth regime or shift toward negative structural change, there exists a problem in the mode of régulation – an employment system that is too centered on the company. In Japan, labor turnover and skill formation had up to that point been carried out within a company or group of companies. This made it difficult to coordinate these activities on an industry or society-wide scale and to transfer employment from low productivity to high productivity sectors throughout the nation as a whole.

The problems that are inherent to coordination or régulation centered around the company have also been raised by others. Hirano (1996), for example, discussed them in the context of welfare services in an aging society, and Isogai (2004) raised them in relation to a new restructuring of labor flexibility beyond the limit of individual companies. The socioeconomic framework of companyist régulation has now transformed itself into a negative factor for the promotion of a new welfare system and skill formation. To be clear, these limitations of companyism by no means imply the effectiveness of market-centered régulation. They are merely the limits of companyism, a specific mode of nonmarket régulation, not the limits of nonmarket modes of régulation in general, as is confirmed by Uni (2003).

What did the application of régulation theory ultimately establish about the cause and character of the long period of stagnation in the Japanese economy since the 1990s? Our studies have identified and assembled several elements or characteristics of this crisis as follows:

1. Crisis of the growth regime

   1.1 Crisis of demand regime: *exhaustion of driving force by final demand factors*, namely, investment, consumption, and export

   1.2 Crisis of productivity regime: absence of an effective mechanism for transferring productive elements from declining to growing sectors in the manufacturing industry

   1.3 Incompatibility of demand regime with productivity regime: higher demand for goods with lower productivity and lower demand for goods with higher productivity (negative structural change)

2. Crisis of the mode of régulation

   2.1 *Incoherence within the companyist mode of régulation*: primarily, incoherence between the wage–labor nexus and international finance

   2.2 *Dysfunction of coordinating mechanisms too centered on companies*: dysfunction in transferring productive elements, promoting skill formation, and supplying welfare services in an aging society

   2.3 Polarization between industries or companies in which the hierarchical market–firm nexus (HMFN) still operates effectively and those in which it is no longer effective: *weakening of the HMFN*

7.4 What Kind of Position Does Japanese Capitalism Occupy in Asia?

7.4.1 Recent Régulationist Studies and Asia

Over the past 10 years since the late 2000s, régulationist studies in Japan have seen further developments both in terms of an expansion of the topics being studied and a deepening of the inquiry being conducted. Even just a glance at the works that have been published is enough for us to see the results of these efforts. Firstly, as texts focusing mainly on theory, we have Yamada (2008), Tohyama (2010), Nakahara (2010), and Wakamori (2013). Secondly, as theoretical/empirical analyses of the issues concerning Japanese capitalism discussed in this chapter, Uni (2009, 2012) develops an analysis focused on growing wage disparity and employment system reform, Nishi (2014) elucidates contemporary transformations in the Japanese economy from the perspective of finance and income distribution, and Ōkuma (2012, 2015) examines the future course of the Japanese economy based on a reconstructed régulation theory with the addition of the environment as a variable. In France, Lechevalier (2011) investigates the neoliberalist turn in Japanese capitalism. Thirdly, in the context of the 21st century that has seen the development of economic globalization and the multinationalization of companies, the analysis of Japanese capitalism cannot be limited to the domestic study of Japan as a single nation. Taking a broader perspective, Yan (2011) presents an analysis of the economic development and institutional changes in China constructed around the concept of "state régulation," and the analysis of the East Asian nations that have formed an international division of labor structure closely integrated with Japan has begun to be undertaken in earnest. Notable publications in this area include Boyer et al. (2012), Uemura et al. (2014), and Yan (2016).

In this section I will briefly summarize the results of régulationist research in Japan in the 2010s, limiting my focus to the analysis of Asian capitalism. That being said, "Asia," for middle-aged and elderly Japanese at least, is a word that comes with a complicated set of emotions. In the Japan that charged into the invasion and colonization of Asia in the early 20th century, and even in the Japan that rapidly realized a high rate of growth after the war, there was a sense in which Japanese saw themselves as "exceptions" in Asia and for a long time embraced a mentality of "out of Asia, into Europe" (and after the war, "out of Asia, into America"). Faced with the reality of long-term stagnation in Japan and rapid growth in Asia since the 1990s, however, what one hears today is a loud chorus advocating an "into Asia" approach of "integrating with a growing Asia." There has been a major shift in how Japanese people look at Asia. Underlying this shift is the marked development of Asian capitalism and the increasingly close economic relationship between Japan and other countries in this region. The closer this relationship becomes, the clearer it is that the nations referred to with the single term "Asian" are truly socioeconomically diverse, and without a deep understanding of this diversity it will be impossible for Japan and Japanese companies to forge favorable relationships with these countries and optimize their decision-making.

In what follows, I will take a brief look at the results of the régulation theory-based research focusing on this diversity of Asian capitalism that has been conducted in Japan in recent years. While it focuses on other countries, at the same time this research also presumably serves to indirectly elucidate the characteristics of Japanese capitalism, not only as typological characteristics in comparison to so-called advanced capitalist countries but also in terms of what distinguishes Japan in an Asian context. In this sense the analysis of Asian capitalism can be described as part of the analysis of Japanese capitalism. It is also a response to the criticism often leveled at régulation theory that it is biased toward "single country analysis" and fails to look at Japan in the context of the global economy.

How is Japanese capitalism positioned within Asia? In response to this question, in Chap. 6 I examined the position and role of Japan from the perspective of trade and investment. Focusing on research on the diversity of Asian capitalism, here I approach this question indirectly by elucidating the typical characteristics of Japanese capitalism within this context.

7.4.2 The Diversity and Characteristics of Asian Capitalism

As I mentioned in Chap. 4, in recent years the theory of diversity of capitalism has been pioneered by Hall and Soskice (2001), but it was Amable (2003) who introduced this debate to the discourse on the capitalist countries of Asia. Both of these analyses were focused on a comparative analysis of capitalisms limited to the major OECD countries, so when it came to the Asian countries included within their perspectives, the former included only Japan and the latter only Japan and South Korea. In his discussion on "five capitalisms," Amable categorizes only Japan and South Korea as belonging to "Asian capitalism," but of course Japan and South Korea are not representative of all of Asia. Recent years have seen startling economic growth in Asian capitalism and the tightening of economic relationships within this region, and when we bear in mind the growing role of Asia in the global economy, it is clear that more detailed research on the state of the various forms of capitalism found in different countries in Asia is required.

On the basis of this awareness, while taking a lot of methodological guidance from Amable (2003) and while citing and drawing comparisons to Walter and Zhang (2012) and Witt and Redding (2013), H. Tohyama and Y. Harada have developed a succession of new analyses of the diversity of Asian capitalism from the perspective of régulation. In doing so they have mainly utilized quantitative methodologies such as multiple factor analysis (MFA) and cluster analysis, gathering a wide scope of data to form the foundation of their approach. They have also studied the various institutions that compose the capitalism of each country, such as companies (Harada 2011; Harada and Tohyama 2012), innovation (Tohyama and Harada

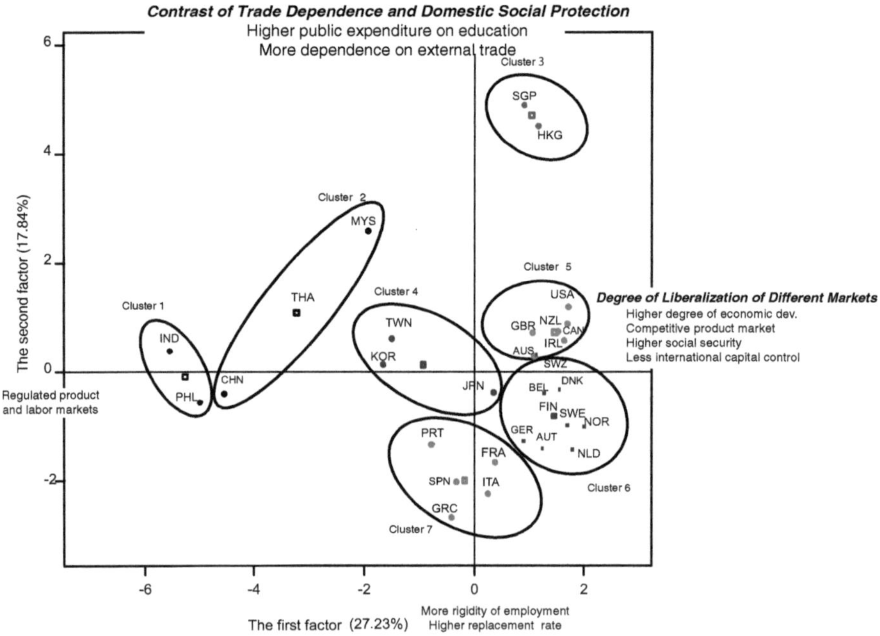

Fig. 7.2 Types of Asian capitalisms and their position in the capitalist world as a whole. (Source: Harada 2011)

2013, 2016), and welfare (Tohyama 2014) from all angles and without limiting themselves to the traditional institutions of labor and finance. In what follows, however, I will do no more than present the conclusions they draw surrounding the diversity of Asian capital.

Figure 7.2 presents the results of their econometric analysis of capitalism in ten countries/regions of East Asia in a chart that includes corresponding data from the so-called "Western" capitalist nations. The details of the axes are given in the chart. Simply stated, the horizontal axis shows the degree of liberalization of different markets. The vertical axis can be interpreted as the contrast between trade dependence and domestic social protection. Generally speaking, in comparison to the West the most noticeable characteristic of the Asian countries is their strong market regulation, but within this context the different forms of capitalism found in Asia can be sorted into the following five categories (Harada and Tohyama 2012).

1. Insular semi-agrarian capitalism: Indonesia and the Philippines
   Characterized by a low standard of economic development, regulated product/labor markets, a low standard of social security, and strict international capital restrictions based on taxation. Not only has direct foreign investment lagged in part because of political instability, but the fact that these countries are made up of many islands makes it easy for them become cut off from economic activity.

2. Trade-led industrializing capitalism: Malaysia and Thailand
   Like the nations in category (1), the degree of liberalization in these countries' markets is not high. But there is more public spending on education and a higher degree of dependence on trade, and employment/working hours are less rigid. Economic liberalization and industrialization are more advanced than in the nations in category (1), and they have been incorporated into global trade networks.
3. City capitalism: Hong Kong and Singapore
   A city-state model of capitalism. The socio-economies in this category are characterized by high economic development, a high degree of liberalization in the domains of product markets, labor markets, and international capital movement, high public spending on education, an extremely high degree of dependence on trade, a low standard of social security, and high profitability in the banking system.
4. Innovation-led capitalism: Japan, Korea, and Taiwan
   What the three members of this group have in common is high economic development and high barriers to entry in their product markets, but in other respects they are quite different. It is therefore impossible to strongly characterize them as a single model, but they share a common history of successful industrialization through an export-led model based on technological innovation.
5. Continental mixed capitalism: China
   In Fig. 7.2 China is included in a group with Malaysia and Thailand, but in an analysis focusing only on Asian economies, China warrants its own category. Chinese capitalism is notably distinguished, for example, by how things like the role of the government in the economy differ from what is seen in other countries. The defining characteristic of the Chinese economy lies in the coexistence of both similarities and major differences from the other categories.

Drawing on the results of this kind of cluster analysis, Uemura qualitatively reorganized these categories (Uemura et al. 2016). Taking the standpoint of régulation theory, he separated the institutional forms (forms of competition, monetary and financial relations, the wage–labor nexus, forms of the state, and the international regime and each nation's place in it) of each of these five types of capitalism and on this basis created a large table sketching out their "modes of régulation" and "growth regimes." The portions of this table directly describing modes of régulation and growth regimes are presented in Table 7.5.

When it comes to these countries' growth regimes, what perhaps characterizes them most strongly is the existence of economies that are easily swayed by demand trends in the global market (Singapore, Hong Kong, Taiwan) and the striking disparity in development between different islands (Indonesia, the Philippines) or regions (China) and in productivity between different sectors (Japan). When it comes to their modes of régulation, these can be seen as having been strongly influenced by the degree of maturity of civil society in the country in question.

Table 7.5 Modes of régulation and growth regimes of five models in Asian capitalism

Models and countries/economies	Mode of régulation	Growth regime
(1) Insular semi-agrarian capitalism: Indonesia, the Philippines	Structural adjustment has been promoted by endogenous crises of the economy and IMF policies. Growth has been promoted by the recent increase in domestic demand. In the Philippines, emigrant workers are part of the growth strategy	The growth regime depends on the export of primary products. Economic growth is supported by income transfer from emigrant workers. There exist growth differentials among islands
(2) Trade-led industrializing capitalism: Malaysia, Thailand	In Malaysia, there is a governance based on segregation and cohabitation of multiple races, and civil society formation is difficult. In Thailand, the informal sector in urban areas has a coordinating function for the labor market	Thailand realized a non-state-led pattern of economic development. Both Malaysia and Thailand have accepted foreign multinationals and have realized export-led growth, being involved in the East Asian production networks
(3) City capitalism: Singapore, Hong Kong	In both Singapore and Hong Kong, the mode of régulation is open, based on the liberalization of the markets. Singapore has developed its market economy, inviting multinationals. Hong Kong is characterized as being part of "one country, two systems"	The growth regime is an open regime with high trade dependency and a high level of financial liberalization. The economy is prone to being influenced by demand fluctuation in the world market
(4) Innovation-led capitalism: Japan	Companyist régulation is weakening, faced by the heterogeneity of firms, but the new mode of régulation has not been established. The hierarchical nexus is eroding due to reorganized subcontracting networks and increasing non-regular workers. Civil society formation has been pursued, but it is still weak	A profit-led and export-led growth regime was established. There are huge productivity growth differentials between the export goods sector and other sectors. Deindustrialization has accelerated since the 1990s
Korea	The mode of régulation is characterized as regulatory relations by large companies and the state. Overseas activities have expanded very rapidly, and state regulation has weakened, creating a more dualistic structure in the domestic economy	The economy showed wage–consumption-led growth in the 1990s, which was transformed into finance-led (profit–export-led) growth in the 2000s
Taiwan	The mode of régulation is a mixture of market-based coordination and public coordination by the state. Low wage growth lags behind productivity growth	Export-oriented industrialization was successful, and export-led growth is seen. The economy is influenced strongly by demand fluctuation in the world market
(5) Continental mixed capitalism: China	There exists "local state capitalism" in provincial governments and city governments which promotes capital accumulation, and this process is coordinated by the state-level régulation. Civil society is still immature	With decreasing wage share and consumption share, the Chinese economy has shown export-led growth, which depends on export demand and vigorous investment. Growth differentials among regions are a serious problem

Source: Author, based largely on Uemura et al. (2016: Table 7.2)

References

Amable, Bruno (2003) *The Diversity of Modern Capitalism*, Oxford: Oxford University Press.

Boyer, Robert (1988) 'Formalizing Growth Regimes,' in Giovanni Dosi, Christopher Freeman, Richard Nelson, Gerald Silverberg and Luc Soete eds., *Technical Change and Economic Theory*, London: Pinter Publishers.

——— (1990) *Nyūmon Regyurashion* (*An Introduction to the Régulation Theory*), Tokyo : Fujiwara Shoten Publishers.

——— (2004a) 'Japon: De la décennie perdue à un impossible New Deal,' *CEPREMAP*, 2004-04.

——— (2004b) *Une théorie du capitalisme est-elle possible ?*, Paris: Odile Jacob.

Boyer, Robert and Michel Juillard (2000) 'The Wage Labour Nexus Challenged: More the Consequence than the Cause of the Crisis,' in Boyer and Yamada (2000).

Boyer, Robert, Hiroyasu Uemura and Akira Isogai eds. (2012) *Diversity and Transformations of Asian Capitalisms*, London and New York: Routledge.

Boyer, Robert and Toshio Yamada eds. (2000) *Japanese Capitalism in Crisis: A Regulationist Interpretation*, London: Routledge.

Ebizuka, Akira, Hiroyasu Uemura and Akinori Isogai (1997) 'L'hypothèse de la « Relation hiérarchisée marché–firme» et l'économie japonaise d'après-guerre : Une analyse en termes d'incitation et de flexibilité,' *L'Année de la régulation*, 1.

Hall, Peter and David Soskice eds. (2001) *Varieties of Capitalism: The International Foundations of Comparative Advantages*, Oxford: Oxford University Press.

Hanada, Masanori and Yasurō Hirano (2000) '"Industrial Welfare" and "Company-ist" *Régulation*: An Eroding Complementarity,' in Boyer and Yamada (2000).

Harada, Yūji (2011) 'Shihonshugi no Tayōsei to Ajia Keizai' (Diversity of Capitalism and Asian Economies), in Fukuyama Shiritsu Daigaku (Fukuyama City University) ed., *Toshi wo Dezain suru (Designing City)*, Fukuyama: Kojima Shoten.

Harada, Yūji and Hironori Tohyama (2012) 'Asian Capitalisms: Institutional Configurations and Firm Heterogeneity,' in Boyer, Uemura and Isogai (2012).

Hirano, Yasurō (1993) 'Sengo Nihon no Keizai Seichō to Chinrōdō Kankei' (Economic Growth and Wage–Labor Nexus in the Postwar Japan), in Robert Boyer and Toshio Yamada eds., *Kiki – Shihonshugi: Regyurashion Korekushon*,1(*Régulation Collection*, vol.1: *Crises of Capitalism*), Tokyo: Fujiwara Shoten Publishers.

——— (1996) *Nihonteki Seido to Keizai Seichō* (*Japanese Institutions and Economic Growth*), Tokyo : Fujiwara Shoten Publishers.

Inoue, Yasuo (1996) *<Seikimatsu Daitenkan> wo Yomu : Regyurashion Riron no Chōsen* (*Reading «the Great Transformation fin de siècle » : A Challenge by the Régulation Theory*), Tokyo : Yūhikaku Publishing.

——— (2000) 'Beyond the East Asian Economic Crisis,' in Boyer and Yamada (2000).

Inoue, Yasuo and Toshio Yamada (2002) 'Demythologing *Régulation*', in Robert Boyer and Yves Saillard eds., *Régulation Theory: The State of the Art*, London and New York: Routledge.

Isogai, Akinori (2004) *Seido Keizaigaku no Furonchia: Riron, Ōyō, Seisaku* (*Frontiers of the Institutional Economics: Theory, Applications and Policies*), Kyoto: Minerva Shobō.

Isogai, Akinori, Akira Ebizuka and Hiroyasu Uemura (2000) 'The Hierarchical Market–Firm Nexus as the Japanese Mode of Régulation,' in Boyer and Yamada (2000).

Itoh, Makoto (1988) *Sekai Keizai no nakano Nippon : Posuto Fōdizumu no Jidai* (*Japan in the World Economy : The Era of Post Fordism*), Tokyo: Shakai Hyōronsha; cf. *Itoh Makoto Chosakushū* (*The Collected Works of Makoto Itoh*), 4, Tokyo: Shakai Hyōronsha, 2010.

Lechevalier, Sébastien (2011) *La grande transformation du capitalisme japonais*, Paris: Presses de Sciences Politiques.

Nabeshima, Naoki (1997) 'La transformation du système financier et la crise contemporaine : Le mode de régulation financière dans le capitalisme japonais,' *Revue d'économie financière*, 43.

——— (2000) 'The Financial Mode of *Régulation* in Japan and its Demise,' in Boyer and Yamada (2000).

Nakahara, Takayuki (2010) *Tairitsu to Chōsei no Seiji Keizaigaku: Shakaiteki narumono no Regyurashion* (*Political Economy of Conflict and Régulation*: *Régulation of the Social*), Kyoto: Nakanishiya Shuppan.

Nishi, Hiroshi (2014) *Shotoku Bunpai, Kin'yu, Keizai Seichō: Shihonshugi Keizai no Riron to Jisshō* (*Income Distribution, Finance, Economic Growth: Theories and Empirical Studies of the Capitalist Economies*), Tokyo: Nihon Keizai Hyōronsha,

Ōkuma, Kazuhiro (2012) 'An Analytical Framework for the Relationship between Environmental Measures and Economic Growth based on the *Régulation* Theory: Key Concepts and a Simple Model,' *Evolutionary and Institutional Economics Review*, 9(1).

——— (2015) *Gurīn Seichō ha Kanō ka*: *Keizai Seichō to Kankyō Taisaku no Seido-Shinka Keizai Bunseki* (*Is Green Growth Possible? Institutional and Evolutionary Economic Analysis on the Economic Growth and Environmental Policy*), Tokyo: Fijiwara Shoten Publishers.

Shimizu, Koïchi (1999) *Le toyotisme*, Paris: La Découverte.

Tohyama, Hironori (1990a) 'Nihon ni okeru Kōdo Seichō to Kiki: Regyurashion Apurōchi ni motozuite' (High Economic Growth and Crisis in Japan : With Special Reference to the Régulation Approach), *Keizai Hyōron* (*Economic Review*), 39(4).

——— (1990b) 'Kōdo Keizai Seichōki ni okeru Chinrōdō Keitai' (The Wage Labor Form in the Period of High Economic Growth), *Keizaigaku Zasshi* (*Journal of Economics*), Osaka City University, 91(1).

——— (2000) 'The Capital–Labour Compromise and the Financial System: A Changing Hierarchy,' in Boyer and Yamada (2000).

——— (2002) '"Kigyōshugiteki Regyurashion" Kasetsu to Sengo Nihon Keizai ni okeru Chingin Kettei' ("Companyist Régulation" Hypothesis and the Wage-Formation in Postwar Japanese Economy), *Keizai Kenkyu* (*Economic Review*, Shizuoka University), 7(2).

——— (2010) *Shihonshugi no Tayōsei Bunseki no tameni: Seido to Keizai Pafōmansu* (*For Analyzing Varieties of Capitalism*: *An Interaction between Institutions and Economic Performance*), Kyoto: Nakanishiya Shuppan.

——— (2014) 'Varieties of Asian Welfare Capitalisms and the Influence of Globalization,' *Journal of International and Comparative Social Policy*, 31(1).

Tohyama, Hironori and Yūji Harada (2013) 'Effect of Institutional Configuration on Innovation Activities in East Asian Firms: A Study of the Institutional Diversity of Asian Economies,' *International Journal of Asian Business and Information Management*, 4(2).

——— (2016) 'Diversity of Institutional Architectures underlying the Technological System in Asian Economies,' *Evolutionary and Institutional Economics Review*, 13(1).

Uemura, Hiroyasu (1990) 'Gendai Shihon Chikusekiron to Shotoku Bunpai : Rijun Shudōgata Seichō to Chingin Shudōgata Seichō' (Contemporary Theory of Capital Accumulation and Income Distribution : Profit-led Growth and Wage-led Growth), *Keizai Hyōron* (*Economic Review*), 39(3).

——— (1992) 'Growth and Distribution in the Post-War Regime of Accumulation : A Theory and Realities in the Japanese Economy,' *Mondes en développement*, 79/80.

——— (1998) 'Sengo Chikuseki Taisei ni okeru Seichō, Bunpai, Kōzō Henka' (Growth, Distribution and Structural Changes in the Postwar Accumulation Regimes), in *Kokusai Keizai Kankyō to Sangyō Kōzō ga Henka suru nakadeno Nihongata Shihonshugi no Chōsei Yōshiki ni kansuru Kenkyū : Shakai-seidoteki Keiryōteki Kenkyū* (*Studies on Transformation of the Régulation Mode of Japanese Capitalism under Changing International Environment and Industrial Structure : A Socio-institutional and Econometric Analysis*), Kagaku Kenkyūhi Hojokin Kenkyū Seika Hōkokusho 1995–1997 (Report of the Research Results by the Grant-in-aid for Scientific Research for 1995–1997), Daihyō (Represented by) Toshio Yamada.

——— (2000) 'Growth, Distribution and Structural Change in the Post-war Japanese Economy,' in Boyer and Yamada (2000).

Uemura, Hiroyasu and Akira Ebizuka (1994) 'Incentives and Flexibility in the Hierarchical Market–Firm Nexus: A Prelude to the Analysis of Productivity Regimes in Japan,' *Japon in extenso*, 31.

Uemura, Hiroyasu, Hiroyuki Uni, Akinori Isogai and Toshio Yamada eds. (2014) *Tenkanki no Ajia Shihonshugi* (*Asian Capitalisms in Transition*), Tokyo: Fujiwara Shoten Publishers.

Uemura, Hiroyasu, Toshio Yamada and Yūji Harada (2016) 'Régulation Approach to Japanese and Asian Capitalisms: Understanding Varieties of Capitalism and Structural Dynamics,' in Nobuharu Yokokawa, Kiichirō Yagi, Hiroyasu Uemura and Richard Westra eds., *The Rejuvenation of Political Economy*, London and New York: Routledge.

Uni, Hiroyuki (1991) 'Sengo Nihon Shihonshugi to Fōdizumu' (Postwar Japanese Capitalism and Fordism), *Keizai Hyōron* (*Economic Review*), 40(11).

——— (1992) 'Sengo Nihon no Chikuseki Taisei' (Regimes of Accumulation in Postwar Japan), *Keizaigaku Zasshi* (*Journal of Economics*), Osaka City University, 92(5/6).

——— (1995) 'Nihon no Yushutsu Shudōgata Seichō' (On Export-led Growth of Japan), *Keizai Riron Gakkai Nenpō* (*The Bulletin of Japan Society of Political Economy*), 32.

——— (1998) *Kōzō Henka to Shihon Chikuseki* (*Structural Change and Capital Accumulation*), Tokyo : Yūhikaku Publishing.

——— (1999) 'Sengo Nihon no Kōzō Henka to Shihon Chikuseki' (Structural Change and Capital Accumulation in Postwar Japan), in Yamada and Boyer (1999).

——— (2000) 'Disproportionate Productivity Growth and Accumulation Regimes,' in Boyer and Yamada (2000).

——— (2002) 'Nihon Keizai no Teiseichō no Gen'in' (Causes of the Slow Rate of Economic Growth of Japan), *Keizai Riron Gakkai Nenpō* (*The Bulletin of Japan Society of Political Economy*), 39.

——— (2003) 'Baburu Hōkai-go no Nihon, Suuēden, Noruuē no Hikaku' (Comparative Analysis of the Economy after the Burst of the Bubble in Japan, Sweden and Norway), *Keizai Riron Gakkai Nenpō* (*The Bulletin of Japan Society of Political Economy*), 40.

——— (2007a) 'Growth Regimes in Japan and the United States in the 1990s,' *Revue de la régulation*, 1.

——— (2007b) 'Export-biased Productivity Increase and Exchange Rate Regimes in East Asia and Europe', *The Kyoto Economic Review*, 76(1).

——— (2009) *Seido to Chōsei no Keizaigaku* (*Political Economy of Institutions and Régulation*), Kyoto: Nakanishiya Shuppan.

——— (2012) 'Increasing Wage Inequality in Japan since the End of the 1990s: An Institutional Explanation,' in Boyer, Uemura and Isogai (2012).

Vogel, Ezra F. (1979) *Japan as Number One: Lessons for America*, Cambridge MA: Harvard University Press.

Wakamori, Fumitaka (2013) *Shin-jiyūshugi, Kokka, Furekishikyuritī no Saizensen: Gurōbaruka Zidai no Seiji Keizaigaku* (*Neoliberalism, State, and Frontier of Flexicurity: Political Economy in the Age of Globalization*), Kyoto: Kōyō Shobō.

Walter, Andrew and Xiaoke Zhang eds. (2012) *East Asian Capitalism: Diversity, Continuity, and Change*, Oxford: Oxford University Press.

Witt, Michael A. and Gordon Redding (2013) 'Asian Business Systems: Institutional Comparison, Clusters and Implications for Varieties of Capitalism and Business Systems Theory,' *Socio-Economic Review*, 11(2).

Yamada, Toshio (1992) 'Heurs et malheurs du mode de régulation japonais,' *Mondes en développement*, 79/80.

——— (1994) *20 Seiki Shihonshugi: Regyurashion de Yomu* (*The 20th Century's Capitalism : An Analysis by the Régulation Approach*), Tokyo: Yūhikaku Publishing.

——— (2000) 'Japanese Capitalism and the Companyist Compromise,' in Boyer and Yamada (2000).

——— (2008) *Samazamana Shihonshugi: Hikaku Shihonshugi Bunseki* (*Various Capitalisms: A Comparative Analysis of Capitalism*), Tokyo: Fujiwara Shoten Publishers.

Yan, Chengnan (2011) *Chūgoku no Keizai Hatten to Seido Henka* (*Economic Development and Institutional Changes in China*), Kyoto: Kyoto University Press.

——— (2016) *Structural Changes in East Asian Labor Markets and Flexicurity Strategy*, Niigata: Niigata University.

Part III
Theoretical Considerations of Contemporary Capitalism

Chapter 8
Stage Theory or Typology?: Methodological Reflections on the Comparative Analysis of Capitalism

8.1 Introduction

The comparison of economic systems is a subject as old as the field of economics. It is fair to say that ever since Adam Smith (1776), every study of economics has incorporated such comparisons. However, the drastic changes in recent world history – such as the development of globalization that is often interpreted as a convergence toward the "one best way" and the transition of formerly socialist countries to market economies – have led to a growing requirement for a self-realized theory of economic systems based on comparative methods and perspectives (Yamada 2006, 2008).

This chapter reexamines the most basic methodological issues in order to advance the study of the comparative analysis of capitalism (CAC). As a prerequisite for contemporary CAC, it is necessary to determine (1) the object of comparison, (2) the aspects of the object that should be the primary focus of analysis, and (3) the proper theoretical framework for the analysis. In this chapter, prior to the concluding remarks in Sect. 8.6, I discuss the following: (1) whether the "market economy" or "capitalism" is the proper primary analytical object (Sect. 8.2), (2) whether the "quantitative" or "qualitative" aspect should be the primary focus (Sect. 8.3), and (3) whether the "stage theory" or the "typology" framework should be used to compare economic societies (Sects. 8.4 and 8.5).

The countries to be studied in CAC have been conventionally divided into three categories according to the stage of development: the advanced capitalist countries who are the main members of the Organization for Economic Cooperation and Development (OECD), the ex-socialist countries who have been in transition to capitalism, and the underdeveloped or developing countries. In addition, region-based categorizations are frequent, for example, Asia (Boyer et al. 2012; Walter and Zhang 2012; Tohyama and Harada 2016), Europe, and Latin America, among others. This chapter focuses on the advanced capitalist countries as the object of comparison.

T. Yamada, *Contemporary Capitalism and Civil Society*, Evolutionary Economics and Social Complexity Science 14,
https://doi.org/10.1007/978-981-13-0517-7_8

8.2 Market Economy or Capitalism?

We define contemporary economic societies as "capitalist" rather than as "market economies." In modern usage, both terms often refer to the same entity, an economic system (in many cases, a national economy) that has been established as a particular historical entity since the modern age. Upon reflection, however, it is clear that the two terms are vastly different (see Table 8.1).

While the term "market economy" attempts to define modern economic societies as consisting only of market relations (commodity exchanging relations), "capitalism" includes the wage–labor nexus as well. To incorporate this nexus alongside market relations means that we must not simply regard the modern society as a space of rational choice by free and equal individuals, but must also take into account the nonsymmetrical character of social relations and the elements of political power. This means that an economic society is not an abstract world composed of timeless and universal laws resembling Newtonian physics but instead that capitalism proceeds toward an uncertain future through an irreversible historic timeline.

In addition, "market economy" presupposes that the economic realm exists independently from the other social realms. However, "capitalism" does not incorporate such exclusive independence of an economic field or market. Although centered on an economic perspective, "capitalism" includes interrelations with other fields such as the polity, society, and ideology. Moreover, while "market economy," through its hypothesis of convergence to an optimal state, understands the economic world as uniform on a global scale, "capitalism" represents the diversity of economic societies in time and space.

Table 8.1 Market economy versus capitalism: two research programs

	Market economy	Capitalism
Concept of market	1. A pure economic abstraction of supply and demand adjustments	1. A nexus of social relations
	2. Horizontal coordination among equals	2. Both horizontal (competition among firms) and vertical relations (capital–labor nexus)
	3. Ideally self-equilibrating	3. Propagation of an unbalanced capital accumulation
Links between various spheres	4. Ideal of total disconnection of the economic sphere (pure economy)	4. The interdependence of economy, society, and polity is intrinsic
Nature of evolutions	5. Implicit conception of "natural equilibrium"	5. Law of accumulation and changing social and economic relations
	6. At best, kinematical time	6. Sense of historical time
Uniqueness/ diversity	7. Ideal of Pareto optimality …… and benchmarking or competition, reducing variety	7. Succession of historical stages and coexistence of various brands of capitalism

Source: Boyer (2007)

Of course, there are some nuances in the use of the term "market economy." For example, Hall and Soskice (2001) use "market economy" almost interchangeably with "capitalism" through reliance on their terms of "liberal market economy" and "coordinated market economy." So while I do not dogmatically insist on these definitions, I prefer "capitalism" to "market economy" for the reasons set forth above.

The question of "market economy" or "capitalism" reflects methodological differences not only in the representation of economic society as a whole but also in the analytical angle and recommended solutions of socioeconomic problems. "Capitalism" represents broader horizons of research than "market economy." If the market economy approach aims at an understanding of precise – and often deductive – laws in a narrowly defined, even fictitious, theoretical world (i.e., a free and perfect market), the capitalism approach intends to grasp realities of actual socioeconomic situations in relation to politics and history. The capitalism approach aims, although it may leave some ambiguous aspects unaccounted for, at a total recognition of economic societies as a whole.

It is here that a method of comparative analysis becomes important. For the market economy approach that follows a deductive method starting from predefined axioms, a method of comparison is not important. For the capitalism approach, on the other hand, it is indispensable. When we aim to find and formulate the laws of economic societies in relation to their polity and culture, comparative analysis is one of the most effective methods available to us. In the capitalism approach, a theory becomes more generalized and perfected only through comparison because the realities of capitalism are too complicated to be deductively described in terms of formalistic definitions. For this reason, a comparative analysis of capitalism is significant. In this regard, the following passage concerning conventional economic theories (the market economy approach) vis-à-vis the régulation approach (one of the capitalism approaches) is very suggestive.

> Whereas conventional economic theories have progressed via intensive elaboration of concepts and the search for axioms, *régulation* approaches have pointed out that any theory has initially a quite limited domain of validity in time and space. Consequently, the international comparisons have been quite helpful in enriching the basic concepts and overcoming the temptation to diagnose a single capitalist configuration for each historical epoch. (Boyer 2007)

8.3 Quantitative or Qualitative Analysis?

Recent literature concerning the main OECD countries indicates potential shifts in the direction of inquiry. The simplest and most appropriate starting point would be a quantitative comparison of their relative economic performance. In this sense, the compilation of economic statistics at national and international levels is the first step in the comparative analysis of capitalism. The representative indicators are GDP, GDP per capita, productivity gains, and economic growth rate. The statistical analyses by Maddison (1982, 1991, 2003) are an example of such results of CAC.

Significant aspects of CAC studies include an abstraction of historical trends or grouping of countries by type based on quantitative indicators and their comparisons. For example, the questions of whether the levels of productivity (Abramovitz 1986; Baumol 1986; DeLong 1988) and the standards of living as expressed by GDP per capita (Baumol et al. 1989) are going to diverge or converge among industrialized countries are often addressed. In neither case, however, have clear answers been forthcoming; when it comes to both productivity and standards of living, the results of econometric comparison depend to a great extent on the range of targeted countries and periods. It is impossible to define the divergence or convergence among countries as a universal historical law solely by means of quantitative comparison.

Furthermore, one can observe comparable macroeconomic performance in the long run even among countries whose institutions differ, such as between the United States and Switzerland and between the main European countries and Japan in the post-WWII era (Amable 2003). This suggests that it is dangerous to infer a qualitative similarity from a quantitative similarity. In short, the quantitative comparison by itself does not tell us much about the substantial similarities and differences among countries or their long-term trends.

It is therefore necessary to advance to the second step, the qualitative comparison or comparative analysis of economic systems. A "system" incorporates "mechanisms" (in régulationist terms, "a growth regime") and "institutions" (also known as "institutional forms" and "modes of régulation"). The study of CAC has developed in tandem with a revival and innovation of institutional economics in recent years. In short, modern CAC has advanced the comparisons and typologies of countries on the ground of a representation in which a country's capitalism or national economy consists of a set of institutions, that is, an ensemble of institutions that are organically entangled.

Here, a new concept of "institutional complementarity" plays a pivotal role. It is defined as follows: "two institutions can be said to be complementary if the presence (or efficiency) of one increases the returns from (or efficiency of) the other" (Hall and Soskice 2001), or "institutional complementarity is present when the existence of the particular form taken by an institution in one area reinforces the presence, functioning, or efficiency of another institution in another area" (Amable 2003). Capitalism is said to become stable and growth promoting due to institutional complementarity. An oft-cited example is the institutional complementarity between the long-term employment system (labor arena) and the main bank system (finance arena) in the postwar Japanese economy (Aoki 1988).

The existence of institutional complementarity implies that a country cannot freely choose individual institutions that are efficient and effective but rather that institutions are integrated in a "system" where they are operating in a complementary manner. This system can be also called an "institutional framework" or "institutional structure." In any case, CAC must incorporate a system comparison or comparative institutional framework.

An institution is an element of a system. A socioeconomic system is composed of many institutions in many institutional arenas. Among those institutions, some are particularly significant from the viewpoint of political economy. For example, Hall and Soskice (2001) emphasize institutions in four arenas: the market for corporate governance or financial systems, industrial relations, education and training systems, and intercompany relations. In Amable (2003), institutions in five arenas matter: product markets, labor markets, finance, welfare, and education. Boyer (2004) distinguishes five arenas of "institutional forms": the wage–labor nexus, competition or interfirm relations, money and finance, the state, and forms of international insertion. The institutional arenas focused on labor, firms, and finance are commonly regarded as important. The importance of welfare, education, and the state varies from scholar to scholar.

8.4 Stage Theory or Typology? (1): The German Historical School and Marxism

The third and most important reflection on the methodology of the comparative analysis of capitalism concerns the theoretical framework of comparison. Even two countries that can be accurately defined as "capitalist" may differ both quantitatively and qualitatively, because capitalism is not uniform. Knowing this, how does one go about understanding the plurality of capitalism? Within what theoretical framework can countries and economies be compared? This issue has loomed large in the history of the social sciences. With such a broad scope of inquiry, I devote two sections to these questions, examining a brief history of social science as it relates to this issue.

There are two typical viewpoints. Either one assumes a tendency to converge among economic systems by viewing any differences as transitory and temporary, or one assumes a divergent or diversified character among economic systems by viewing differences as necessary and durable. The first viewpoint defines these differences in terms of stages of economic development. The second viewpoint emphasizes that socioeconomic differences are not merely a difference in the stage of development. Ultimately, the question is whether we should adopt a convergence perspective or a divergence perspective. That is, should we subscribe to stage theory or typology? The social sciences have long concerned themselves with such issues (see Table 8.2). In this section, I will examine the perspectives of the German Historical School and Marxism.

The issue of whether economies converge or diverge was first examined in a dramatic fashion in 19th-century Germany. List (1841), the founder of the German Historical School, proposed the "national economy" view, which differs from the cosmopolitan and universal economic laws and consequent argument favoring free trade advanced by the British Classical School. For List, human history consisted of five stages: original barbarism, the pastoral condition, the agricultural condition, the agricultural–manufacturing condition, and the agricultural–manufacturing–commercial condition, and each national economy develops by succeeding to ever-

Table 8.2 Two types of perspective on the plurality of capitalism

Schools or periods	Issues	Stage theory/convergence perspective	Typology/diversity perspective
German historical school	Human history	List (1841): stage theory of economic development	Weber (1904, 1921): "ideal types" denying a general law of historical development
		Hildebrand (1864), Schmoller (1884), Bücher (1893)	
Marxism	Human history	Historical materialism: Asian, classical, feudal, modern bourgeois, and socialist modes of production	
*Marx	Development of capitalism	Convergence-biased view emphasizing "the great civilizing influence of capital" (Marx 1857–58) and that an advanced country is the future image of a less advanced country (Marx 1867)	Suggestions on an original path of historical development in Russia (Marx 1881)
*Marxism in the 20th century	Transformation of capitalism in the 20th century	Lenin (1917): stepping up of stages in capitalism along with its own intensifying contradictions, defining imperialism as "the highest stage of capitalism"	
*Japan in the 1930s	Debate on Japanese capitalism	*Rōnō* school: feudal remnants are results of Japan's backwardness in the developmental stages of capitalism	*Kōza* school: feudal elements are a necessary constituent peculiar to Japanese capitalism
*Japan in the postwar era	Historical character of Japanese capitalism	Uno (1980): convergence of Japanese capitalism with capitalism in general, emphasizing the stage theory	Ōtsuka (1965): typological originality of Japanese capitalism constructed on industrialization without modernization
Social sciences in the postwar era	Advanced capitalist countries	Shonfield (1965): convergence to a mixed economy	Goldthorpe (1971, 1984): diversification into neoliberal and corporatist approaches
		Kerr et al. (1960), Kerr (1983): convergence to an industrial society	
	Developed and underdeveloped countries	Rostow (1960): convergence to a high mass consumption society, based on unilinear path view of stage-of-growth	Frank (1969a, b): polarized or double-tracked development into center and periphery
Current arguments	Convergence or non-convergence to the market-led model	Many international organizations: efficiency of market-led model and a necessary convergence to it	Albert (1991), Hall and Soskice (2001), Amable (2003), Boyer (2004): varieties/diversity of capitalism, denying a convergence to the market-led model

Source: Author

higher stages. List was very cognizant of the differences between English and German capitalism, understanding them, above all, from a stage theory perspective by emphasizing advanced ("normal") nationality versus backward nationality. While the Great Britain of List's time was already in the agricultural–manufacturing–commercial condition, Germany was only in the agricultural–manufacturing condition. For Germany to attain the former condition, List insisted upon the necessity of an industrial protection policy and protectionism in trade, both of which ran counter to the British Classical School's free trade doctrine. Once it reached the final stage of development, however, List believed Germany should then become an economy underpinned by free trade and unrestricted competition.

List understood the differences between Great Britain and Germany as pertaining to their developmental stages, stressing the present necessity of a protectionist policy for Germany in order to catch up to Great Britain. List's stage theory of economic development thus derived from a strong, practical concern – the modernization of Germany, which at that time was behind Great Britain economically. After List, the German Historical School developed various stage theories of economic development, for example, those of Hildebrand (1864), Schmoller (1884), and Bücher (1893). However, these theories gradually lost their practicality and became abstract and speculative. Finally, in the midst of the "method debate" (*Methodenstreit*) involving C. Menger and others, M. Weber (1904, 1921) shifted the perspective from stage theory to typology by forging a concept of "ideal types." Weber emphasized the individualist nature of the historical society by denying the existence of a general law of historical development.

What is the contribution to this issue of Marx, who also lived in the 19th century? As is well known, Marx's historical materialism saw human history as a succession of Asian, classical, feudal, and modern bourgeois modes of production, and he believed that the last would be replaced by a socialist or communist model. With regard to the question of diversity in modern capitalism, Marx was inclined to see differences among countries as pertaining to the stage of development. According to Marx, all of the so-called backward countries, including Germany, would soon approach the most advanced form of capitalism—that is, that of England—by virtue of "the great civilizing influence of capital" (Marx 1857–1858). In the preface to *Capital*, Marx says that "the country that is more developed industrially only shows, to the less developed, the image of its own future" (Marx 1867). That is, an advanced country is the future image of a less advanced one. Here the differences between England and Germany are understood not only from a stage theory perspective but also from a strong convergence-biased point of view. We can conclude that Marx's basic viewpoint vis-à-vis the plurality of capitalism mirrors the stage theory perspective.

In his argument on Russian rural communes (Marx 1881), however, Marx also evinces a perspective that takes into account original paths of historical development in different countries, that is, a perspective incorporating national or regional diversity in capitalism.

After Marx's death in 1883, Marxists in the 20th century faced inconsistencies between the theory-based world depicted in Marx's *Capital* and the actual world developing in front of them. The revisionism and imperialism controversies of the early 20th century represented their initial struggles with the new realities. The core question they faced was how they were to explain an imperialism-based transformation in capitalism. Lenin (1917) defined imperialism as "the highest stage of capitalism." He predicted the collapse of capitalism by defining imperialism as a new and final stage of capitalism, known as "moribund capitalism." The imperialist or monopolistic stage of capitalism was seen as differing from the free competition stage seen in the 19th century.

Ever since he proposed it, Lenin's stage theory perspective has significantly influenced the Marxist school of thought. For a long time after Lenin, Marxism fell into a cognitive trap, assuming that capitalism proceeds by "stepping up" from a stage of free competition to that of monopoly capitalism, and, finally, to state monopoly capitalism, and that the contradictions inherent in capitalism would become more and more severe with this "stepping up" and lead to its breakdown. In general, based on its concerns with the historical law of capitalist development, Marxism is inclined to consider the plurality of capitalism from the viewpoint of stage theory, and, as such, it tends to lack a perspective vis-à-vis the diversity among capitalist countries in the contemporary world.

Bringing our focus back to Japan, this country has experienced tremendous controversy over its "stage" or "type" of capitalism. The first Japanese language translation of *Capital* appeared in the 1920s. However, the capitalist world depicted in *Capital* differed greatly from Japan's socioeconomic realities. The greatest issue was how to evaluate the "feudal remnants" that existed extensively in Japan at the time. Were they something transitory that would disappear along with the capitalist development of Japan or something structural that would survive as long as the country remained capitalist? Were they a result of Japan's backwardness in the stages of capitalism or a necessary element peculiar to Japanese capitalism? These questions provoked intense disputes among Japanese Marxists in the 1930s as they were closely related to their practical interests in working out a revolutionary strategy. The *Rōnō* school considered "feudal remnants" a product of Japan's backwardness in terms of its stage of development, insisting that Japan would converge with the advanced capitalist countries in proportion to the development of its capitalism. On the other hand, the *Kōza* school stressed the impossibility of "feudal remnants" dissolving under capitalism and therefore asserted that they would inevitably survive to create a distinctive type of Japanese capitalism (see Chap. 1 of this book).

These same opposing viewpoints were reproduced in the post-WWII social sciences. On the one hand, Uno's (1980) political economy proposed the convergence of Japanese capitalism with capitalism in general from a stage theory angle, while on the other hand, Ōtsuka's (1965) economic history pointed out the typological originality of Japanese capitalism by contrasting "industrialization with modernization" (the West) with "industrialization without modernization" (Japan).

8.5 Stage Theory or Typology? (2): Social Sciences in the Post-WWII and Modern Eras

In the several decades following WWII, the advanced countries, whether victor or vanquished, entered an era known as the "golden age of capitalism," during which they experienced unprecedented rates of economic growth. Economic systems had obviously changed from those that had existed in the early 20th century. Shonfield (1965) found the root causes of this economic prosperity to lie in the new role of governments actively intervening in the private economy. From this viewpoint, he compared capitalist countries such as France, the United Kingdom, West Germany, and the United States. Government intervention was high in France, for example, compared to that seen in the United States. France recovered remarkably quickly from its devastation during the war and had strong economic performance that surpassed that of the United States. Shonfield concluded that France developed not in spite of its anti-market principles, but precisely because of them. Here we can perhaps say that he found a type of capitalism different from that in the United States, but he himself emphasized the fact that, in the middle and long term, modern capitalism had transformed itself into a mixed economy that included both market principles and government intervention. American capitalism should also converge to a mixed economy. Shonfield thus proposed a kind of convergence perspective – convergence to a mixed rather than to a market economy.

In the 1960s, Kerr defined the dominant trend of the times as "industrialization" or "industrialism" (Kerr et al. 1960; Kerr 1983). His viewpoint – by which he sought to overcome Marxist thought, which emphasized class struggles and social conflicts – was that, with the development of industrialization, capitalist countries would become similar to one another in terms of technical structure, education systems, and social stratification. Thus, according to Kerr, every society would finally converge to a system called "industrialism," regardless of the means used to achieve this end or the fact that the concrete form this system would take might vary in each case. In an industrialist society, neither the state nor the market dominates, and countries gradually become more homogeneous with regard to technology or education systems. In short, class struggles would end, and history would be motivated by a universal and ahistorical factor – technical and economic rationality. History may not have followed a Marxist path from capitalism to socialism, but all of the world's economic societies were indeed evolving into industrial ones. The engine driving this industrialist convergence resided in technology.

Countering this industrialist view of convergence is the Corporatism Theory that has been developed mainly in Europe (Goldthorpe 1971, 1984). The term "corporatism" here refers to a system in which governments organize formal or informal arrangements for consultation and negotiation among employers' associations, union federations, and government to deal with problems in macroeconomic policy.

The important role of labor unions is stressed. Increased movements toward corporatism since the 1970s, especially in Nordic countries and Austria, diminished the validity of industrialist theory, which had predicted the dissolution of class struggles. The rise of corporatism during the crisis of Fordism in the 1970s and 1980s implied a diversification into at least two responses, one based on neoliberalism and the other on corporatism. According to Goldthorpe, capitalist societies are not converging, but rather diverging.

In shifting our attention from developed countries to developing ones, we find that nearly at the same time as the works of Shonfield and Kerr, Rostow published a book entitled *The Stages of Economic Growth* (1960) in which he undertook a new "stage-of-growth analysis." He established a convergence view based on stage theory, while the convergence view of Shonfield and Kerr is not necessarily founded on a firm stage theory conception of history. Rostow's aim was to prevent underdeveloped countries from transforming themselves into socialist nations by showing them a route to an American-style society. This aim was indicated by his book's subtitle, *A Non-Communist Manifesto*. In place of the Marxist stages of development, Rostow offered five stages of growth: traditional society, preconditions for takeoff, takeoff, the drive to maturity, and the age of high mass consumption. The takeoff stage is the most critical. China and India at Rostow's time were attempting to "take off," and many other underdeveloped countries remained at the preconditions stage. Every country could thus be placed along a continuum anchored by a traditional society on one end and a high mass consumption society on the other. Although he admitted the existence of some peculiarities that stem from traditional societies and the political choices of each country, on Rostow's unilinear path of development differences among countries dissolve into differences in their stage of development. Thus, underdeveloped countries have a promising future if they wish to converge to an American-style mass consumption society but only if they successfully pass through the takeoff period first. Here we see the typical stage theory view of history and its strong bias toward a convergence view, wherein stage differences will eventually disappear.

On the other hand, as a perspective of "polarized development" or "double-tracked development," dependency theory runs counter to the thinking of Rostow (Frank 1969a, b; Amin 1970). "Underdevelopment" is, according to Frank, not equal to "undevelopment." While the metropolitan centers of industrialized capitalist countries have advanced from "undevelopment" to "development," many third world countries have been obliged to follow a course from "undevelopment" to "underdevelopment." This is the "development of underdevelopment." Economic development and underdevelopment are two sides of the same coin, and they are inseparable in modern world history. Dependency theory, showing two divergent courses in history or two diversified types of capitalism – "development" and "underdevelopment" – revealed the illusionary character of Rostow's arguments. These arguments, based on a unilinear stage-of-growth view of history, had promised underdeveloped countries an affluent future resembling that of contemporary American society.

Over the last two or three decades, in the midst of a flurry of financial liberalization and globalization, we have seen the increasing influence of the argument for the efficiency of the market-led economic model *à l'américaine* and the necessary convergence of the rest of the world to it. Although the strength of this argument was weakened by the bankruptcy of Lehman Brothers in 2008 and the global economic crisis that followed, the market-based type of convergence view persists among economists working at global institutions, governments, and central banks even today. Moreover, many academic and educational institutions of economics are still dominated by the neoclassical school that focuses only on the market economy (not capitalism) and insists, intentionally or not, on the efficiency of, and the necessary convergence to, the American economic model.

Opposition to this view had, of course, been raised earlier, and many criticisms of this convergence view have been developed under the name of the Varieties of Capitalism (VOC) approach, Comparative Institutional Analysis, and the Comparative Analysis of Capitalism (Hall and Soskice 2001; Aoki 2001; Amable 2003). These comparative approaches establish the existence of types of capitalism other than the American type and posit not only their raisons d'être but also their efficiency and fairness as economic models. The question of "stage theory vs. typology" or of "convergence view vs. diversity view" persists as a preeminent issue. Beyond a mere parallelism, however, there are important lessons we must extract from the historical retrospective examined in these two sections.

8.6 Conclusion

In this chapter, we have considered some basic methodological issues in the comparative analysis of capitalism: market economy or capitalism, quantitative analysis or qualitative analysis, and, most importantly, stage theory or typology. Comparative analysis is useful and indispensable when we intend to analyze not just market economies but capitalist economies that are made up of market relations, the capital–labor nexus, and power relations. The first step in the comparative analysis of capitalism lies in a quantitative comparison of countries based on statistical data. In the second step, the comparison must be developed into a qualitative analysis that investigates the socioeconomic systems composed of the complementary institutions. Lastly, we have to extract lessons from an extensive body of research from the modern social sciences concerning stage theory and typology to determine the appropriate theoretical framework of comparison.

As we have seen, stage theory understands differences between economies more in terms of a time horizon and typology understands these differences more in terms of a space horizon. Stage theory is inclined to view differences as accidental and transitory, typology as necessary and persistent. Stage theory therefore has an affinity for the convergence view and typology for the divergence view. In other words, stage theory emphasizes the belief that "Country *A* will soon reach a similar condition to country *B*." In recent years, market fundamentalism has also stressed this aspect of necessary convergence to "the one best way," positing that all other countries, by dissolving their peculiarities and distortions, can and should emulate the American model.

We can learn a great deal from stage theory in that it places a great emphasis on historical changes. At the same time, it does have some weaknesses. First, stage theory is likely to assume the convergence view. Second, stage theory is rather indifferent to the varieties of capitalism that exist concurrently. Third, stage theory often falls into a teleological interpretation of history. For example, 20th-century Marxism insisted that capitalism would "step up" by stages, intensify its contradictions, and ultimately collapse, paving the way for the advent of socialism. For Marxism, ascending the ladder of development implied taking necessary steps to reach the ultimate goal, which was socialism. In the case of Rostow, the society of high mass consumption was considered the final goal of history. We must not accept the teleological view of history offered by stage theory, regardless of our respect for its attention to capitalism's temporal variability. Rather than take an arbitrary view like "stepping up in stages" or "reaching the final objective of history," we need to embrace some new key concepts that can align with historical changes in capitalism.

Can typology meet this need? It tackles head-on the issue of the national or spatial diversity of capitalism, and as such should be put to better use as a critical lens through which we can examine the view of convergence to the American model or the unilinear theory of development that has arisen in recent years. However, typology in itself is not necessarily sufficient. First, classifying countries into certain types very often means fixing each country to a particular type, and this leads to the depiction of the world map as static and unchangeable. Second, world history is likely to be understood as a parallel arrangement of several types of capitalism, consequently resulting in a relative view of history or, eventually, in a "discontinuance of history" perspective. For example, as is often pointed out, dependency theory, which insists on the polarized development of world history, has lost its explanatory power with the emergence of countries like the newly industrialized Asian economies, which have escaped from underdevelopment. We need to maintain a perspective that is mindful of the spatial diversity of capitalism, and this is a virtue of typology. Nonetheless, how do we go about restoring a dynamic conception of history?

How do we transcend the abstract opposition of stage theory vs. typology? Alternatively, how do we integrate them? One key to the answer may reside in a construction of theories of institutions and institutional change. Such theories have so far been developed mainly in political science, particularly in a branch of this discipline referred to as "historical institutionalism" (Mahoney and Rueschemeyer 2003; Streeck and Thelen 2005; Thelen 2004, 2014). This will be the subject of the following chapters.

References

Abramowitz, Moses (1986) 'Catching Up, Forging Ahead, and Falling Behind,' *Journal of Economic History,* 46(2).

Albert, Michel (1991) *Capitalisme contre capitalisme*, Paris: Seuil.

Amable, Bruno (2003) *The Diversity of Modern Capitalism*, Oxford: Oxford University Press.

Amin, Samir (1970) *L'Accumulation à l'échelle mondiale*, Paris: Editions Anthropos.

Aoki, Masahiko (1988) *Information, Incentives, and Bargaining in the Japanese Economy*, Cambridge and New York: Cambridge University Press.

——— (2001) *Towards a Comparative Institutional Analysis*, Cambridge MA: MIT Press.

Baumol, William J. (1986) 'Productivity Growth, Convergence, and Welfare: What the Long Run Data Show,' *American Economic Review*, 76(5).

Baumol, William J., Sue A. Blackman and Edward N. Wolff (1989) *Productivity and American Leadership: The Long View*, Cambridge MA: MIT Press.

Boyer, Robert (2004) *Une théorie du capitalisme est-elle possible?*, Paris: Odile Jacob.

——— (2007) 'Capitalism Strikes Back: Why and What Consequences for Social Sciences?,' *Revue de la régulation*, 1. Online. Available at: http://regulation.revues.org/2142

Boyer, Robert, Hiroyasu Uemura and Akinori Isogai eds. (2012) *Diversity and Transformations of Asian Capitalisms*, London and New York: Routledge.

Bücher, Karl (1893) *Die Entstehung der Volkswirtschaft*; Primary Source Edition, Nabu Press, 2013.

DeLong, J. Bradford (1988) 'Productivity Growth, Convergence, and Welfare: Comment,' *American Economic Review*, 78(5).

Frank, Andre Gunder (1969a) *Latin America: Underdevelopment or Revolution: Essays on the Development of Underdevelopment and the Immediate Enemy*, New York and London: Monthly Review Press.

——— (1969b) *Capitalism and Underdevelopment in Latin America: Historical Studies of Chile and Brazil*, Revised Edition, New York and London: Monthly Review Press.

Goldthorpe, John H. (1971) 'Theories of Industrial Society: Reflections on the Recrudescence of Historicism and the Future of Futurology,' *Archives européennes de sociologie*, 12(2).

——— ed. (1984) *Order and Conflict in Contemporary Capitalism: Studies in the Political Economy of Western European Nations*, Oxford: Clarendon Press.

Hall, Peter A. and David Soskice eds. (2001) *Varieties of Capitalism: The Institutional Foundations of Comparative Advantages*, Oxford: Oxford University Press.

Hildebrand, Bruno (1864) 'Naturalwirtschaft, Geldwirtschaft und Kreditwirtschaft,' *Jahrbücher für Nationalökonomie und Statistik.*, Bd.2

Kerr, Clark (1983) *The Future of Industrial Societies: Convergence or Continuing Diversity?*, Cambridge MA, Harvard University Press.

Kerr, Clark, John T. Dunlop, Frederick H. Harbison and Charles A. Myers (1960) *Industrialism and Industrial Man: The Problems of Labor and Management in Economic Growth*, Cambridge: Harvard University Press.

Lenin, Vladimir Il'ich (1917; English Edition 1964) *Imperialism: The Highest Stage of Capitalism*, in *Collected Works*, 22, Moscow: Progress Publishers.

List, Friedrich (1841; English Edition 1977) *The National System of Political Economy*, Reprint, Fairfield: A. M. Kelly.

Maddison, Angus (1982) *Phases of Capitalist Development*, New York: Oxford University Press.

——— (1991) *Dynamic Forces in Capitalist Development: A Long-run Comparative View*, New York: Oxford University Press.

——— (2003) *The World Economy: Historical Statistics*, Paris: OECD Publications.

Mahoney, James and Dietrich Rueschemeyer eds. (2003) *Comparative Historical Analysis in the Social Sciences*, Cambridge: Cambridge University Press.

Marx, Karl (1857-1858; English Edition 1973) *Grundrisse: Foundations of the Critique of Political Economy (Rough Draft)*, Harmondsworth: Penguin Books. This is the English translation of *Grundrisse der Kritik der politischen Ökonomie (Rohentwurf) 1857–1858*, Berlin: Dietz Verlag, 1953.

——— (1867; English Edition according to the Fourth German Edition 1906) *Capital: A Critique of Political Economy*, New York: Modern Library, Random House.

——— (1881; English Edition in Collected Works 1989) 'Drafts of the Letter to Vera Zasulich,' in *Karl Marx and Friedrich Engels Collected Works*, 24, Moscow: Progress Publishers.

Ōtsuka, Hisao (1965) 'Modernization Reconsidered: With Special Reference to Industrialization,' *The Developing Economies*, 3(4).

Rostow, Walt W. (1960) *The Stages of Economic Growth: A Non-Communist Manifesto*, London: Cambridge University Press.

Schmoller, Gustav von (1884; English Edition 1897) *The Mercantile System and its Historical Significance*, New York: McMillan. This is the English Translation of 'Das Merkantilismus in seiner historischen Bedeutung: Städtische, territoriale und staatliche Wirtschaftpolitik,' in 'Studien über die wirtschaftliche Politik Freidrichs des Grossen,' *Jahrbuch für Gesetzgebung, Verwaltung und Volkswirtschaft im deutschen Reiche*, Bd.1.

Shonfield, Andrew (1965) *Modern Capitalism: The Changing Balance of Public and Private Power*, Oxford: Oxford University Press.

Smith, Adam (1776), *An Inquiry into the Nature and Causes of the Wealth of Nations*, 2 vols., London; in *Glasgow Edition of the Works and Correspondence of Adam Smith*, II, Oxford: Clarendon Press, 1976.

Streeck, Wolfgang and Kathleen Thelen eds. (2005) *Beyond Continuity: Institutional Change in Advanced Political Economies*, Oxford and New York: Oxford University Press.

Thelen, Kathleen (2004) *How Institutions Evolve: The Political Economy of Skills in Germany, Britain, the United States, and Japan*, Cambridge: Cambridge University Press.

——— (2014) *Varieties of Liberalization and the New Politics of Social Solidarity*, New York: Cambridge University Press.

Tohyama, Hironori and Yūji Harada (2016) 'Diversity of Institutional Architectures underlying the Technological System in Asian Economies,' *Evolutionary and Institutional Economics Review*, 13(1).

Uno, Kōzō (1980) *Principles of Political Economy: Theory of a Purely Capitalist Society*, Sussex: Harvester Press.

Walter, Andrew and Xiaoke Zhang eds. (2012) *East Asian Capitalism: Diversity, Continuity, and Change*, Oxford: Oxford University Press.

Weber, Max (1904) 'Die "Objektivität" sozialwissenschaftlicher und sozialpolitischer Erkenntnis,' *Archiv für Sozialwissenschaft und Sozialpolitik*, 19.

——— (1921) *Wirtschaft und Gesellschaft*, 2. Aufl., Mohl Tübingen; 4. Aufl. 1964.

Yamada, Toshio (2006) 'What is the Comparison of Economic Systems?,' *The Journal of Comparative Economic Studies*, 2.

——— (2008) *Samazamana Shihonshugi: Hikaku Shihonshugi Bunseki* (*Various Capitalisms: Comparative Analysis of Capitalism*), Tokyo: Fujiwara Shoten Publishers.

Chapter 9
Economic Crises and Growth Regimes

9.1 Dynamics of Capitalism in Time and Space

The financial crisis of 2008 developed into the so-called Euro-zone crisis. Triggered by the unexpected bankruptcy of Lehman Brothers in September 2008, the financial crisis soon developed into a global economic crisis involving the manufacturing sector, bringing about a social crisis affecting employment and various aspects of life. The days of panic have passed – owing to unconventional counter-crisis measures immediately taken by governments, central banks, and world organizations – but the pace of recovery has been very slow and uneven. In some Euro-zone countries, however, the crisis has entered a new phase: a sovereign–debt crisis. Worse still, in Europe and the United States, increasing controversy over immigration seems to have strengthened the trend toward protectionism in trade and national/racial chauvinism. The financial crisis that began in 2008 is still continuing, albeit having taken on new forms and aspects.

In the midst of this crisis – which has been deemed to be of the "once-in-a-century" variety – we saw a breakdown of the American model of financial capitalism headed by investment banks. What type of capitalism was this financial capitalism, or finance-led growth model, before it collapsed? Before the US economy became finance-led, what type of capitalism had prevailed in that country? In the near future, what type of socioeconomic system will replace the finance-led model? These questions presuppose historical changes in American capitalism itself, and we are thus faced with questions concerning the *historical change* or *dynamics in time* of capitalism.

What is the economic state of other countries? Japan and Germany, for example, have also suffered from changes brought about by the financial crisis. These two countries, however, have not adopted the finance-led model *à l'américaine*; rather, they have followed an export-led or industry-led capitalism model. They have not been on a market-led, but rather a state-led or company-led trajectory. What about

T. Yamada, *Contemporary Capitalism and Civil Society*, Evolutionary Economics and Social Complexity Science 14,
https://doi.org/10.1007/978-981-13-0517-7_9

the Nordic, East Asian, and Latin-American countries and emerging countries such as Brazil, Russia, India, and China (the BRICs)? Additionally, why have Euro-zone countries shown such a variety of responses to the Euro-zone crisis? The models inherent in these countries' economies can never be equated with the American model, regardless of talk of "globalization" and "convergence across the world" among growth models. Euro-zone countries vary greatly in terms of their economic structures. These are questions of *national diversity* or the *dynamics in space* of capitalism.

Capitalism thus varies according to when (in time) and where (in space) it is found. Capitalism is never uniform, but rather multiform and plural. The current world economic crisis poses anew questions pertaining to the "variability of economic and social dynamics in time and space" (Boyer 1990) or to the plurality of capitalisms that exist in different temporal and spatial contexts. Capitalism historically has varied its growth regimes because of major crises, and, at the same time, capitalist economies coexist and confront each other as a variety of growth models within a contemporary world, thereby engendering new dynamics. It is therefore quite nonsensical to advocate "a general law of the market economy" without referring to these dynamics in time and space. Today, in the midst of a major structural crisis, we require an economics of "structural change" or "dynamics"; we must not be satisfied with an economics of "equilibrium" or "statics."

By focusing on *growth regimes*, in this chapter we investigate the plurality or variability of what can be called "capitalism," which has, in general, been brought into relief by economic crises. First, we examine historical structural changes among the growth regimes of hegemonic countries (Sect. 9.2), as well as the spatial diversity of growth regimes/strategies in the era of structural crisis that can be seen at present. Through these examinations we arrive at an understanding of the geopolitical and hierarchical dynamics that exist within the current global economic space (Sect. 9.3). This chapter concludes by referring to the significance of the "growth regime approach" when it comes to how the temporal and spatial dynamics of capitalism are to be understood (Sect. 9.4).

9.2 Growth Regimes and Structural Changes Over Time

9.2.1 Structural Crises and Changes of Growth Regimes

As we saw in the previous chapter, in order to understand the dynamics of capitalism in time and space, we have to transcend the abstract opposition of stage theory versus typology. To begin with, as a new conception of dynamics in time, in place of the framework of "stages of development and stepping up" proposed by stage theory, I propose a new conceptual framework: "growth regimes and their structural changes" or "growth regimes and their succession." "Growth regime" or "accumulation regime" is a régulationist concept that designates a regular configuration of macroeconomic variables in a particular country and at a particular time as a whole.

According to régulation theory, for a growth regime or macroeconomic framework to become firmly established, it needs to be sustained by an adequate "mode of régulation" – a set of social "rules of the game" comprising various institutions and values. The combination of a growth regime and a mode of régulation constitute a "mode of development." The viability and coherence of a growth regime and its mode of régulation determine the character and stability of a particular capitalist society, that is, of a particular mode of development (see Chap. 4, Sect. 4.2).

In addressing growth regimes and the structural changes therein, the concept of "structural crisis" is key (Boyer and Saillard 2002). When we use the word "crisis" to refer to all kinds of difficult phases within a capitalist economy, it is useful to distinguish at least two types of crisis on the basis of degree and character. One is a *cyclical crisis*, which corresponds to the troughs of Kitchin or Juglar cycles. This type of crisis is a temporary downswing phase where tensions and disequilibria accumulated during periods of expansion are wiped out. After a period of reckoning, the economy recovers quasi-automatically and soon reenters a prosperity phase.

The other type is a *structural crisis*. Unlike a cyclical crisis, this type of crisis imposes structural changes on the conventional economy. Here the economy encounters difficulties inherent in its fundamental structure and therefore cannot reestablish a stable growth trajectory without the old socioeconomic structure being transformed into a new one. This kind of crisis emerges through a malfunction in the preceding growth regime and/or mode of régulation. The economy cannot heal itself by appealing to the so-called logic of the market, and it requires a radical reformation of existing institutions and policies. In the history of capitalism, we typically observe structural crises lasting 10–20 years after periods of durable growth stretching from 20 to 30 years.

We can thus identify two types of crisis: cyclical and structural. The latter is far more important in understanding historical changes in capitalism. In fact, capitalism has changed its growth regime and mode of régulation repeatedly through structural crises, and these structural crises have determined the major changes in its history. While traditional economics may address cyclical crises to a certain extent, it does not address structural crises at all. Adopting the perspective of "growth regimes and their structural changes" instead of the teleological perspective of stage theory employed in traditional economics is useful in conceptualizing historical changes in capitalism.

Framed in terms of this understanding of the concept of "structural crisis," in what sort of historical topology is the current global economic crisis situated? It is often said that the present crisis is exceptional, a "once-in-a-century" event. However, a glance at the last 100 years reveals both the Great Depression of the 1930s and the Stagflation Crisis of the 1970s. These too were major crises on par with the current one, and by definition, then, none is truly "exceptional." We must therefore be honest with ourselves in examining the successive occurrence of structural crises in the last 100 years: first in the 1930s, then in 1970s, and now since 2008. More accurately, by introducing the durable growth subperiods that precede the structural crises, we can understand the global history of capitalism as an alternation of growth and crisis or the transformation of growth regimes.

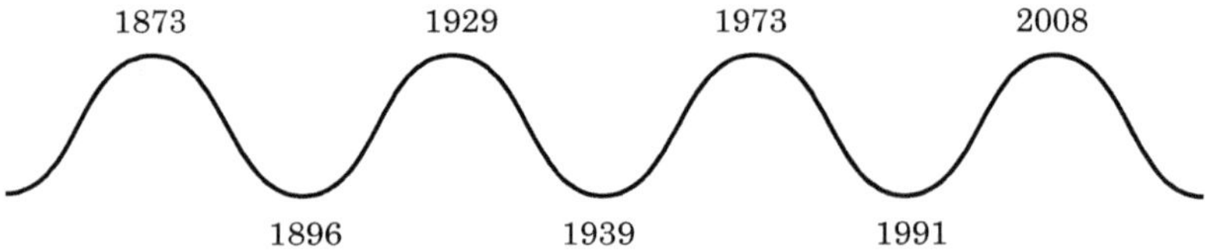

Historical period	Victorian Prosperity	Roaring Twenties	Golden Age of Capitalism	New Economy
	Great Depression fin de siècle	Great Depression in the 1930s	Stagflation Crisis	Global Financial Crisis
Growth Regime	Profit and Investment-led	Intensive without mass consumption	Wage and consumption-led	Finance-led
Mode of Régulation	Market competition	Market competition	Capital–Labor alliance	Stockholder sovereignty
Mode of development	British	Transitory	Fordist	Finance-led

Fig. 9.1 Four historical growth regimes in hegemonic countries (Source: Author)

Growth regimes, however, also vary in the spatial dimension; they differ not only historically but also geographically. Therefore, as a first step, it is better to confirm historical changes in growth regimes by focusing on those of the hegemonic country of the era in question. The growth regime of the hegemonic country imposes itself on other countries, regardless of whether it is successfully imitated or adopted elsewhere, and determines the state of the contemporary world. This is why we should begin by focusing on the growth regimes of hegemonic powers.

Figure 9.1 shows the state of hegemonic power in the history of capitalism over the last 150 years, divided into four periods (Yamada 2013). "Hegemonic power" refers to the United Kingdom in the 19th century and the United States from the second half of the 20th century until today. The first half of the 20th century reflects a period of hegemonic transition from the United Kingdom to the United States (in Fig. 9.1 the United States is taken to represent the hegemonic nation during this period). Recalling Kondratieff's long waves, each period has an upswing wave (i.e., subperiod of durable growth), followed by a downswing wave (i.e., subperiod of structural crisis). There are four subperiods of durable growth: Victorian Prosperity (the United Kingdom in the mid-19th century), the Roaring Twenties (the United States in the 1920s), the Golden Age of Capitalism (the United States after WWII), and the New Economy (the United States from the 1990s to 2008). The four subperiods of structural crisis are the *fin de siècle* Great Depression, the Great Depression of the 1930s, the Stagflation Crisis of the 1970s, and the Global Financial Crisis that began in 2008.

Viewed in terms of régulationist concepts, these four periods represent four modes of development; upswing and downswing waves correspond to the rising and declining subperiods of each mode of development. The four successive growth regimes can be characterized as "profit- and investment-led," "intensive without mass consumption," "wage- and consumption-led" or "Fordist," and "finance-led." The post-WWII Fordist regime was supported and guided by a capital–labor alliance type mode of régulation and the finance-led regime in recent years by a stockholder sovereignty type. The four modes of development can be labeled in chronological order the "British," "Transitory," "Fordist," and "Finance-led" types. In short, capitalism has developed by changing its mode of development (i.e., growth regime and/or mode of régulation) about every half-century. The capitalism of the hegemonic power has thus experienced structural changes every several decades, developing itself through a succession of growth regimes and modes of development. Such changes form the essence of the historical dynamics of capitalism.

9.2.2 *The Growth and Crisis of the Fordist Regime*

Hereafter I will discuss only the period from the mid-20th century to the present while focusing on the United States as the hegemonic power. As has already been discussed in Chap. 4, during the post-WWII period, an economy called "Fordism" – featuring mass production and mass consumption – was established in the United States. Its macroeconomic framework was characterized by a wage and consumption-led growth regime based on a capital–labor compromise as its mode of régulation (see Fig. 4.2).

Here, high productivity gains in the manufacturing sector were the driving force behind the entire economy. Productivity gains were distributed not only as profits, but also in the form of real wage hikes. Real wage hikes, in turn, stimulated individual consumption demand for products such as electrical appliances, cars, and houses. The increased levels of consumption also led to more investment. The increased level of investment, coupled with consumption, led to an increase in aggregate demand (i.e., economic growth) on the one hand, and productivity gains on the other. The resulting growth in GDP led to further productivity gains via improved economies of scale. This chain of events, often referred as a macroeconomic virtuous circle comprising *productivity–wage–consumption–investment–demand–productivity*, codified a growth regime characterized by mass production and mass consumption. A growth regime led not by profit and investment but by wages and consumption was established for the first time in the history of capitalism. This growth model not only continued for nearly 30 years in the United States but also spread, to a greater or lesser extent, to other advanced capitalist countries (Aglietta 1979; Boyer 1988). This is the macroeconomic configuration of the post-WWII high rate of economic growth often referred to as the "Golden Age of Capitalism" (Marglin and Schor 1990).

How did this growth regime persist for roughly 30 years? By setting up new institutions and a new mode of régulation. In the post-WWII era, many institutions were established, including a collective bargaining system, minimum wage system, social security system, managed currency system, consumer loan system, Keynesian economic policies, and a stable international economic system as manifested in the IMF and GATT (General Agreement on Tariffs and Trade). The most decisive moment in the history of the formation of these institutions was the establishment of a capital–labor compromise through collective bargaining. This was a compromise that involved the acceptance of simple, Taylorist labor by workers and the provision of productivity-indexed wages by managers. Capital and labor, in spite of their traditionally antagonistic relationship, became allies at this crucial juncture. Workers accepted Taylorism in order to embrace the Fordist mass production system. In exchange, managers did not monopolize productivity gains, but rather allocated some portion of them to wage hikes. A capital–labor alliance consisting of *the acceptance of Taylorism in exchange for the provision of productivity-indexed wages* thus coordinated and guided an economy led by wages and consumption. In short, the Fordist growth regime in the postwar United States was established under this capital–labor alliance mode of régulation.

Fordism, however, soon found itself embroiled in a structural crisis. In response to various adverse events and circumstances, such as the dollar shock instigated by President Nixon, oil shocks, and stagflation in the 1970s, governments began to adopt neoliberalist policies in the 1980s. Behind these events lay a breakdown of the Fordist growth regime and mode of régulation. First, workers no longer accepted the Taylorist production method, which imposed upon them an increased intensification and fragmentation of labor. Having gained access to mass production goods, workers demanded more diversified consumption goods and services. These are impossible to produce using Fordist methods, which focus on a single kind of product. This sequence of events resulted in a malfunctioning of the mechanism by which gains in productivity were being attained. Second, the success of Fordist industries catalyzed higher levels of urbanization, which in turn drove higher demand for services and benefits in areas such as education, medical care, and retirement that was impossible to satisfy via Fordist wages indexed to productivity. This represented an inherent malfunction in the productivity–distribution mechanism. The mode of régulation based on the capital–labor alliance collapsed, as did the growth regime led by wages and consumption.

9.2.3 The Growth and Crisis of the Finance-Led Regime

In the midst of the Fordist crisis that began in the 1970s, the United States initially adopted a strategy of internationalization, thereby prioritizing companies' level of competitiveness. On the one hand, this led to wage austerity and a degradation of employment in lieu of the Fordist high-wage compromise. On the other hand, American consumers enjoyed access to low-priced imported goods. At the same time, the United States went on to liberalize the finance sector, giving this sector an elevated position of importance in the economy. The preeminence of finance even spread to workers as pension funds became more common. In addition, under the neoliberalist project, finance had effectively come to be seen as a magic wand that could take the place of the social security system, increase access to educational opportunities, medical care, and housing and ultimately wipe out poverty (Boyer 2011). The United States had intended to survive the crisis by executing two strategies, namely, internationalization and, perhaps more decisively, financialization. In the 1990s the revived United States was no longer an industry-led economy that could be characterized as Fordist, but rather had transformed itself into a finance-led economy of a very different nature.

We have already presented, as Fig. 4.5 in Chap. 4, a very simplified schematic of the finance-led mode of development (see also Aglietta 1998; Boyer 2000; Yamada 2013). As a growth regime, this model's driving force is an increase in asset prices (stock and housing prices), which leads to an increase in financial returns (income and capital gains). Increased financial returns, through the asset effect and facilitated by households having easy access to credit (e.g., subprime loans), stimulate consumption. Company investment is driven by the reduced financing costs that follow from high stock prices. At the same time, it must be noted that the high return requirements of financial circles may lead to limited investment. If aggregate demand consists of only two components, consumption and investment, then their increase means an increase in aggregate demand (i.e., economic growth), and this then leads to higher company profits. Higher profit levels give rise to a self-fulfilling expectation of further profits that drives asset prices higher.

By thus establishing a virtuous circle of *asset prices–financial returns/investment–consumption–demand–profits–asset prices*, the American economy experienced a revival that lasted for about 20 years centered around the year 2000. In this finance-led model, in contrast to the Fordist economy that had preceded it, higher asset prices including asset bubbles serve as the main driving force in the economy rather than gains in productivity. The growth regime is no longer led by wages, but by financial returns.

A new macroeconomic loop requires a new mode of régulation to guide and coordinate it. The new mode of régulation in this case is often called the "stockholder sovereignty type," as shown in Fig. 9.1. It is equivalent to so-called "corporate governance," particularly by stockholders. Under the watchword of "corporate governance," an institutional apparatus is established that connects an increase in asset prices to an increase in financial returns, leading to a domination of management by finance. Moreover, the formation of a stock option system demonstrates the creation of a compromise between management and finance; this new compromise occupies a dominant position among all of the institutions in the economy. A stockholder sovereignty type of régulation in place of the capital–labor alliance type of régulation that had preceded it and a finance–management compromise in place of the capital–labor compromise found in Fordism have assumed central positions in the socioeconomic landscape. In lieu of the previous capital–labor alliance, the finance–management coalition forms the "dominant social bloc" (Amable 2003).

Unlike Fordism, the finance-led model is characterized by nonuniversality and instability. Regarding nonuniversality, it can be pointed out that this model was only adopted in the United States and, to a lesser extent, the United Kingdom. In other countries, such as Japan, Germany, and Sweden, the driving force of the economy does not reside in the finance sector. Although these countries have been more or less obliged to adopt financial liberalization policies and "global standards" under strong pressure exerted by the finance-led model, they have not adopted the finance-led model itself. Concerning the aspect of instability, the formation and bursting of asset bubbles are part and parcel of the model, primarily because it is driven by increasing asset prices. Bubbles inevitably burst, leading to a financial crisis which in turn manifests as a banking crisis, exchange rate crisis, stock market crisis, and the like. In this era of global finance, asset bubbles have succeeded each other one after another all over the world and even in the United States, which experienced the information technology bubble in the 1990s and early 2000s and more recently the housing bubble. The finance-led type of capitalism is thus closely tied to bubble economies and is destined for instability as a growth regime (Orléan 1999).

The finance-led model of capitalism, having flourished in spite of its intrinsic lack of stability, appears to have reached a turning point with the bankruptcy of Lehman Brothers; after roughly 20 years of durable growth, this model seems to have entered a period of structural crisis. Sketching the broad mechanism of this crisis (Fig. 4.5), one can see that previous virtuous circles break down and reverse direction, becoming vicious. Falling asset prices come to serve as the driving force that destroys the previous stability that had been built upon their rise; financial returns decrease, leading to substantial financial losses that result in the bankruptcy of various financial institutions and eventually overall paralysis in the financial system. Excess leverage and consumption, sustained by increasing asset prices, also slow down. This breakdown induces a contraction of investment, which, together with that of consumption, dents aggregate demand and, consequently, profits and expectations for profitability. All of these factors reinforce a decline in asset prices.

To sum up, all macroeconomic variables, which formerly drove higher levels of wealth performance in a positive chain reaction, now destroy the very wealth they had created as this process plays out in reverse. There was no chance that the economy would automatically recover from this kind of crisis, and in fact it barely escaped total collapse even with the employment of "nonconventional" economic measures. The exceptional government programs enacted to rescue financial institutions, however, have resulted in fiscal or sovereign–debt crises in many Southern European countries, and fiscal crises have in turn further deepened the crises relating to financial institutions and the financial system as a whole.

We are still in the midst of a structural crisis, out of which the affected economies can only be led by a new growth regime and a new mode of régulation based on radical structural change. When we adopt the framework of "growth regimes and their structural changes" rather than "stages of development and stepping up," we understand this to be indicative of a historical change in capitalism that focuses on the hegemonic power.

9.3 The Comparative Approach and the Spatial Dynamics of Capitalism

9.3.1 The Typical Country Approach and the Comparative Approach

In the previous section, while focusing on hegemonic powers, we traced the structural changes and succession of growth regimes in the history of capitalism. In so doing we derived a new historical perspective that takes the place of stage theory. However, this perspective does not yet suffice to answer our initial question: what are the temporal and spatial dynamics in which contemporary capitalism operates in the era of the current global economic crisis? Countries other than the United States and the United Kingdom, even if greatly affected by the financial and hegemonic power of these countries, have not fully adopted the Anglo-Saxon model; on the contrary, some countries have successfully developed their own original, alternative models of capitalism. Not only in advanced countries but also in moderately and less-developed countries, capitalism is now developing in varied and diversified forms. These new forms influence one another, and we must therefore examine the spatial dynamics of capitalism.

Political economists have traditionally examined the spatial configuration of capitalism at a certain point in time. Adam Smith, criticizing the mercantilist policies of his era, compared Europe and North America in his discussion of the "natural course of things" leading toward a wealthy society (Smith 1776). In the previous chapter, we took a look back at how the plurality of economic societies was addressed by the social sciences from the 19th to the 20th century. However, compared to the 18th and 19th centuries – or even to the mid-20th century – the number of capitalist countries has today increased remarkably, thus enlarging the so-called capitalist zone. In particular, compared to the 1950s and 1960s when developed capitalist countries were generally limited to North America, Europe, and Japan, there has been an explosion of capitalism, and capitalist countries now comprise those considered NIES, the ASEAN countries, the formerly socialist countries, and various other countries in Latin America, Oceania, and Africa. In addition, much attention has been paid to the BRIC countries as emerging capitalist nations or countries with promising new market economies. With an increasing number of countries adopting various types of capitalism – and with the size of the capitalist zone growing ever larger – the variety of growth regimes or of development models has become increasingly notable.

Faced with a number of different variations of capitalism, it is not sufficient to adopt a *typical country approach* in analyzing the capitalist world. The typical country approach, conventionally adopted in political economy, is an analytical method in which one analyzes the most advanced and dominant country in the contemporary world, styling it as an ideal type of capitalism. According to this approach, the essence of capitalism can be understood by analyzing a typical advanced country in isolation without comparing it to other countries. Here one may find a way of thinking that is akin, either implicitly or explicitly, to stage theory or the convergence view. These approaches hold that differences among capitalist economies stem from their being at different developmental stages, and that moderately and less-developed economies will eventually catch up to and converge with the "typical" economy being analyzed. The United Kingdom served as the main capitalist archetype in the 19th century, while the United States was assigned this role in the 20th century. Today, in the case of neoclassical economists who resort to a theory of the so-called market economy, for example, it is obvious that the United States is being considered the "typical country."

The typical country approach, despite its failings, has been useful in understanding certain elements of capitalism. In the current environment of capitalist diversity, however, simply analyzing the American economy will not confer much information vis-à-vis how other countries are likely to develop. To understand this more diversified capitalist milieu, another approach must be explored: the *comparative approach*. New techniques such as Comparative Institutional Analysis (Aoki 2001), the Comparative Economic System approach, and the VOC (Varieties of Capitalism) approach have recently been developed for this purpose. The diversified types of capitalism and growth regimes that exist around the world not only confront and complement each other but also form a kind of hierarchical geopolitical order. Although it is very difficult to disentangle these complex spatial dynamics as a whole, a good first step may be to classify growth regimes or economic societies in terms of a typology in order to facilitate comparisons. Through such comparisons we can arrive at a preliminarily understanding of the confrontation–complementation relationships among types of growth regimes and the dominance–subordination relationships that arise between them. Next I will survey the main results of the comparative analysis that has been conducted on advanced forms of capitalism in recent years, and then summarize these findings to present a brief sketch outlining the spatial dynamics of the contemporary world economy.

9.3.2 The Diversity of Advanced Capitalist Countries

VOC is a well-known comparative analytical approach applied to the main OECD countries at the end of the 20th century. Hall and Soskice (2001) expressed criticism of the view of convergence on the American model and classified the advanced capitalist countries into two types: Liberal Market Economies (LMEs) and Coordinated Market Economies (CMEs). The Anglo-Saxon countries headed by the United States belong to the LMEs, while the CMEs are composed of Continental European countries headed by Germany, the Nordic countries, and Japan. This approach finds that both types of capitalism have not only recorded nearly equivalent economic performance but also have their own proper *raison d'être* because their respective industries' comparative advantage is completely different. These findings challenge the prevailing opinion that the American model is the most efficient, and therefore all advanced capitalist economies must necessarily converge on it.

The VOC approach had a strong impact in that it proposed, based on its comparative analysis, a spatial configuration of advanced capitalist countries in a simple two-type classification. This is why this approach has been used to deliver a sharp criticism of the convergence view. But this analytical framework also has numerous problems. First, do Germany, Sweden, and Japan, which were grouped in the same category, really have identical economic systems? Second, given that France and Italy are classified among neither the LMEs nor CMEs, is the typology that regards these two powers as exceptions or intermediate cases sound and valid? To respond to these questions, Amable (2003) and Boyer (2004) presented a full analysis from the point of view of the régulation approach.

Here I summarize only Amable's core conclusions. Concerning the main OECD countries at the end of the 1990s, he distinguishes five types of capitalism: market-based, Asian, Continental European, social democratic, and Mediterranean models. As for the results of his cluster analyses, I have already introduced them in Chap. 4, Sect. 4.4.2, presenting his seminal schematization as Fig. 4.6. Here I will limit myself to summarizing the essence of his qualitative analyses. Proposing a framework of five institutional domains, product market, labor market, finance, welfare, and education, he lays out each model's institutional characteristics as follows (Table 9.1).

The "market-based model" includes the United States and other Anglo-Saxon countries. Here the competitive pressures in the product market are intense, and this leads to the labor market becoming more flexible and shedding various types of regulation. In other words, low-wage, short-term, unstable jobs proliferate. As a trade-off, the period of unemployment tends to be short, and there are many opportunities for reemployment. In response to these circumstances, the stock market forms the core of corporate finance, which provides speedy but not terribly patient investment. Welfare systems are slow to develop, and the risk to individuals of investing in a specialized skill is high, so there is a high capacity for innovation in fields in which the formation of generalized skills through a highly competitive education system plays a central role, such as biotechnology, information technology, and aerospace technology.

The "Asian model" applies to Japan and South Korea. The socio-economy is organized around large companies; in Japan, for example, large corporations have led the socio-economy while constructing close relationships with *keiretsu*, company groups, industry organizations, financial institutions, and governments. This social organization, which has been referred to as "meso-corporatism" or "companyism," has in some respects been destroyed by the long period of stagnation and progress of globalization since the 1990s, but both labor markets and product markets are still to some extent controlled by large companies as they were in the past. The custom of long-term employment for the core workers at large companies, at least, has been preserved, and thus for these workers investment in skills specific to their companies remains advantageous. Social security at the level of the state has stalled at a low level. A comparative advantage is maintained in industries such as electronics, automobiles, and machine tools.

Table 9.1 Five models of advanced capitalism

Models of capitalism	Institutional domains					Industries with a comparative advantage	Representative countries
	Product markets	Labor markets	Finance	Welfare	Education		
Market-based model	Deregulated; high competitive pressure	Flexible in terms of employment and wages	Stock market based; capital that reacts swiftly but lacks patience	Liberal welfare state; residualist and at a low level in the United States	Competitive education system; centered on general skills	Biology Information Aerospace	USA GBR
Asian model	"Governed" rather than regulated competition centered on large firms	Regulated labor markets centered on large firms; protection of regular employment	Bank-based; Long-term finance by main banks, although this trend is declining	Low level of social security	Private tertiary education system; in-house training by firms	Electronics Machinery Automobiles	JPN KOR
Continental European model	Competitive to mildly regulated	Coordinated labor markets; variance in the degree of employment protection	Financial-institutions-based; patient capital	Corporatist model; relatively high level of welfare	Public education system; emphasis on secondary education	–	GER FRA
Social democratic model	High international competitive pressure due to small countries depending on foreign trade	High labor flexibility; active labor market policies	Bank-based	Universalist model; high level of welfare	Public education system; high public expenditure on tertiary education	Medical care Environment Wood-related	SWE FIN
Mediterranean model	Regulated; public sector	Regulated; employment security instead of social security	Bank-based	Limited welfare state; emphasis on old-age expenditures	Weak education system; low enrolment ratio	Textiles Leather	ITA SPN

Source: Author, based largely on Amable (2003: Table 5.2)

Next comes the "Continental European model." It includes most of the countries located at the center of the European continent, such as Germany, France, and Austria. These nations belong to the group of countries with advanced social security institutions, but their social welfare systems are not as extensive as those in the social democratic model (Northern Europe). Instead, their employment security is quite strong. In other words, the labor market is not very flexible, and technical education is not very well established. And while individual countries may have industries in which they are leaders, such as the aviation and military supply industries in the case of France and the chemical and pharmaceutical industries in the case of Germany, it is impossible to find a single industry in which all countries adopting this model share a strong competitive advantage.

The primary examples of the fourth model, the "social democratic model," are of course the nations of Northern Europe. Most of them are small nations dependent on trade, and as the pressure of foreign competition is very strong, labor flexibility is also quite high. What characterizes this model, however, is that this flexibility is not left up to market adjustments, but rather realized through institutional schemes such as a high level of public technical education, active labor market policies, moderate employment security, and a high level of social security (see also Fujita 2014). Strong industries include those related to health and welfare, the environment, and timber.

The fifth model, the "Mediterranean model," operates in Southern European nations such as Italy, Spain, Portugal, and Greece. Here both product markets and labor markets are strongly regulated, and while employment security is robust in comparison to the Continental European model, social security is inferior. Higher education is not well developed, and industries that generally depend on low-wage, low-skill labor predominate. In terms of trade, these countries specialize in "low-tech" products such as textiles, clothing, and leather.

So even looking only at so-called advanced capitalist nations, we can thus discern five distinct models in operation around the world, and there is no indication of other countries converging on the American model. The diversity of capitalist models would presumably become even richer if we included Asian countries undergoing significant growth (Harada and Tohyama 2012). What sort of spatial dynamics might we be able to describe if we further expanded our field of view to include the world economy as a whole?

9.3.3 Seven Types of Economy in the World Economic Space

The 2008 crisis spread from its epicenter, the United States, to the rest of the world, giving rise to the Euro-zone crisis and a downswing in the world economy as a whole. The Euro-zone crisis, arising out of a unique problem stemming from the use of a single currency, has revealed the structural fragility of some Southern European economies and a North–South division within the zone. On account of this crisis, the relative position of advanced capitalist countries has declined; no longer can any of them cope with economic crises without cooperation from emerging market economies and major petroleum exporters such as the BRICs. This new dynamic can be observed in the expansion of world organizations to include emerging economies as well as the traditional industrialized nations, as seen in the expansion of the G7 to the G20.

As a result, comparative analyses that center on advanced economies alone are, in and by themselves, no longer sufficient to provide an understanding of the dynamics of the post-2008 capitalist space. It is essential to analyze global spatial dynamics while considering the entire world, headed by the BRICs, oil-producing countries, formerly socialist and transitional economies, and OECD countries. As long as the targets of analysis extend to the global dimension, it is inevitable that detailed arguments will be largely sacrificed. Nevertheless, the essential step now is to sketch a post-2008 world economic map, however rough it may be. By consulting the recent literature, we will first identify the diversity of growth models or economic societies in today's world and then establish a hierarchy among them.

When it comes to the global range of growth models and strategies, Boyer (2011) proposes a very interesting framework, classifying them into seven types. His discussion mainly aims to achieve a "bird's-eye view" of the confrontation–complementation relationships in the world economy, rather than analyze the precise mechanisms inherent in each type. These seven types are distinguished in terms of their growth strategies or socioeconomic characteristics rather than in terms of strictly defined growth regimes or developmental modes. Nevertheless, Boyer's seven-category typology can be readily adapted to our present discussion. I present it below, with a few modifications.

1. Dominant financier type: the United States and United Kingdom

   This type is a finance-led economy that promotes economic growth by creating financial liberalization/innovation and providing global financial intermediations. In addition, the United States has been the world's "consumer of last resort." Overall, the finance-led economies of the United States and United Kingdom still dominate the world's market-based economies.
2. Innovative industrialist type: Japan, Germany, the Netherlands, and Sweden

   This type of growth strategy maintains its economic expansion through the production and export of high-quality manufactured products, but it falls into crisis when world trade contracts. The success of this kind of export-led economy is contingent upon the nonvolatility of exchange rates and the favorable growth of the world economy. An absence of these factors leads to its demise. Today, the most urgent task confronting countries with this type of economy may be strengthening connections with countries that possess a developmentalist type of continental economy such as China, India, and Brazil, which have together become the growth engine of the world economy. The NIES countries in East Asia can also be considered to have economies of this type.
3. Developmentalist type: China, India, and Brazil

   These economies, often called "continental economies," have (and will continue to have) extremely large domestic markets, and they also adopt and adapt vigorously developmental policies. Among them, China – having thus far adopted a strategy of export-led growth – needs to transform its strategy into one fueled by domestic demand-led growth. In addition, unlike the case of some Eastern European countries, countries featuring this type of economy have been very prudent in opening themselves to capital markets, and have thus been able to mitigate for themselves the adverse effects of the world financial crisis. Some of the ASEAN countries, although they do not have domestic markets as large as those of the three aforementioned nations, may have economies that approximate this type, given their adoption of developmentalist policies.

4. Rentier type: Saudi Arabia, Russia, and Venezuela

   This type of economy depends largely on rent revenue, i.e., sales of petroleum, natural gas, and the like. Within this type of economy, growth will be greatly influenced by the revival of the American and Chinese economies. The large amount of rent (savings) gained owing to favorable terms of trade for fuel resources goes ultimately to the United States, thus compensating its current deficits. This means, conversely, that savings in these countries are not directed to their own domestic investments and do not assist in cultivating domestic industries.

5. Dependent financier type: Iceland, Hungary, Greece, and Ireland

   Having had economic growth dependent on large amounts of debt in foreign or quasi-foreign currencies, economies of this type have experienced a serious economic crisis due to the devaluation of their currencies following capital flight in the wake of the 2008 crisis. Not only Hungary but also many other Eastern European and Baltic countries have found themselves in a similar position. In peripheral countries within the Euro-zone like Greece and Ireland, the fragility of financial dependence has become evident in the form of a sovereign–debt crisis rather than an exchange rate crisis.

6. Disarticulated type: many Latin-American countries, including Mexico and Argentina

   Following the failure of the import substitution model, countries of this economic type continue to find themselves in a state of socioeconomic disarticulation, suffering from unfavorable international incorporation, crises of state bankruptcy, and increased inequality. They have failed to create modern export sectors that would have facilitated national economic growth, and at the same time have lost economic autonomy and stability on account of their insertion into the international economy.

7. Preindustrial type: many African countries (but not South Africa)

   Generally speaking, in countries with this type of economy there is no, or only very little, of the fundamental infrastructure that is indispensable to economic development. Poverty and inequality prevail in these nations, and global capital has no interest in them. Such economies are, in a sense, disconnected from the capitalist world; their political systems hinder the development of entrepreneurship and productive capitalism. Many African countries are of this type, while South Africa is a notable exception on the continent that does not fall into this category.

Roughly speaking, the contemporary world economic space comprises these seven types of economy, and they confront and complement one another in terms of trade, finance, capital flow, emigration/immigration, and, of course, international politics. Each type has its own interests and policy objectives. The dominant financier type, for example, provides the international public good of global financial intermediation and sees its own interests in greater financial liberalization and innovation. The innovative industrialist type, which depends mainly on exports, requires a world economy that is open to the free trade of manufactured goods. It also requires stability of finance, including the stability of exchange rates. Financial stability is also indispensable for rentier-type countries. These seven types of growth strategy thus demonstrate not only the world's diversity from a wider viewpoint but also the relationships of confrontation–complementation that stem from this diversity itself.

9.3.4 Hierarchy and Dynamics of the World Economic Space

The global economy is not structured as a mere *gestalt* that features confrontation and complementation among growth strategy types; its diverse types of economy can also be differentiated in terms of hierarchical order. This touches upon a second issue, which concerns the spatial dynamics of the world economy. The hierarchical structure of the world economy has already been conceptualized, for example, through Wallerstein's (1979) arguments regarding the capitalist world system. He defines this system as possessing a three-layered structure consisting of a core, semiperiphery, and periphery. The "core" undertakes economic activities that yield a great deal of surplus, and the "periphery" has a notable lack of such activities. Moreover, any surplus held by the periphery is exploited by the core through a mechanism of "unequal exchange," discussions of which often take place within the context of dependency theory. But the decisive merits of the world system theory lie in its understanding of the world economy as possessing a triad structure that features a "semiperiphery."

The semiperiphery situates itself in a "middle stratum" between the upper core and the lower periphery. Politically, it plays the role of buffer between the other two; economically, it plays the role of the receptor of industrial sectors that are thrown out of the core areas due to wage hikes. The semiperiphery has a more or less even distribution of core and peripheral activities; it profits from its cost advantage vis-à-vis the core and from its revenue advantage vis-à-vis the periphery. The world system cannot exist without the semiperiphery, regardless of which countries belong to it at any given time. In a period of world economic expansion, the semiperipheral countries fall into deeper dependency vis-à-vis the core countries. In a period of contraction, on the other hand, some of the former may elevate their positions and join the latter, and vice versa. In general, the semiperipheral countries have shown a strong ability to profit from circumstances brought about by the downswing phase of economic activities – in other words, they strengthen their presence in periods of structural crisis in the world economy (Wallerstein 1979; Arrighi and Drangel 1986).

This geopolitical triad structure that focuses on the concept of "semiperiphery" can assist us in acquiring a better understanding of the hierarchical structure that includes the seven aforementioned types of growth strategy. As shown in Fig. 9.2, roughly speaking, the dominant financier and innovative industrialist types constitute the core of the contemporary world political economy, while the dependent financier, disarticulated, and preindustrial types constitute the periphery. Being midway between these two strata, the developmentalist and rentier types occupy the semiperiphery. Of course, the borderline between the core and the semiperiphery, like that between the semiperiphery and the periphery, is ambiguous; some countries that belong to dependent financier and disarticulated types would be better classified as part of the semiperiphery. Conversely, some countries of the rentier type or in the ASEAN category might be more accurately characterized as belonging to the periphery.

Both before and after 2008, the United States has been in a position of hegemonic power. The core also continues to be composed of countries with dominant financier and innovative industrialist types of economies, but the dominance of the core has declined throughout the crisis. In contrast, some countries of a developmentalist or rentier type have elevated their positions from the periphery to the semiperiphery, while some other countries of these types have more strongly consolidated their position within the semiperiphery, often challenging the hegemonic and core countries. As has been pointed out, such changes have manifested as the expansion of the G7 to the G20, where new member countries are mainly of the developmentalist or rentier type, headed by the BRICs. On the other hand, some countries may have fallen from the semiperiphery into the periphery during the crisis, as might be the case for some countries of the dependent financier or disarticulated type. In the era of a structural crisis – or the era of a long downswing phase in global economic activity – the semiperipheral countries tend to strengthen their power and position, although a few of them may fail to do so and collapse (Arrighi and Drangel 1986).

In the current world economic crisis, the seven growth types are likely to be restructured and reorganized into the three strata shown in Fig. 9.2. This is the most recent set of dynamics in space, or geopolitical configuration, that has been clarified in the world economy owing to the economic crisis. The crisis has greatly changed the power balances among the growth types as well as each country's position in the world system, in some cases causing a shift in whether a country belongs to the core, semiperiphery, or periphery. We must not allow ourselves to become mired in the static view of history into which the conventional typology has often fallen. A structural crisis radically transforms the geopolitical position of each country and its spatial and hierarchical position among growth regime types. Structural crises thus lead not only to historical transformations in hegemonic countries' growth regimes but also to changes in relationships among growth regime types in the world economic space.

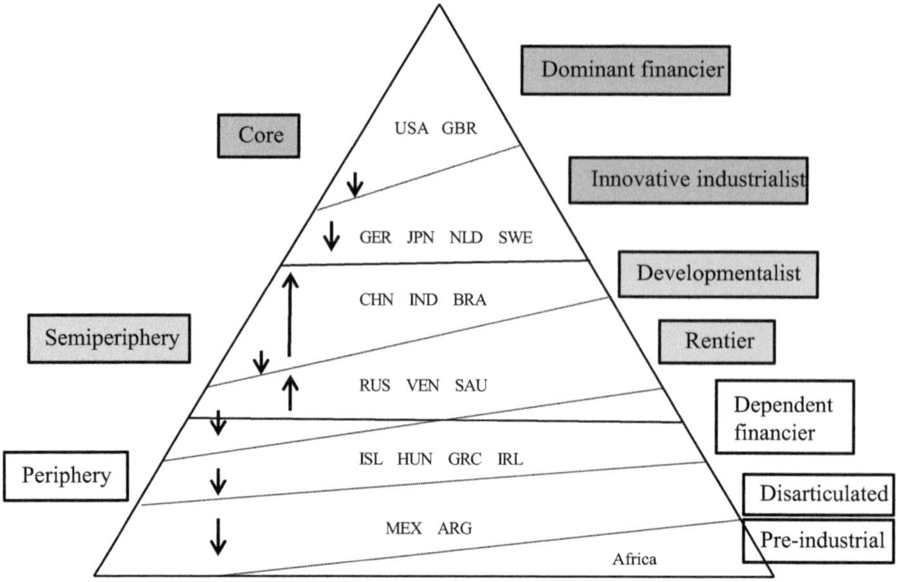

Fig. 9.2 Hierarchical structure of the world economic space. (Source: Author)

9.4 Concluding Remarks

In this chapter I have traced the dynamics of capitalism in time and space. Specifically, I have developed, based on reflections on the abstract opposition between stage theory and typology (see Chap. 8), a historical perspective of growth regimes and their structural changes in capitalism focusing on hegemonic power. I have also developed an argument concerning the diversity of growth regimes/strategies that leads to an understanding of the hierarchy inherent in the world economic system. We can provisionally call this perspective the "growth regime approach." I have stressed the significance of the concepts of "growth regime" and "structural crisis" in understanding capitalism. *Structural crisis* is an especially decisive moment that brings about great transformations in time and space in the world economy, as evidenced in the most recent crisis.

As for the concept of "growth regime," notwithstanding its theoretical importance that has already been emphasized, it must be admitted that there is an essential aspect of history that could be overlooked by examining this concept in isolation. While this concept is well suited to understanding the particular macroeconomic characteristics of various societies, including Fordist, finance-led, market-led, and social democratic growth regimes, a study of growth regimes does not necessarily cover the entirety of a historical era, which can consist of a wide array of socioeconomic models or growth regimes. The concept of growth regime in itself does not illuminate for us the main *trends* in world history. World history manifests as not only the alternation and diversity of growth regimes but also – and above all – as the rise and fall of sociopolitical trends, including the dominant ideologies and policy-based thinking of each era. Such trends, in this sense, correspond to Przeworski's (2001, 2014) concept of "policy regime," which we will examine in the next chapter.

To conclude, what we can say for the moment is as follows. What is important in understanding capitalism is to comprehend historical trends as a whole, as well as structural changes within each country and the typological diversity among countries. Indeed, today's global economic crisis suggests that world history should be understood as *a series of paradigmatic changes in historical trends that incorporate structural changes and a diversity of growth regimes*. It is in this context that the importance of the *growth regime approach* becomes evident.

References

Aglietta, Michel (1979) *A Theory of Capitalist Regulation: The US Experience*, London: NLB.

——— (1998) 'Le capitalism de demain,' *Notes de la Fondation Saint-Simon*, 101.

Amable, Bruno (2003) *The Diversity of Modern Capitalism*, Oxford: Oxford University Press.

Aoki, Masahiko (2001) *Towards a Comparative Institutional Analysis*, Cambridge MA: MIT Press.

Arrighi, Giovanni and Jessica Drangel (1986) 'The Stratification of the World-Economy: An Exploration of the Semiperipheral Zone,' *Review*, 10(1).

Boyer, Robert (1988) 'Formalizing Growth Regimes,' in Giovanni Dosi, Christopher Freeman, Richard Nelson, Gerald Silverberg and Luc Soete eds., *Technical Change and Economic Theory*, London and New York: Pinter Publishers.

——— (1990) *The Regulation School: A Critical Introduction*, New York: Columbia University Press.

——— (2000) 'Is a Finance-led Growth Regime a Viable Alternative to Fordism?: A Preliminary Analysis,' *Economy and Society*, 29(1).

——— (2004) *Une théorie du capitalisme est-elle possible?*, Odile Jacob, Paris.

——— (2011) *Les financiers détruiront-ils le capitalisme?*, Paris: Economica.

Boyer, Robert and Yves Saillard eds. (2002) *Régulation Theory: The State of the Art*, London and New York: Routledge.

Boyer, Robert, Hiroyasu Uemura and Akinori Isogai eds. (2012) *Diversity and Transformations of Asian Capitalism*, London and New York: Routledge.

Fujita, Nanako (2014) 'Historical Evolution of Welfare Policy Ideas: The Scandinavian Perspective,' in Magara (2014).

Hall, Peter A. and David Soskice eds. (2001) *Varieties of Capitalism: The Institutional Foundations of Comparative Advantages*, Oxford: Oxford University Press.

Harada, Yūji and Hironori Tohyama (2012) 'Asian Capitalisms: Institutional Configurations and Firm Heterogeneity,' in Boyer et al. (2012).

Magara, Hideko ed. (2014) *Economic Crises and Policy Regimes: The Dynamics of Policy Innovation and Paradigmatic Change*, Cheltenham and Northampton: Edward Elgar.

Marglin, Stephen A. and Juliet B. Schor eds. (1990) *The Golden Age of Capitalism: Reinterpreting the Postwar Experience*, Oxford: Clarendon Press.

Orléan, André (1999) *Le pouvoir de la finance*, Odile Jacob, Paris.

Przeworski, Adam (2001) 'How Many Ways Can Be Third?,' Andrew Glyn ed., *Social Democracy in Neoliberal Times: The Left and Economic Policy since 1980*, Oxford: Oxford University Press.

——— (2014) 'Choices and Echoes: Stability and Change of Policy Regimes,' in Magara (2014).

Smith, Adam (1776) *An Inquiry into the Nature and Causes of the Wealth of Nations*, London; in *Glasgow Edition of Works and Correspondence of Adam Smith*, II, Clarendon Press, 1979.

Wallerstein, Immanuel (1979) *The Capitalist World-Economy*, Paris and Cambridge: Maison des Sciences de l'Homme and Cambridge University Press.

Yamada, Toshio (2013) 'The Crisis of 2008 and the Dynamics of Capitalism in Time and Space,' in Kiichirō Yagi, Nobuharu Yokokawa, Shinjirō Hagiwara and Gary Dymski eds., *Crises of Global Economies and the Future of Capitalism*, London and New York: Routledge.

Chapter 10
The Neoliberal Regime and its Possible Crisis: A Reflection from the Viewpoint of Institutional Change

10.1 Policy Regime and Growth Regime

After the Lehman Shock of 2008 and the ensuing global financial crisis, many political economists have pointed out the limitations of neoliberalism and market fundamentalism or confirmed a crisis of finance-led capitalism. Today, however, 10 years after the Shock, neoliberal ideas and policies, including political control being exercised by Wall Street in the United States, seem to be as dominant as ever in spite of their serious failures. It also does not seem that the form of capitalism dominated by finance has disappeared. Worse still, we may now be witnessing a new wave of chauvinism and trade protectionism, especially in the US and some of the countries belonging to the EU. Are there any signs of the sprouting of strong new politico-economic systems or ideas that will replace those of neoliberalism? Ten years after the shock, frankly speaking, it is difficult for us to be sure about the direction in which the current regime is evolving. We must therefore consider both the tenaciousness and variability of institutions and regimes. This leads us to the question of what determines institutional change and how it occurs.

This chapter, keeping the problems of today's neoliberalism in mind, proposes some basic theoretical elements concerning the possible crisis of the neoliberal regime. The word "regime" refers to a political, economic, and ideological system with some coherence, domestically or internationally. A regime consists of institutions that, as a whole, are complementary and hierarchical to one another.

Two concepts of regime are relevant to us: policy regime and growth regime. The first concept, "policy regime," was proposed by Przeworski (2001, 2014). He proposed it after observing that, in advanced countries, major political parties, regardless of their partisan stripes, propose similar policies. According to him, in modern democratic politics, a party comes into office by making a major successful policy innovation, and the major opposition parties, in spite of their criticism of the incumbent party during election campaigns, will implement similar policies if elected.

T. Yamada, *Contemporary Capitalism and Civil Society*, Evolutionary Economics and Social Complexity Science 14,
https://doi.org/10.1007/978-981-13-0517-7_10

The difference between parties thus becomes so small that one can identify a movement of convergence toward a new state of policy equilibrium: a "policy regime." As long as a particular policy regime prevails, there occurs only an alternation of partisan control without changes in policy. A policy regime lasts for decades, and it changes infrequently. In the case of democratic countries after WWII, Przeworski identifies two policy regimes: the *Keynesian* policy regime in the period of high economic growth following WWII, and the *neoliberal* policy regime beginning in the 1970s or 1980s.

This concept of policy regime is very attractive because it offers signposts to aid in understanding the main trends in world history. It can be paraphrased as a medium to long-term historical trend or tide in politico-economic systems and policy thought. A policy regime represents a historical era or trend, and its change a swing or turn in the tide of world history. The transformation from Keynesian to neoliberal policy regime, for example, corresponds to our conception of the transformation of growth regime from Fordism to a finance-led regime in the case of the hegemonic power (see Chaps. 4 and 9). Przeworski emphasizes the fact that policies that have succeeded in a (hegemonic) country will be imitated by other countries, which will in turn lead to the medium and long-term synchronization of policies across countries. This chain of events can explain, above all else, the seemingly worldwide spread of a particular policy ideology during a given era. In short, the concept of policy regime elucidates major historical trends or politico-economic paradigms that the concept of growth regime happens to overlook.

Nevertheless, it must be admitted that the concept of policy regime cannot by itself help us understand the socio-economic diversity among countries within any historical period. Despite an inclination, according to Przeworski, among countries to synchronize or converge in terms of policy, in reality countries do not all converge to the same regime or policies. Although countries are greatly influenced by the policy innovations of hegemonic countries, they do not and cannot realize the same growth regimes and growth strategies. While countries can share a particular trend to some extent, they do not completely converge to the same model or strategies, being distributed as they are in a wide range of institutions and structures.

In order to achieve a greater understanding of this diversity, the concept of "growth regime" is necessary. This concept originates in French régulation theory, and generally implies a set of overall regularities in macroeconomic variables of a particular country at a particular time. A growth regime may generate a vigorous "mode of development" when supported by proper institutions and "mode of régulation," while a regime that does not possess this kind of support will decline and fall into crisis. The concept of "mode of régulation" must be understood not only from an economic but also a political viewpoint. As Amable and Palombarini point out, "For the theory of régulation, institutions are a product of 'political compromises' or 'institutionalized compromises'; this has prevented the adoption of the

Table 10.1 Growth regimes and policy regimes

	1950s–1960s	1970s/1980s–
Policy regime	*Keynesian*	*Neoliberal*
Growth regime		
Growth regime in the hegemonic country	*Fordist* or *industry-led*	*Finance-led*
Spatial diversity of the growth regime/socio-economic model		
(1) Hall and Soskice (2001) on main OECD countries		LMEs CMEs
(2) Amable (2003) on main OECD countries		Market-based Asian Continental European Social-democratic Mediterranean
(3) Boyer (2011) on the world as a whole		Dominant financier Innovative industrialist Developmentalist Rentier Dependent financier Disarticulated Pre-industrial

Source: Author

functionalist hypothesis characterizing almost all economic theories. The analysis of institutional change would thus impose an explanation of the social and political impact of an economic trajectory." (Amable and Palombarini 2005: 249)

In this chapter I use the term "growth regime" expansively, that is, almost with the connotation of a "mode of development." Table 10.1, based on the studies of Hall and Soskice (2001), Amable (2003), and Boyer (2011), shows existing growth regimes or socio-economic models. Here I will mainly cover the finance-led growth regime, focusing on the US, the hegemonic country.

In this discussion, "regime" therefore designates either the concept of a "policy regime" that describes a trend in world history or a "growth regime" that covers the spatial varieties of capitalism. As was mentioned above, in this context a regime, be it a policy regime or growth regime, consists of a coherent body of institutions. Regime changes therefore presuppose changes in the regime's core institutions, and regime crises involve crises of core institutions as well. After some theoretical discussion on institutional changes (Sects. 10.2, 10.3, and 10.4), this chapter proposes a critical perspective on the current neoliberal policy regime and finance-led growth regime (Sect. 10.5), before concluding with some remarks on the driving principles in world history (Sect. 10.6).

10.2 Path Dependence and Regime Crisis

Path dependence theory has greatly influenced discussions of institutional change in recent years. In effect, when we extract an essential historical understanding undergirding theories of policy regimes and growth regimes, we can find in them a kind of theoretical configuration of path dependence. For example, Przeworski's policy regime theory examines historical evolutions within the following framework: policy innovation (assumed to occur in a period of crisis) → state of policy equilibrium (policy regime) → new policy innovation. In the case of régulation theory, at least in its original form, growth regime theory assumes a similar historical trajectory: structural crisis → durable growth (growth regime) → new structural crisis.

A historical pattern can be defined as follows. In the first stage, conventional institutions are reexamined and signs of new institutions emerge during a critical epoch (period of crisis). Next comes the forging of proper institutions and policies supporting economic development and political stability (period of durable growth or political equilibrium). Finally, with the passage of time, these measures reach an impasse, resulting in a new epoch of regime crisis and institutional innovation (new period of crisis).

As this shows, the historical perspective of policy and growth regime theories, intentionally or not, stands, to some extent, on the model of path dependence theory. In this sense the latter is situated as a starting point for understanding changes in institutions and regimes. There is already an extensive body of literature featuring various opinions in many academic disciplines on path dependence theory. In this chapter I focus on the development of this theory only with respect to the study of institutions, especially in the academic tradition of "historical institutionalism," an approach that has greatly extended path dependence theory.

The characteristics of path dependence theory from a historical perspective are, *grosso modo,* summarized as follows. A historical path begins with an epoch called a "critical juncture" in which many possibilities for the future vie with each other and jostle amidst chaos and disorder. Over time, however, either one or a small number of possible paths, often resulting from relatively small events, will be taken by the society in question. What institution or path will be chosen is, in many cases, dependent on "contingent" or "exogenous" shocks. But once a path is chosen, it creates "positive feedback" or "increasing returns," reproducing itself for a relatively long period, and institutions and paths thereby lock in particular patterns. This is the stable period for institutions. Eventually, however, the path becomes unstable owing to the emergence of a new situation, leading to a period of abrupt path collapse and a search for new approaches, that is, a new period of critical juncture (Pierson 2000; Mahoney 2000; Deeg 2001).

Path dependence theory, therefore, still understands history in line with the original framework described above: critical juncture → developmental trajectory (reproduction of path) → critical juncture. Its historical perspective is well summarized as "long continuities" periodically interrupted by "radical shifts" (Pempel 1998: 3; Thelen 2004: 28). The merits of path dependence theory in the field of

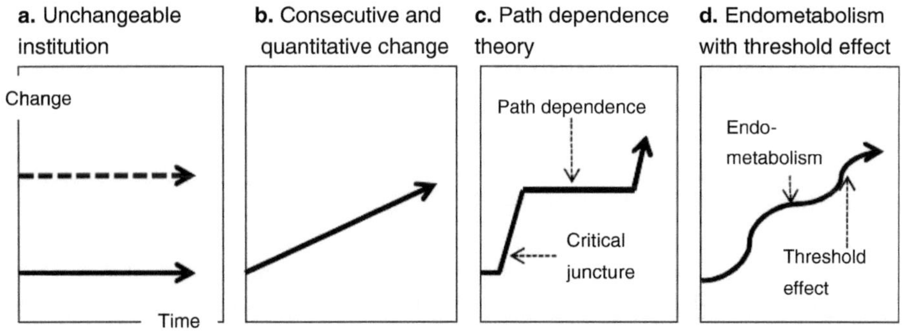

Fig. 10.1 Various views on institutional change: (**a**) unchangeable institution, (**b**) consecutive and quantitative change, (**c**) path dependence theory, (**d**) endometabolism with threshold effect. (Source: Author)

institutional studies include: (1) it facilitates a dynamic, historical understanding of institutions (in other words, it provides a theory of institutional change) by moving away from the kind of static, unchangeable view of institutions often presupposed in the comparative analysis of institutions (Fig. 10.1a); (2) it discusses changes in history, including qualitative transformations of economic societies, instead of providing an uninterrupted, monotonous view of history that simply involves consecutive, quantitative and often linear variations (Fig. 10.1b); (3) it distinguishes between the generating and existing causes of institutions by clearly distinguishing between periods of critical juncture and reproduction (Fig. 10.1c), leading to a rejection of the functionalist explanation of institutions that insists that the existence of institution A is due to its function A'; and (4) it allows for a discussion of different types of capitalism through its emphasis on concrete historical events and their path-establishing roles.

Although path dependence theory has facilitated a discussion of institutional change, its understanding of institutional change is not necessarily persuasive. Among the many critiques of this theory, the following are the most relevant: (1) it identifies causes of institutional change solely in exogenous or contingent shocks; (2) it does not focus on the importance of big events early in a sequence, but emphasizes only small events (Schwartz 2001; Deeg 2001); (3) it detects moments of institutional change, not "gradual" and "endogenous" change, but "radical" change, at a critical juncture; and (4) as Thelen (2003, 2004) points out, it involves a mechanical dichotomy that divides history into periods of institutional change (critical juncture) and institutional stability (reproduction) (Fig. 10.1c).

These four points must be superseded by a more developed discussion of institutional change (e.g., Fig. 10.1d). Path dependence theory, in spite of its cultivation of a historical view that is punctuated by regime crises, does not suggest how a regime crisis occurs. In the next section I therefore consider the essence of institutional change by examining discussions of the types of institutional changes that can occur.

10.3 Endometabolism of Institutions and Types of Institutional Change

10.3.1 Beyond Thelen's Classification

One could obtain many classifications of institutional change from various criteria. The most well-known typology was principally proposed by Kathleen Thelen. This typology classifies institutional change into four types from the point of view of its "process" (incremental or abrupt) and "result" (continuity and discontinuity): (a) "reproduction by adaptation" (*incremental* process of change with a *continuous* result of change), (b) "survival and return" (*abrupt* process with a *continuous* result), (c) "gradual transformation" (*incremental* process with a *discontinuous* result), and (d) "breakdown and replacement" (*abrupt* process with a *discontinuous* result) (Streeck and Thelen 2005: 9; Thelen 2009: 475).

(a) "Reproduction by adaptation" describes a state in which established institutions, while adapting themselves to the developments of their era, maintain, reproduce, and preserve themselves. (b) "Survival and return" refers to cases in which, although there is a transitory institutional change owing to an attempt at abrupt institutional transformation, the attempt soon falters and the original institutions return. In reality, however, as long as the "result" remains "continuous" neither of these are cases of institutional change but rather of institutional persistence. In Thelen's classification we therefore find only two types of actual institutional change: (c) "gradual transformation" and (d) "breakdown and replacement." "Gradual transformation" refers to a situation in which, notwithstanding a partial and gradual process of changes, the accumulation of changes over a long period of time results in a "discontinuous" breakdown of the initial institutions. This is the situation to which Thelen attaches particularly great importance. "Breakdown and replacement" designates a type of change in which institutions suffer sudden transformations leading to states of affairs that are disconnected from those that had preceded them. This is a type of change in which previous institutions are replaced almost at a stroke in a critical moment, as might be seen in the case of a war, a great depression, or a revolution. In Thelen's classification as a whole, institutional changes are thus essentially distinguished only by whether they are "incremental" or "abrupt," a typology too simple to be effective.

I therefore intend to construct a slightly more detailed typology. Keeping Thelen's viewpoint that classifies the "process" of institutional change into "gradual" and "abrupt (radical)" categories, we must also pay attention to the "causes" of institutional change. Although there may be many causes of institutional change, here I categorize them into "endogenous" and "exogenous" from a much wider point of view. Just as it is not easy to distinguish between "gradual" and "radical" concerning the actual process of institutional change, so too is it difficult to distinguish "endogenous" from "exogenous" with respect to the causes of institutional

Table 10.2 Types of institutional changes: processes and causes

		Causes of change	
		Endogenous	Exogenous
Process of change	Gradual	*Endometabolism*: Gradual transformation of the institution by means of its own functioning (a)	*Hybridization*: Gradual penetration and mixture of foreign and international influences (c)
		Modes of change: Layering, drift, conversion	
	Radical	*Threshold effect*: Internal collapse of the institution after reaching the threshold of endometabolism (b)	*Big events*: International shocks, wars, revolutions, etc. (d)
		Mode of change: Displacement	

Source: Author

change, because causes normally arise within complicated relationships. I nonetheless attempt to present my typology in the simplest way possible as shown in Table 10.2 ("Mode of change" headings are included in this table in anticipation of the discussion in the next section).

10.3.2 Endometabolism and the Threshold Effect

The most important and core cause of institutional change is "endometabolism" (a), that is, a gradual institutional change with an endogenous cause. Endometabolism is a concept to which the régulation school has been more or less attached, and is in general defined as "the process by which the functioning of the structure alters the structure itself" (Boyer and Saillard 1995: 337). In the field of political economy, it is defined as "the transformation of a mode of development under the impact of its proper internal dynamics" (Boyer 2004: 197), or "the inner development of tensions within a given architecture" (Boyer 2005: 70). Adding some complementary explanations, in the context of the régulation school the concept of "endometabolism" was first focused on by Frédéric Lordon in 1993. Later, he wrote, "In order to represent the régulationist insight completely, a means of formalising endogenous processes of structural change is needed. This type of change, given the distinctive term endometabolism […], where structural deformations are gradually generated from a repetition of conjuncture over a long period, is especially resistant to formalisation" (Lordon 1995: 178). By incorporating the concept of endometabolism, régulation theory acquired a more effective view of history that surpasses the somewhat mechanical views (such as the theory of punctuated equilibrium) found in path dependence theory.

In short, just as a living thing alters, through everyday metabolic functions, its biological structure, passing from infancy to youth to prime-of-life to old-age over the medium to long term, an institution gradually changes itself based on its own dynamics. This is the endometabolism of an institution.

When we understand an "institution" broadly within the framework of "institutional structure," the whole configuration of endometabolism becomes clearer. By functioning, the institution alters not only (1) itself but also (2) the external environment surrounding it and (3) the various strategies of agents who act under it and other existing institutions. An institution modifies its institutional structure by way of its endometabolism. By way of the institutional environment, the process moves to the institution itself, and finally to the strategy of actors. The "strategy of actors" refers to the intentions and behaviors adopted by various socio-economic groups interested in the institution concerned and is often fortified by the formation of a political coalition. This kind of political factor becomes very important in institutional change or endometabolism.

The endometabolism of an institution, however, often precipitates drastic collapse or leads to a regime crisis once it reaches a certain threshold. Having maintained overall stability in spite of its endometabolism, an institution may eventually plunge into a period of instability, that is, radical and nonlinear institutional change of endogenous cause. This is called the "threshold effect" (b) in Table 10.2 and Fig. 10.1d. It is also discussed using terms such as "cut-off point," or "tipping point" (Pierson 2004: 84). Arriving at a threshold effect, one often witnesses not only an economic crisis but also a political crisis, including a split in the hitherto dominant political coalition. For example, the stagflation crisis in the 1970s was an episode of radical change that was brought about by exceeding a certain threshold of the endometabolic alteration of the Fordist growth regime (Boyer 2004: 195–196), resulting in a breakdown of the Fordist capital–labor alliance. Endometabolic alterations in contemporary socio-economies can be seen, for instance, in urbanization, globalization, deindustrialization, financialization, and an aging society. Some advanced capitalist countries have gone beyond a kind of tipping point, leading to drastic nonlinear transformations.

Considering this threshold effect, path dependence theory, which presupposes that a critical juncture (radical change) occurs only exogenously, must be criticized for missing major aspects of change. As Schwartz and Deeg note, "In formal path dependence, critical junctures cannot emerge from the normal processes of change inside a path. … The new critical juncture arose endogenously (and dialectically) from the path's own internal logics, rather than arising exogenously" (Schwartz 2001: 11–12). "Contrary to the theory of path dependence which asserts that only exogenous change can move actors off a current path, an exogenous shock is *not* the only way a path gets disrupted, i.e., a process of fundamental institutional change is initiated. … Ultimately, a mixture of endogenous and exogenous pressures led to a series of path-changing initiatives" (Deeg 2001: 10–11).

10.3.3 Hybridization and Big Events

The third type of institutional change is "hybridization" (c), a gradual institutional change with an exogenous cause. While endometabolism has its origin inside the same space, hybridization designates an institutional change caused by an interaction with another space, such as a foreign country or the international environment. Here I would like to limit the usage of the word "hybridization" to the case of exogenous and *gradual* change. For example, although a country may make an effort to imitate, import or transplant a foreign institution, the precise replication of this external institution often turns out to be impossible. Instead, as time goes by we find a mixture of traditional and foreign institutions, giving rise to an original institution. This is well illustrated in postwar Japan by the birth of the Toyota production system. This was an original system, notwithstanding Toyota's initial intention to learn and introduce the Ford system from the US.

As the last type of change, we can point to "big events" (d), such as a war, a revolution, a great depression or recession, large-scale political changes in foreign countries, natural disasters, and various international or non-economic shocks. These can result in a radical institutional change with an exogenous cause. As examples we can cite, among other such events, the Great Depression of the 1930s, World War II, the Nixon Shock, the Oil Shocks, the Asian Currency Crisis, and the 2008 Financial Crisis. In reality, however, it is impossible to mechanically distinguish exogenous (big) and endogenous (threshold effect) events, because this determination depends on the point of view or time horizon of the observers. For example, on the one hand the Nixon Shock may be categorized as a "big event" if it is taken as an unexpected surprise, but on the other hand it can also be seen as a "threshold effect" if one considers it in the context of the medium to long-term period of the continuous decrease of the gold reserve in the United States and the gradual devaluation of the dollar. The same is true of the other examples. What should also not be forgotten is that the threshold effect and big events often accompany a regime crisis.

As for the régulation school's view of the main causes of the transformation of the mode of régulation, while showing some shifts in emphasis over time this school attaches importance to both endogenous threshold effects and exogenous big events. For example, Boyer writes,"After having privileged the initial conception – necessity of a radical change to explain a transformation of the mode of *régulation* – the studies have progressively explored the possibilities of endometabolism, that is, brutal alteration of the mode of *régulation* under the effect of the accumulation of a series of marginal changes" (Boyer 2004: 205), and later notes, "When the *régulationist* scholars did their groundbreaking research, first on the United States, then on France, they were surprised to find that the war and major crises had been crucial episodes in the changes of regimes of accumulation and modes of *régulation*. These episodes were seen to have been nothing less than social laboratories" (Boyer 2013: 13). The latter passage clearly shows that the régulationists have never ignored the crucial role of big, radical events on the transformation of the growth regime or mode of régulation.

10.4 Gradual Change of Institutions and Political Elements

10.4.1 Modes of Gradual Institutional Change in Thelen

In the preceding discussion we have made the *gradual* change of institutions, "endo-metabolism" (a) and "hybridization" (c) in Table 10.2, our starting point for understanding institutional change. However, this does not mean that radical changes or critical junctures emphasized by path dependence theory do not matter. While of course there are exceptional "big events" that occur out of the blue, critical junctures often correspond to a tipping point where gradual changes reach a certain critical mass.

The gradual nature of institutional change was emphasized early on by North (1990). Defining institutions as "the rules of the game," North at the same time paid attention to the tenaciousness of "informal constraints" (routines, customs, traditions, conventions and cultures) in comparison with "formal rules" (constitutions, statute, common laws, specific bylaws and individual contracts), and emphasized the adhesiveness or non-variability of the former. Consequently, even if formal rules are changed, or radical institutional changes are put into effect through revolution, conquest and so on, the changes eventually become incremental because of the tenacious nature of informal constraints (North 1990: Ch. 10). Here too we see a discrepancy between the institution itself and its interpretation or enforcement by actors.

In recent years, Thelen's discussions of the gradual nature of institutional change are particularly suggestive. Thelen (2004: 30–31) presents her methodological viewpoint as follows. First, criticizing discussions that draw a sharp line between the analysis of institutional stability and that of institutional innovation and that regard all changes as exogenous, she presents instead a pattern of incremental change. Second, disagreeing with the functionalist theories of institutional origins and the punctuated equilibrium theories of institutional change, as well as with the tendency toward "automaticity" of institutional reproduction sometimes implied in the logic of path dependence (especially of increasing returns), she shows how elements of stability and change are often inextricably intertwined. Third, in line with power-distributional theories she underscores the contested nature of institutional development and the important role of changes in political coalitions.

One of Thelen's most important contributions to the discussion of institutions resides in her typology of the modes of gradual institutional change. Regarding gradual institutional change, she first proposed two modes: "layering" and "conversion" (Thelen 2003: 225–230, 2004: 35–36). "Institutional layering" means adding or superposing new institutions over old ones without dismantling them. "Institutional conversion" designates a situation in which, even when the environment around conventional institutions have changed, the institutions themselves are not replaced but rather reinterpreted and differently enforced without formal or legal changes. In this case, the role and function of the institution concerned naturally become different from what they had been in the past.

She then goes on to further classify various modes of gradual change by adding some new types. These include the "drift" and "displacement" of institutions, which are perhaps the most important among the new supplementary modes described in Streeck and Thelen (2005: 31). "Institutional displacement" refers to an abolition of the old institution and introduction of the new, that is, a substitution of the new for the old institution. However, this mode is perhaps better classified as radical change than as gradual change. In contrast, "institutional drift" refers to a situation in which, although the environment has changed, the institution remains invariable and constant, resulting in an unsuitable institution. In this case, the institution loses its enforcement power and becomes ineffective. This is also a kind of gradual and substantial institutional change.

Based on the above understanding, Thelen classifies various modes of gradual institutional change from the standpoint of characteristics of the political context, that is, strong or weak veto possibilities, and of the targeted institution, such as high or low levels of discretion in interpretation and enforcement (Thelen 2009: 489; Mahoney and Thelen 2010: 19).

10.4.2 Three Aspects of Institutional Structure and their Discrepancies

Having presented a standpoint that finds the essence of gradual institutional change in "endometabolism" and "hybridization," here I would like to analyze the modes of institutional change differently from the Thelen typology. On what differences in the endometabolism of institutions are the three modes of incremental change (layering, conversion, and drift) based? As shown in the previous section, the endometabolism of an institution includes, through the functioning of the institution, an alteration of (1) the environment surrounding it (the context in which it is embedded), (2) the institution itself, and (3) the strategies of various actors (in other words, their interpretation, enforcement, and approval/disapproval of the institution). When we grasp the institution more broadly as an institutional structure that consists of three aspects, "environment" (context surrounding the institution), "institution" (institution as a text) and "application/enforcement" (interpretation and application of this text by actors, or a kind of textual criticism of the institution), the modes of gradual institutional change can be conceptualized as differences or discrepancies among them. This is described in Table 10.3.

Suppose that in an initial period (Period 1) an institutional structure I_1 includes an institution a within an environment A that is interpreted and enforced in the manner α. Here, α is assumed to be the most authentic and suitable form of application of institution a. This is expressed as I_1 (A, a, α). In this state, there is no discrepancy between the three aspects, and the institution is reproduced steadily. However, the institution is always in the process of endometabolism. In the second period (Period 2), in which the endometabolic process has reached a certain point, the institutional

Table 10.3 Modes of institutional change viewed within a framework of institutional structure

	Period 1	Period 2	Modes of change	Process of change
Environment	A	B		
Institution	a	b	Displacement: I (B, b), I (B, b, β)	Radical
	a	$a + b$	Layering: I (B, $a + b$)	Gradual
	a	a	Drift: I (B, a)	
Enforcement	α	β	Conversion: I (B, a, β)	

Source: Author

environment changes from A to B. In this period, the environmental change includes a great transformation of the context as a whole, as well as the emergence of new circumstances around individual institutions. One may see this not only in terms of a change on the part of the environment but also when a gap between an institution and the environment opens up due to alterations of the institution itself. In any case, some kind of significant change in the institutional context is expressed as B.

If a new institution b is then promptly established to cope with the new environment, leading to the emergence of a new institutional structure expressed as I_2 (B, b) or I_2 (B, b, β), this is an instance of the "displacement" of an institution. As I have already pointed out, institutional displacement should be considered a radical rather than gradual change, and as such is not our main object here. It is in cases in which the old institution a is not replaced by a new one b that gradual change becomes relevant. This is also the case when the existing institution a exhibits considerable tenaciousness.

To begin with, one can imagine a situation in which, under a new environment B, a new institution b is added to the old one a, such that b is superposed on a. In short, this is the case in which a new institution b is established corresponding to a new environment B, but in which the traditional institution a also survives. In such cases a and b often coexist in either confrontational or complementary relationships. This situation of I (B, $a + b$) is institutional "layering."

Next, when, without such coexistence, the old institution a still survives in the changed environment B, we see an institutional "drift" that can be expressed as I (B, a). This case may arise due to the ignorance and incompetence of policymakers or through the rejection of institutional reforms by interest groups that benefited from the old institution. Institutional drift naturally brings about substantial dysfunction.

Even in this situation, however, if there is some room for discretion regarding the application/enforcement of the institution, or if there are powerful interest groups that can impose their own interpretation of an institution on politics and society, then the old institution a can be changed by interpreting institution a as β, which involves adapting it to environment B. This is the third case of gradual institutional change, that is, institutional "conversion," formulated as I (B, a, β).

We can therefore understand the gradual change of an institution as creating intermediate states between the two ideal configurations of an institutional structure, I_1 (A, a, α) and I_2 (B, b, β). The tenacious character of an institution produces these forms. What is important to note here is that it is in fact these intermediate forms that are the normal states of an institution, and also that each intermediate form, although maintaining a medium or short-term stability, will gradually but steadily proceed toward an endometabolic change. The normal essence of an institution or regime lies in its gradual change, notwithstanding its apparent stability.

As shown, an institution changes gradually through endometabolism and hybridization. When this gradual change arrives at a tipping point or encounters abrupt big events, the transformation of the institution may become radical. Whether gradual or radical, it is the agents or actors who are active under the institution in question that ultimately define institutional change. It is through the activities of the actors within institutions that institutions themselves are incrementaly reformed and that the environment surrounding them changes. In turn, the strategies of actors change to correspond to environmental changes, and, through this process, a new and different enforcement or interpretation of institutions emerges. Institutions that have been stably reproduced as a whole in spite of incremental reforms may therefore eventually become unstable and break down.

At this point, political moments become pivotal. At least with respect to institutions that are economically important, the role of politics is crucial. That is, actors reexamine and revise their strategies under new environmental conditions. They then organize or reorganize a new "social coalition" or "political coalition," aiming at the realization of institutions conforming to their new strategies or at removal of institutions unfavorable to them (Amable 2003: Ch. 2; Thelen 2014: 10). Of course, the degree and forms of organization are quite various, from concrete collusion to implicit and transitory coordination, or from a relationship of sharing the same philosophy to one of explicit bribery. In any case, actors aim at organizing the majority or dominant social group in order to serve their own interests. In the process a reorganization of group members or recombination of coalitions naturally occurs.

10.5 The Economic Background and Political Influence of Neoliberalism

10.5.1 Deindustrialization, Globalization, and Financialization

So far we have reviewed theories regarding the elements and modes that determine changes in institutions and regimes. Based on this discussion, in this section I propose a critical perspective on the current neoliberal regime, focusing on its economic background and political moments.

The neoliberal policy regime was erected on the grave of the previous Keynesian policy regime, and, especially in hegemonic countries, the finance-led growth regime was likewise erected on the grave of the Fordist growth regime. Of course, this establishment of new regimes was never an automatic or necessary development, but a consequence, on the one hand, of the clear and particular intentions of dominant social groups and the re-composition of a political coalition to realize their will. On the other hand, however, we must not overlook the objective changes in institutional structure that, due to the endometabolic process of the Keynesian–Fordian regime, have greatly altered the existing institutional contexts in advanced capitalist countries. Fordism has undermined its own foundational environment precisely because of its success.

Let us start with the latter factor in this change before examining the former. As a result of the development of Fordist institutions and growth regimes, the advanced countries initially experienced progress in industrialization. This resulted, on the one hand, in an intensification of international competition propelled by overcapacity in production, and, on the other, in a slowdown in productivity gains and acceleration of wage increases and inflation. Influential international events like the Nixon Shock and Oil Shocks in the 1970s encouraged these tendencies. Before long, out of fierce international competition there emerged a multinationalization of companies and a *globalization* of the economy. Advanced countries conducted *deindustrialization* with the slowdown of industrial productivity and the rise of newly industrialized economies. As a result of both of these factors, the *financialization* of the economy arose, mainly in the hegemonic countries. Globalization, deindustrialization and financialization imply a great transformation of the economic context. This transformation was also a consequence of the Fordist growth regime reaching its threshold of endometabolic changes.

Deindustrialization produced a drop in the number of organized workers in large manufacturing companies and also a drop in the unionization rate, resulting in a sharp decline in the power of the working class (Crouch 2004: Ch. 3; Glyn 2006: Ch. 5). Employment shifted to the service sector. Along with the tertialization of employment, the interests of employees diversified and split, owing to the smaller size and uncertainness of management characteristics in the service sector and to the diversification of forms of employment, including non-regularization. The so-called "unity" of laborers disappeared.

In addition, engineers and civil servants had in the past also banded together with "laborers" in a narrow sense. Moreover, there existed a broad "capitalist–citizen accord" (Bowles et al. 1990: 57) or "state–citizen accord" that involved not only wage-earners but also, through the welfare state, the non-active population. The "Fordist coalition" or "Keynesian coalition" of the postwar period consisted of this kind of wide alliance of workers, citizens, and capitalist managers. This coalition has collapsed, however, with the decline of laborers' power due to the deindustrialization of the economy and the non-regularization of employment. Here we see people having become "losers" as workers.

The intensification of international competition and the *globalization* of the economy have also drastically changed institutional environments. Here it must be noted that imported consumption goods sold at cheap prices, as a result of more openness to foreign trade, merely made up for the wage stagnation caused by the decline of labor's power. These goods were principally provided by the newly industrialized countries, headed by China. People in the advanced countries, as "consumers" that enjoy cheap imported goods, have thus regained what they lost as "laborers" (Reich 2009: Ch. 2; Boyer 2011: 25); they have become "winners" as consumers. At the same time, there has appeared, beyond a simple trade relationship between the advanced and emerging countries, a new political and economic context—the multinationalization and strengthening of giant companies in the advanced countries.

Multinational companies, together with financial businesses that have rapidly expanded thanks to the development of new financial technologies and instruments, have substantially driven the globalization of the economy. The development of global financial businesses and the *financialization* of the economy has involved many workers. The aging of societies has increased the number of people who live on pensions, and this mass of retired workers has become, in a manner of speaking, "rentiers." Here we see an increase in the influence of pension funds. For their part, active workers have compensated for the stagnation in their wage income by gaining various financial incomes, especially in good times. People have thus begun to appear as "investors" instead of as "workers" (Reich 2009: Ch. 2). These people are now (at least temporarily) "winners" as investors.

Today people have come to be defined as "consumers" and "investors" more than as "workers." This also implies that they assume the role of "debtor." Crouch ironically expresses this as "privatized Keynesianism," stating: "Instead of governments taking on debt to stimulate the economy, individuals and families did so, including poor ones" (Crouch 2011: 114). The emergence of the masses taking on these new characteristics has supported the neoliberal or finance-led regime from a distance.

10.5.2 The Political Influence of the Neoliberal Coalition

The endometabolism of the Fordist regime thus ultimately resulted in the emergence of preconditions for deindustrialization, globalization, and financialization. However, as suggested at the beginning of this section, these preconditions have been realized in a particular, concrete direction only through the support of neoliberal policies and ideas instead of Keynesian ones. Above all, they have been realized by establishing a new political coalition that promotes these policies and ideas, a "neoliberal coalition." This neoliberal coalition has promoted its own interests powerfully and strategically by not only founding new institutions favorable to itself but also by gradually changing existing institutions.

Contrary to its superficial discourse of "free competition," "efficiency of the market" (deregulation) and "retreat of the state" (privatization, tax reduction), the core substance of neoliberalism resides firmly in a movement toward restoring power to the upper classes (Harvey 2005: 19, 38, 156). This restoration of power is above all founded on establishing a system in which financial returns increase explosively: a finance-led growth regime. In effect, neoliberalism, although having produced only poor results in terms of productivity gains and economic growth, has achieved a great deal with respect to the distribution of wealth to the upper classes.

As is very well-known, the consequences of this regime are currently a huge concern around the world, with the issue of "increasing inequality" becoming central (Piketty 2014). The upper classes have undoubtedly restored their economic power.

At the center of the upper classes are situated the super-rich, including the top managers of global financial businesses and giant multinational companies. The alliance of these two groups makes up the core of the neoliberal coalition. Surrounding them are middle class executives, bureaucrats, accountants, lawyers, consultants, economists, journalists, the self-employed, and so on (Harvey 2005: 33–34). Despite including this second rank of members, the neoliberal coalition remains a minority when contrasted with that of Fordism; the range of this coalition is very narrow. As is pointed out by Bresser-Pereira (2014: 60), "The new neoliberal class coalition that had become hegemonic in the 1980s was a narrow one, comprising the rentier capitalists, the highly paid financiers and traders that managed their wealth, and the top executives of the major multinational enterprise." However, one of the advantages of the neoliberal coalition lies in its having successfully drawn in many consumers and investors as members of the most external circle in the coalition's concentric structure (Martinelli 2014: 295).

The interests of these consumers and amateur investors do not necessarily correspond with those of the core players. Rather, the former often become victims of neoliberal policies. But those who work in manufacturing, as well as in various jobs and professions that have been created mainly in the service sector, cannot avoid having close ties to the giant global companies that supply cheap consumption goods. They are also obliged to deal with the financial markets that offer apparently attractive opportunities for financial (investment) income. The neoliberal coalition has thus succeeded in establishing a wide membership, so long as it can keep within its fold the ambiguous strata of consumers and investors that support the core of the coalition.

Though the neoliberal coalition is very fragile at its outer edges, its core is very strong because of its political power. This is the decisive advantage of this coalition. Big companies have now obtained not only economic but also political power (Reich 2009: Ch. 4; Crouch 2004: 105, 2011: 94–95). That is, big companies, to gain economic advantages over their rivals, have strengthened their influence in the field of political decision-making, thus entering into a political competition. This is mediated by money in the hands of companies and the powerful lobbying it funds, leading to institutional changes including the previously described layering, drift and conversion. With respect to the role of politics, politicians have become more and more reliant on political funds offered by companies, particularly within the context of ever growing campaign budgets (Martinelli 2014: 297). Naturally, it becomes impossible for such politicians to implement policies that are contrary to big companies' interests. Here we witness the establishment of a finance–manager–politician complex. In short, money dominates politics, and politics becomes an instrument serving the privileged classes. This is the reason the politico-economic regime of neoliberalism has been able to remain standing today, even after the recent global financial crisis.

10.5.3 A Crisis of Democracy and Possible Crisis of Neoliberalism

Neoliberalism, behind its facade of "free competition" and "retreat of the state," has survived by means of hidden strategies, such as "political monopoly" and "takeover of the state." Neoliberalism has resulted, therefore, not merely in increasing inequality economically, but also in the dysfunction or breaking down of democracy politically. This has already been pointed out by many commentators. For example, Robert B. Reich, detecting "the triumph of capitalism and the decline of democracy" under neoliberalism, criticizes this trend as follows. "We in our capacities as consumers and investors have done significantly better. In our capacities as citizens seeking the common good, however, we have lost ground" (Reich 2009: 7, 50). Moreover, as Colin Crouch warns, "If the wealthy interests are able to convert wealth into political power – as is very often the case – they are able to distort both the market economy and democracy" (Crouch 2013: vii).

The neoliberal regime is therefore fundamentally incompatible with democracy; on the contrary, it appears as a moment destructive to democracy. In addition, the finance-led regime, as long as it is driven by financial bubbles, is always economically unstable. The existing neoliberal coalition is constantly exposed to the risk of a split due to its unstable dynamics. However, from a more fundamental point of view, an authentic regime crisis of neoliberalism, if it does in fact arise, will occur only when citizens reclaim political power and restore their democratic authority.

Neoliberalism, after having experienced the economic crisis of 2008, is now precipitating an accelerating decline of political democracy. If a movement of revendication by civil society reaches a certain level in opposition to increases in inequality that are too large and democracy that is too dysfunctional, the regime crisis that ensues will become not only "economic" but also "political." The conditions requisite for this regime crisis include the formation of a new political coalition for a new civil society. In any case, the contradiction between neoliberalism and democracy has the potential to lead to a deep structural crisis of the existing regime.

10.6 Concluding Remarks

We have examined, based on the analytical angle of gradual institutional change, a possible crisis of the neoliberal policy regime or finance-led growth regime. Although certain institutions clearly possess a tenacious character and institutional change may be gradual, there is no doubt that it will occur over the medium and long term. This is also the case for policy regimes and growth regimes, as is demonstrated by the shifts from the Keynesian to the neoliberal policy regime and from the Fordist to the finance-led growth regime.

When we engage in this kind of historical reflection, we can posit the "capital principle" and the "society principle" as two moments that drive "history." The "capital principle" is the world of human activity evoked by words like "money," "finance," "profit," "externality," "world," and "transformation," while the "society principle" is the world of "land," "labor," "lifestyle," "everydayness," "solidarity" and "stability." While the terminology used may differ, placing these two principles at the foundation of social/historical understanding is something that has in fact been proposed by most thinkers who have engaged with these topics. Polanyi (1957), for example, grasps modern history as a "double movement" of "the principle of economic liberalism" and "the principle of social protection." And when Braudel (1979) discusses "material civilization, economy, capitalism," a society principle and capital principle are presumably implied within "material civilization (economy)" and "capitalism" respectively.

Once we establish the society principle and the capital principle, it becomes apparent that modern society (or indeed, human history) has developed in the midst of a conflict between these two principles. While opposing each other they complement each other, while coming together they repel each other, and in this way modern history (and more broadly human history) obtains its driving force. The society principle provides stability but easily falls into stagnation. To break out of this stagnation people throw themselves into the capital principle, seeking money and the outside world. The new products and innovation the capital principle engenders captivate people and bring about changes in society and the world. In this way the capital principle is a principle of enterprise and innovation and at the same time a principle of instability and inequality. People seek change in the midst of stability and stability in the midst of change. History develops within the dialectic of these two principles.

Modernity is an era in which the capital principle became vastly more dominant than the society principle. The capital principle then became independent of the society principle and came to subsume and dominate it even further. To borrow Polanyi (1957)'s phrase, the market (capital) became "disembedded" from society. But while modern capitalist society is a society in which the principle of capital completely covers society as a whole, it is not as though the society principle has been completely extinguished. And on the flipside of the enormous capacity for change of the capital principle is its inevitable tendency to charge ahead recklessly without the capacity to stop itself or even slow itself down. The ability to put the brakes on this runaway train exists only in the society principle. The capital principle must be controlled by the society principle. In other words, the capital principle must be régulated by the society principle. Looking back over modern history from this perspective, it becomes apparant that eras of capital principle dominance have alternated with eras of society principle dominance. In the 19th century, for example, the capital principle rose to prominence under the name of "liberalism," while in the middle of the 20th century the society principle made a comeback in the form of "Keynesianism" before once again falling under the sway of the capital principle with the rise of "neoliberalism" beginning at the end of the 20th century.

In other words, today's neoliberal policy regime and finance-led growth regime are systems in which to a large extent the capital principle is running wild. The postwar Keynesian policy regime and Fordist growth regime, in contrast, were to a certain extent able to control the runaway recklessness of the capital principle, and as a result the postwar era was able to realize, in developed countries at least, high levels of economic growth and development of the welfare state. This society principle was heavily concentrated in "the state" or "the government," however, and was only ever realized "from above" through these institutions. What is incumbent upon us today, in this era of the thoroughly dominant capital principle of "neoliberalism," is of course to emphasize the necessity and importance of a policy shift being undertaken by governments, and, in accordance with this, or indeed in addition to this, to restore the society principle through the formation of civil society from the bottom up. If today's dominance of neoliberalism is deepening not only an economic crisis but a crisis of democracy as well, then surely we have no choice but to search for a new system, a new mode of régulation, and a new growth regime by reforming democracy through the formation of civil society "from below."

References

Amable, Bruno (2003) *The Diversity of Modern Capitalism*, Oxford: Oxford University Press.

Amable, Bruno and Stefano Palombarini (2005) *L'Economie politique n'est pas une science morale*, Paris: Raisons d'Agir.

Bowles, Samuel, David. M. Gordon and Thomas. H. Weisskopf (1990) *After the Waste Land: A Democratic Economics for the Year 2000*, New York and London: M. E. Sharpe, Inc.

Boyer, Robert (2004) *Une théorie du capitalisme est-elle possible?* Paris: Odile Jacob.

——— (2005) 'Coherence, Diversity, and the Evolution of Capitalisms: The Institutional Complementarity Hypothesis,' *Evolutionary and Institutional Economics Review*, 2(1), October.

——— (2011) *Les financiers détruiront-ils le capitalisme?* Paris: Economica.

——— (2013) 'Capital in the Twenty-First Century: A Regulationist View,' *Revue de la Régulation*, 14, Autumn, URL: http://regulation.revues.org/10618

Boyer, Robert and Yves Saillard eds. (1995) *Régulation Theory: The State of the Art*, London and New York: Routledge.

Braudel, Fernand (1979) *Civilisation matérielle, économie et capitalisme*, Paris: Armand Colin.

Bresser-Pereira, Luiz Carlos (2014) 'The Hegemony Constraints in the Neoliberal Years of Capitalism,' in Magara (2014).

Crouch, Colin (2004) *Post-Democracy*, Cambridge: Polity.

——— (2011) *The Strange Non-death of Neoliberalism*, Cambridge: Polity.

——— (2013) *Making Capitalism Fit for Society*, Cambridge: Polity.

Deeg, Richard (2001) 'Institutional Change and the Uses and Limits of Path Dependency: The Case of German Finance,' *Max-Plank-Institut für Gesellschaftsforschung Discussion Paper*, 01/6, November.

Glyn, Andrew (2006) *Capitalism Unleashed: Finance, Globalization, and Welfare*, Oxford: Oxford University Press.

Hall, Peter and David Soskice eds (2001) *Varieties of Capitalism: The Institutional Foundations of Comparative Advantages*, Oxford: Oxford University Press.

Harvey, David (2005) *A Brief History of Neoliberalism*, Oxford: Oxford University Press.

Lordon, Frédéric (1995) 'Formalising Regulationist Dynamics and Crises,' in Boyer and Saillard (1995).

Magara, Hideko ed. (2014) *Economic Crises and Policy Regimes: The Dynamics of Policy Innovation and Paradigmatic Change*, Cheltenham and Northampton: Elgar.

Mahoney, James (2000) 'Path Dependence in Historical Sociology,' *Theory and Society*, 29(4), August.

Mahoney, James and Kathleen Thelen eds. (2010) *Explaining Institutional Change: Ambiguity, Agency and Change*, New York: Cambridge University Press.

Martinelli, Alberto (2014) 'A Political Analysis of the Global Financial Crisis: Implications for Crisis Governance,' in Magara (2014).

North, Douglass C. (1990) *Institutions, Institutional Change and Economic Performance*, Cambridge and New York: Cambridge University Press.

Pempel, T. J. (1998) *Regime Shift: Comparative Dynamics of the Japanese Political Economy*, Ithaca and London: Cornell University Press.

Pierson, Paul (2000) 'Increasing Return, Path Dependence, and the Study of Politics,' *American Political Science Review*, 94(2), June.

——— (2004) *Politics in Time: History, Institutions, and Social Analysis*, Princeton and Oxford: Princeton University Press.

Piketty, Thomas (2014) *Capital in the Twenty-First Century*, Cambridge and London: The Belknap Press of Harvard University Press.

Polanyi, Karl (1957; Second Paperback Edition 2001) *The Great Transformation: The Political and Economic Origins of Our Time*, Boston: Beacon Press.

Przeworski, Adam (2001) 'How Many Ways Can Be Third?' in Andrew Glyn ed., *Social Democracy in Neoliberal Times: The Left and Economic Policy since 1980*, Oxford: Oxford University Press.

——— (2014) 'Choices and Echoes: Stability and Change of Policy Regimes', in Magara (2014).

Reich, Robert B. (2009) *Supercapitalism: The Battle for Democracy in an Age of Big Business*, New edition, London: Icon Books.

Schwartz, Herman (2001) 'Down the Wrong Path: Path Dependence, Markets, and Increasing Returns,' Unpublished Manuscript, University of Virginia.

Streeck, Wolfgang and Kathleen Thelen (2005) 'Introduction: Institutional Change in Advanced Political Economies,' in Streeck and Thelen eds, *Beyond Continuity: Institutional Change in Advanced Political Economies*, Oxford and New York: Oxford University Press.

Thelen, Kathleen (2003) 'How Institutions Evolve: Insights from Comparative Historical Analysis,' in James Mahoney and Dietrich Rueschemyer eds., *Comparative Historical Analysis in the Social Sciences*, Cambridge: Cambridge University Press.

——— (2004) *How Institutions Evolve: The Political Economy of Skills in Germany, Britain, the United States, and Japan*, Cambridge: Cambridge University Press.

——— (2009), 'Institutional Change in Advanced Political Economies,' *British Journal of Industrial Relations*, 47(3), September.

——— (2014) *Varieties of Liberalization and the New Policies of Social Solidarity*, New York: Cambridge University Press.

Chapter 11
Transition Economies and State Capitalism

11.1 Introduction: The Past and Present of Transition Economics

Almost 30 years have passed since socialism collapsed and the transition to capitalism began. It is perhaps more common to refer to this as a "transition to market economies" than as a "transition to capitalism." But since the actual substance of "market economies" is nothing other than capitalism, including in China, here I use these terms interchangeably. In any case, today formerly socialist nations are referred to as "countries transitioning to a market economy," and in the field of economics there has been an ongoing attempt to analyze this major turning point in world history under the rubric of "transition economics."

Over the past 30 years the issues discussed in transition economics have spanned a wide range of topics, and the main points of argument have shifted with the passage of time. Nakagane (2010) presents a truly comprehensive and incisive account of these developments. I defer to him regarding the details of this discourse, but even I, a scholar from another field observing transition economics from the outside, can vividly recall some of its most contentious debates.

At the start of the transition period, the fiercest dispute revolved around transition strategies and whether "shock therapy" or "gradualism" should be employed. The question was how various elements of transition, including moving from planned economies to market economies, from systems of state ownership to systems of private ownership (privatization), and from single-party dictatorships to multiparty democracies, should be carried out and in what order. On this point the failure of Russia, which employed a radical shock therapy approach, is often contrasted with the success of high growth seen in gradualist China. It is obvious that an immediate move to free markets without any institutional reforms is doomed to fail, but we cannot simply say that gradualism is therefore always the correct choice; as is demonstrated by the fact that Chinese labor market reforms occurred quite

T. Yamada, *Contemporary Capitalism and Civil Society*, Evolutionary Economics and Social Complexity Science 14,
https://doi.org/10.1007/978-981-13-0517-7_11

rapidly, there are presumably various options depending on the historical and institutional context of the nation in question.

The debate in transitional economics eventually shifted toward the question of how to evaluate the results of transitions from one system to another. Detailed studies of each country or region's economic performance (growth rate, inflation, industrial structure, distribution problems, economic openness to other countries, and so on) were compiled, the tools of fine-grained analysis were applied to the actual circumstances surrounding the institutional reforms (marketization, privatization, and democratization) that form the core of transition between economic systems, and work along these lines continues to be carried out today. Various types of statistical indices regarding institutional reforms have been conceived, the diversity of transition economies has been confirmed through quantitative and qualitative comparisons of individual countries, and attempts have been made at categorizing these types of transitional economies. Very broadly speaking, it would seem that at this point institutional reform is progressing in the Baltic and central/eastern European states, is delayed in China, Vietnam, and central Asia, and is somewhere in the middle in Russia and south-eastern Europe.

Along with a certain amount of progress in transitioning to new systems, problems of "corruption" have arisen anew. When it comes to systemic transition on such a large scale, the emergence of some institutional gaps is inevitable no matter what form it takes, and even if institutional reforms are carried out there is no guarantee that the resulting institutions will be effective in practice. In such cases rent-seeking activities are undertaken behind the scenes, and corruption is rampant throughout politics, business, and the bureaucracy. The problems the former socialist countries who tried to tear down their authoritarian political and economic systems and replace them with free, fair, and transparent alternatives are facing today are the connections, both open and covert, between politicians, businesspeople and bureaucrats and the elite classes taking all sorts of profits and benefits for themselves – problems that, ironically enough, are no different from what occurred under the old regime. Have the transitional nations that set out toward a "market economy" in fact only arrived at "state economies" rife with corruption?

When it comes to the two largest transitional countries, Russia and China, from the 2000s onwards, that is, in Russia under President Putin and China under Presidents Hu Jintao and Xi Jinping, it is said that the state is once again strongly intervening in economies that were supposed to have been marketized, and the influence of state companies has grown even though privatization was supposed to have been progressing. In Chinese, the phrase is "*guo jin min tui* (the state advances, the private sector retreats)." To put it another way, "capitalism" has been developed while being tightly bound up with the "state." At some point people began to refer to this situation that has emerged in recent years as "state capitalism," and this has now become one of the focal points of transition economics.

11.2 Ian Bremmer's *The End of the Free Market*

The debate over state capitalism in recent years was ignited by Ian Bremmer (2009a, b, 2010). Bremmer, an American political scientist born in 1969, founded the Eurasia Group, a political risk consulting company, and continues to serve as its president in addition to his work as a scholar. His book *The End of the Free Market* speaks of the dangers of the rise of state capitalism and the threat it poses to what he calls "free-market capitalism," and has received a particularly large response in the English-speaking world.

Let me begin by introducing this text. What does Bremmer mean by "state capitalism"? According to him, capitalism in the present era can be broadly divided into two categories: "free-market capitalism" and "state capitalism." Free-market capitalism, also called "mixed capitalism," is characterized by competition in free markets and limited governmental intervention. It can be subdivided into two models, Anglo-Saxon and European, and includes Japan as well as the so-called developed nations of Europe and America. In his use of "free-market capitalism," however, Bremmer seems to mainly have the United States in mind. State capitalism, an approach that exhibits fundamental differences from free-market capitalism, is a system in which capitalism and market economies are developed on the basis of strong economic intervention by the state.

Generally speaking and broadly defined, "state capitalism" can be used to refer to any implementation of capitalism that is strongly bound up with the state, but Bremmer's specific definition is slightly more limited. He defines state capitalism as a system in which the state (politics) is in a position of guidance in regard to capitalism (the economy), and politicians use markets to pursue their own "political gain." "This book defines twenty-first-century state capitalism as 'a system in which the state plays the role of leading economic actor and uses markets primarily for political gain'" (Bremmer 2010: 33). Here "political gain" refers to the interests of the class that holds political control, and in concrete terms amounts to maintaining, preserving, and expanding this ruling class's power and maximizing the wealth (rent) they are able to obtain by wielding it. Bremmer's true intention in thus defining state capitalism as a system for the pursuit of "political gain" is to emphasize that it is different from free-market capitalism in which government intervention is seen as being done in order to support economic growth, promote public welfare, and increase the prosperity of the citizens of the state in question. In any case, what Bremmer calls state capitalism is a system that has rent-seeking as its ultimate goal and uses markets toward this end.

According to Bremmer, this state capitalism model can be seen in the Arab nations surrounding the Persian Gulf (Saudia Arabia and the United Arab Emirates) in addition to China and Russia, and also in nations such as India, Brazil and Indonesia. In other words, the BRIC nations that have received particular attention as emerging market economies are all the products of state capitalism-type development. And following the 2008 financial crisis, as a result of faith in American-style free market capitalism having been lost, movements to emulate state capitalism have spread in other developing countries. In practice this has meant that government wealth, investment, and ownership has recovered markedly, and the use of industry tied to government has been expanded.

Concretely speaking, then, by what means do people in political authority steer state capitalism? By controlling several types of intermediary organizations – state-owned enterprises (SOEs), national champions, and sovereign wealth funds (SWFs) – people in authority possess strong influence, and are able to reap large rewards, without engaging in their day-to-day management. Well-known examples of the first category of intermediary organizations, SOEs, include Russia's oil and natural gas corporations (e.g. Gazprom) and China's power, finance and automotive corporations (e.g. State Grid Corporations of China and the China FAW Group Corporation). Three quarters of the world's oil reserves are under the ownership of SOEs. The second category, national champions, is comprised of large private corporations that receive government investment and support and acquire a dominant position in the export market. Examples of this type of corporation include mining and steel corporations in Russia and Aviation Industries of China (an aerospace corporation) and Lenovo (an information and communications device manufacturer) in China. Organizations in the third category, SWFs, are run by the government and are intended to collect extra funds and invest them strategically. The number of such organizations has therefore been rapidly increasing – mainly in Russia and China, of course, but also in countries with emerging export economies. These funds manage enormous amounts of money, but their disclosure of information is inadequate and the details of their actual status remain out of view.

At the end of Bremmer's book he discusses the threat of state capitalism and its shortcomings, and concludes by stating his view of the future. State capitalism's threat lies in its undermining of the market principle through the manipulation and intervention in markets of those who wield political power. Regarding how this ultimately threatens the living standards and security of people living in free-market countries, Bremmer writes, "The risk for the United States – and for free-market democracies generally – is that distortions created by state capitalism will ensure that the pie isn't expanding quickly enough to accommodate all the new mouths it will soon be expected to feed. That will threaten not just standards of living, but eventually perhaps the security of the world's free-market democracies" (ibid. 151). He also notes that state capitalism has numerous shortcomings. State capitalism, which is characterized by government intervention, preeminence of the bureaucracy, and corruption, lacks the power to innovate, and since it is not a system that aims to improve the welfare and fair treatment of the citizenry cannot obtain the sympathy of the majority. Bremmer concludes by saying that this state capitalism will no doubt come to an end eventually, "but it's likely to be around for decades to come" (ibid. 183).

This is the main thrust of Bremmer's *The End of the Free Market*. Simply stated, it views global capitalism in terms of a straightforward dichotomy between "free-market capitalism" and "state capitalism" – or indeed a "good guy/bad buy" view of history – and there are many tired aspects of its arguments that transparently praise "market fundamentalism" or the view that markets are infallible. Should American-style free-market capitalism really be considered such an ideal system? On this point one need only consider, for example, how thoroughly politics has been controlled and corrupted by corporate money and lobbying in neoliberal America and the extent of the decline in public welfare and civil democracy this has wrought (Reich 2009). If the state capitalism Bremmer describes is a system in which "the economy is controlled by politics" (power becomes wealth), then it can also be said that today free-market capitalism has transformed into a system in which to no small extent "politics is controlled by the economy" (wealth becomes power). We thus have no choice but to adopt a stance that distinguishes itself from both state capitalism and American-style free-market capitalism.

Having stated these reservations, one aspect of Bremmer's work I would praise is his defining the readily apparent state capitalism in nations such as China and Russia more narrowly as a system in which "political gain" is pursued by those who wield political power. There is in fact over a century's worth of discourse on concepts surrounding "state capitalism" in the social sciences (see Sect. 11.5), but I think Bremmer's definition does an excellent job of capturing the character of what has been occurring in recent years in most of the nations with transitioning economies we are currently examining – not only in transition economies but also in the fields of emerging market economies and energy export economies. And while Bremmer gives this concept the nuance of being a "stage" in the sense that he looks forward to the eventual triumph of free-market capitalism and decline of state capitalism, for the time being he employs it as a "type" concept presented as a parallel to free-market capitalism. As noted above, however, as a theory of "types" of capitalism it is overly simplistic.

11.3 The Response to Bremmer's Theory of State Capitalism

As I stated at the beginning of the previous section, Bremmer's *The End of the Free Market* elicited a strong reaction. Particularly in Britain and the United States it was introduced and reviewed in major newspapers such as *The New York Times*, *The Washington Post*, and *The Wall Street Journal* and magazines of politics, economics, and international relations such as *Forbes* and *Foreign Affairs* (Janjigian 2010; Cooper 2010; Levingston 2010; Stewart 2010). The magazine *The Economist* also put together a special report on the issues it raised in 2012 (Economist 2012).

Most of the positions presented in these publications shared Bremmer's fear of the threat of the rapid expansion of state capitalism, and with a particular focus on debating the "Chinese" model" and "Beijing consensus" in regard to China they also expressed concern that this was becoming a new model of development for developing nations. While expressing these fears that state capitalism could disturb free markets and the global economy, ultimately they expected free markets to triumph. This was the general tone of the discussion.

According to *The Economist*, care must also be taken concerning the strength and sophistication state capitalism possesses today compared to in the past. "First, it is developing on a much wider scale: China alone accounts for a fifth of the world's population. Second, it is coming together much more quickly: China and Russia have developed their formula for state capitalism only in the past decade. And third, it has far more sophisticated tools at its disposal" (Economist 2012). Regarding the third point, it was pointed out, for example, that state-run companies were now being listed on stock markets and their management was being entrusted to professional managers and financial strategists rather than bureaucrats and the well-connected.

Many other arguments were made along the same lines. Schuman (2011), while noting that state capitalism may demonstrate better economic performance than free market capitalism in the wake of the 2008 financial crisis, maintains that the economic distortions and corruption that exist under state capitalism will constrain it and that going forward this system will require powerful market reforms. Aligica and Tarko (2012) emphasize that however strong state capitalism might appear today, it is nevertheless a rent-seeking system, and like rent-seeking systems of the past is ultimately destined to collapse. Lubman (2012) views the lack of transparency of Chinese state-run corporations that are expanding abroad as problematic, while Dyer (2010) predicts that in the future today's China of "Market-Leninism" will face a problem of innovation.

This view of state capitalism as a threat or as having no potential for the future has of course elicited criticism and approaches that distanced themselves from these positions. Under the ironic title, "We're All State Capitalists Now" (Ferguson 2012), the British historian Niall Ferguson asserts that to a greater or lesser extent every country has its state capitalist aspects, and that depending on how you look at the indices America can be seen as more state capitalistic than China. It goes without saying that the state has a certain role to play in the economy, so he admonishes against the loose use of this term. On this basis he concludes that what is important is the role the state must play in improving economic efficiency and controlling rent-seeking behavior (corruption) and the elucidation of measures to be taken to this end. Campbell (2012) is sympathetic to this position. Taking a different approach, Kurlantzic (2012), conscious of a tendency in the discourse to cast doubt on state capitalism's capacity for innovation, warns against underestimating this type of capitalism's ability to innovate.

Author of *Markets over Mao* Nicholas Lardy (2014) asserts that the driving force behind the rapid development of the Chinese economy has been, and will continue to be, the vitality of private markets, and criticizes theories of state capitalism that advocate state guidance and the dominance of state-run corporations. He claims that instead of "the state advances, the private sector retreats," in fact "the private sector advances, the state retreats." Responding to Bremmer from the Chinese perspective, Li and Shaw (2013) offer a defense of the Chinese model. According to them, in order to understand Chinese-style state capitalism you must extend your inquiry to China's unique view of the state, the capabilities of a one party state and a culture that assimilates foreign ideas, and a unique relationship between the state and the market. On this basis they conclude that in the future the Chinese Communist Party will establish a political and economic system with a distinctly Chinese flavor in the midst of competition among diverse forms of capitalism.

In addition, while there are few points on which they directly engage with Bremmer's argument, Aglietta and Bai (2013) take up the problem of the lack of civil society in China, while Haley and Haley (2013) examine trade policies and the support given to industry by the Chinese government. Musacchio and Lazzarini (2014) examine state capitalism in Brazil, while Nölke (2014) looks at China, Russia, India, South Korea and Thailand in addition to this country. Notable texts written in French include Bergère (2013) on China and Sapir (2013) on Russia.

11.4 The Relationship Between the State and Capitalism

The concept of "state capitalism," as Bremmer himself notes in presenting it, has a long history, and has been employed by many theorists with different implications. In order to situate Bremmer's conception within this context, in the next section I will trace the conceptual history of state capitalism and in this section I will lay the groundwork for this by briefly discussing the relationship between the state and capitalism.

The role of the state in the development of capitalism, and the relationship between capitalism and the state: when we think about these old and yet new problems we are reminded of the classic theories of economic development formulated by economic historians. Specifically, Gerschenkron (1962), known for the theory of "the advantages of backwardness," asserts that in the 19th century, when it came to the nations that were "backward" in comparison to Britain, in France and Germany "banks" played a large role in industrialization, while in Russia, which was even more backward, the lack of an orderly financial system meant that it was the "state" rather than banks that played a pivotal role in its development. Rostow (1960), on the other hand, devoted all of his energy to the eradication of communism. His theory of "stages of economic growth" describes development in stages toward an American-style society of mass consumption, and expresses fears that a state with an authoritarian dictatorship in the name of communism could become a tool for realizing something like Japan's Meiji restoration in China, a nation whose "take-off" toward becoming a modern society had been delayed.

These are arguments concerning the role of the state in the development of industry in so-called "backward" or "developing" countries, so what about Britain, the "leading" nation of that era? Did capitalism in Britain develop "spontaneously" without any help from the state? Bremmer himself denies this. Recall the existence of the East India Company. While a corporation, the East India Company received various special privileges under its charter from the British crown, and existed as a "national champion" with a monopoly on Asian trade from the 17th century to the middle of the 19th century. As this demonstrates, in Britain during the infancy of capitalism the government (state) was an active leader, encouraging the development of industry, promotion of exports, discovery of new markets, and strengthening of the military, thereby serving as a lever for the primitive accumulation of capital. This is generally referred to as "mercantilism," but it could also be called "state capitalism" in a broad sense of the term.

Looking at things in this way, we begin to suspect that perhaps "capitalism" has been connected to the "state" and dependent on its support since its inception. It would seem that capitalism, regardless of whether its development is early or late, is something that at a certain phase (stage) of its history requires special policy protection from the state. As though to provide support for this view, in the midst of his internal criticism of the "world-systems" analysis Mielants (2007) acknowledges the "origins of capitalism" in merchants seizing control of the state and through so doing enacting systemic policies for the accumulation of wealth. Unlike in the East, where power continued to be held by aristocrats and officials, in the West political power was seized by the merchant class, and this is what accounts for capitalism having developed earlier in the latter region. As a result, capitalism would never have arisen without the state (although state assistance alone was not enough; the broad formation of new institutions, including a change in people's ways of thinking, was also needed). To this extent, capitalism was by nature state capitalism from the moment of its birth.

To recognize this broad definition of state capitalism is, to begin with, a good antidote to facile theories of free-market capitalism, because the latter are often built on the following sort of underlying assumption or article of faith. "Market economies are something that have arisen 'autonomously' or 'spontaneously' in the course of human history, and the fairest and most efficient system is one that leaves everything up to the free competition of the market. When particular organizations such as the government or other groups put pressure on the market, free competition is constrained, the system of prices is distorted, and the welfare of society is harmed. As for the transition of socialist countries to market economies, if we remove the malignant obstacle of a planned economy and state ownership that is staring us in the face, the spring of the market economy will well up naturally at our feet." In such assertions we can discern the mistaken belief that capitalism is innately free-market capitalism. But without even having to cite the failure of the "shock therapy" approach tried in Russia in the 1990s, looking at the state of affairs in which, in the midst of neoliberalism's dominance, the "takeover of the state" by multinationals and financiers under the auspices of calls for the "withdrawal of the state" is progressing, it is clear that capitalism is not inherently equivalent to free markets.

11.5 Aspects of the Concept of State Capitalism

As noted above, the state has been an entity essential to the development of capitalism, but the extent of the relationship between the two has differed depending on the era and country in question. In very general terms, while it may be fine to label capitalism with strong state interference or control "state capitalism," when this term is established as a concept in the social sciences a more specific connotation is required, and discourse on state capitalism with a variety of conceptual connotations has in fact been conducted over the past century. Several such types of state capitalism theory come to mind, including Bremmer's, and rather than displaying a consistent conceptual lineage these various approaches can more accurately be described as having arisen out of the differing aspects of the eras and issues to which they have been addressed.

First came the concept employed in Marxism from the end of the 19th century to the beginning of the 20th century. The use of "state capitalism" as a technical term is said to have begun with an address given in 1896 by Wilhelm Liebknecht, one of the founders of Germany's Social Democratic Party. There are also examples of this term being used by other figures such as Rudolf Hilferding, Karl Kautsky, and Nikolai Bukharin, and while they did not necessarily use it with the same connotation, the most well known of these varying definitions was that of Lenin.

In Lenin's view, while the Russian Revolution (1917) had succeeded and the transition to socialism had begun, thanks to its backwardness Russia contained a mixture of various economic *uklad* (economic institutions or modes of production), including patriarchal agricultural economies, small-scale commodity production, private capitalism, and socialism. According to Lenin, in addition to the above there was also the *uklad* of "state capitalism," comprised of the leasing of state property to concession projects (e.g. oil) with foreign capital, cooperatives, and capitalists. Here state capitalism was not a concept that described the system as a whole, but rather referred to one economic institution within a broader socio-economic structure. At the same time, Lenin valued this institution very highly as "a step toward socialism" that constituted the most complete material preparation for the transition from capitalism to socialism (Lenin 1965: 295).

Looking at Lenin's concept of state capitalism again from today's perspective, it seems to be quite a peculiar definition. For one thing, while the concept of state capitalism has often been employed in Marxist or other anti-capitalist thought and social movements, in such cases it has always been used with a negative (or at best neutral) nuance. In Lenin's conception of it, however, as a "step toward socialism" state capitalism was assigned a highly positive meaning from his point of view. For another thing, while by using state capitalism as a concept within a "stage" theory Lenin shared something in common with most other approaches to this concept, he nevertheless displayed a marked difference from these other approaches insofar as he positioned its "stage" as the ultimate phase of capitalism or the gateway to socialism.

Second, there is an approach that conceives of the political and economic institutions of the collapsed Soviet Union as "state capitalist." In other words, this view holds that while the Soviet Union is normally said to have been an example of "socialism" or "state socialism," it was actually state capitalism, and moreover an extremely particular and early stage form of capitalism. But as a result of this form of state capitalism becoming a constraint on the subsequent development of productive forces, this state capitalism fell apart at the end of the 20th century with the collapse of the Soviet Union. Ōtani et al. (1996), published after the so-called "collapse of socialism," is a representative text of this understanding as it was expressed in Japan.

According to Ōtani, Soviet society from Stalin's declaration of the rush toward socialism in 1936 to its collapse in 1991 was not socialism but a "unique type of state capitalism." This "unique type" was a mode of production that "forcibly furthered the accumulation of capital administratively through command-like, barrack-like policies on the basis of the authority of the party/bureaucrats" (ibid. 22); in other words it was a primitive accumulation state, but its uniqueness lay in its having carried out its expansion mainly in the sector of heavy industry with state capital's violent accumulation as its axis. This system had a certain amount of success, and in the 1950s gave rise to a new stage of productive forces, but unable to respond to the further challenges of productive forces under its primitive accumulation-type state capitalism, in spite of numerous partial reforms (from the Liberman reforms to perestroika) it ultimately collapsed in 1991. This understanding is presumably the greatest common denominator of the various approaches that assert that the economic system of the Soviet Union was state capitalism.

Here I will state my reservations about this "Soviet Union = state capitalism" formulation. If we adopt a view in which the collapse of the Soviet Union is positioned as the collapse of primitive accumulation state capitalism, we can expect an understanding of history in which free competition capitalism began during the Yeltsin administration. In fact, presumably with the period after the collapse of the Soviet Union in mind, Ōtani writes that now the "dismantling of state capitalism itself" (Ōtani et al. 1996: 28) has been brought about, and "what has emerged on the stage is a genuine bourgeois society upholding 'freedom and democracy'" (ibid. 34). If so, how are we to position what is now referred to as "state capitalism" when characterizing the Putin administration? There is no need to insist on Bremmer's conception of state capitalism, but how are we to evaluate the statist tendencies characteristic of the Putin government? Can we say that the Putin administration has escaped primitive accumulation state capitalism and is pointing the way toward "genuine bourgeois society," or is it engaged in a kind of rollback of "freedom and democracy"? Standing within a reality in which the Putin era is already much longer than the Yeltsin era, how does the "Soviet Union = state capitalism" view position the state capitalism of today's Russia within the context of stages of development?

A similar understanding can also be found overseas in Chattopadhyay (1994) and Screpanti (2001: 276–9). The "Soviet Union = state capitalism" theory was not a view that only emerged after the collapse of the Soviet Union; when we trace its origins, we see that following Stalin's declaration of the establishment of socialism it was constantly being put forward in opposition to this claim by, among others, Rana Dunayevskaya, Tony Cliff, and Charles Bettelheim.

Also, in the 1970s Ikumi (1979) asserted that "what constitutes today's socialism…contains nothing that is fundamentally different from capitalism." He did not use the phrase "state capitalism," and his thought differed from that of the three names mentioned above, but he describes the Soviet Union of that era as a variant of "capitalism without civil society" (first comes the state and its guiding/ruling groups, then civil society being oppressed below) and positions it in opposition to the "capitalist civil society" of the West.

Regarding the third conception of state capitalism a brief mention will suffice. It arises within the theories of comparative economic systems or the diversity of capitalism. For example, Schmidt (2003), who compares the forms of capitalism found in Britain, Germany and France, defines these as "market capitalism," "managed capitalism," and "state capitalism" respectively, with the term "state capitalism" being used here as a conception of "type" to describe what sets French capitalism apart among Western European countries. Other writers have used the description "state-led" regarding France. "State-led" has also been used in reference to nations such as China and Malaysia in comparisons of types of Asian capitalism (Walter and Zhang 2012).

As we have seen, in the history of the theoretical discourse the concept of "state capitalism" has had varying content depending on the era and field of study in which it is employed. When it comes to the latter, the concept has been introduced in Soviet economics, development economics, comparative economics, and transition economics, and while its connotation has differed in each of these fields, it has only very rarely (as in the case of Lenin) been viewed positively, and in the remaining majority of cases has been assigned either a negative or neutral significance. And while originally this concept was discussed mostly within the context of Marxism, today it has gone beyond this framework and appears within a broader spectrum of intellectual discourse. Regarding the question of whether state capitalism represents a "stage" or a "type" of capitalism, both Lenin and those who assert that the Soviet Union = state capitalism (such as Ōtani) hold that it is a stage, but when it comes to the nature of this stage there is a stark contrast between Lenin, who believed it was the final stage (doorway to socialism), and those like Ōtani for whom it was the beginning of capitalism. Assertions that it was a type of capitalism, on the other hand, arose naturally enough from the discourse on comparative economic system theory, and were also made by Ikumi in his broad examination of world history in the 1970s.

To once again position Bremmer's theory of state capitalism within this context, it addresses development economics (or perhaps more precisely emerging market economics) and transition economics, and is argued from within a liberal, non-Marxist intellectual perspective. To the extent that it takes a very negative view of state capitalism and asserts that it must eventually disappear it is a "stage" view, but at the same time it also treats state capitalism as a "type" by placing it in contrast or opposition to free market capitalism. In any case, Bremmer frames it as a rent-seeking system designed to control the economy through politics, and emphasizes that in recent years this system has been spreading quickly in various nations, particularly the BRIC countries, and is having a negative effect on a global scale.

11.6 State Capitalism as a Mode of Régulation

Now let us analyze state capitalism under Bremmer's narrow definition, and, understanding it as a system in which markets are used in order to allow those in power to extract economic and political rent, follow this line of thinking a bit further regarding China as an example of a major country with a transition economy. Bremmer is vociferous when it comes to the current state of state capitalism and the global "threat" it poses, but says little about why it arose and has continued to exist as a socioeconomic system. In order to answer this difficult question, we must presumably consider state capitalism as "mode of régulation" and then analyze what sort of "growth regime" it gives rise to and how the country in question's economic growth is realized along with its accompanying contradictions. This is the perspective of régulation theory. What I can present here is only the starting point of an initial methodological perspective.

Even if it is a fact that entering the 21st century a trend toward a state capitalism of '*guo jin min tui*' (the state advances, the private sector retreats) came to the fore, we cannot discuss the Chinese economy exclusively in these terms. Katō et al. (2013) is a useful text that describes the characteristics of the modern Chinese economy around an axis of the concept of state capitalism. I will proceed by borrowing the points it argues. This text identifies four characteristics of the Chinese economy: (1) cutthroat, no-holds-barred market competition; (2) a mixed system with a heavy emphasis on state-owned corporations; (3) competition for growth among local governments; and (4) the formation of interest groups of bureaucrats/the party's ruling class. Among these, point (4) is directly related to Bremmer-type state capitalism, but what characterizes the Chinese economy is in fact the dense, multilayered interrelation of these four elements.

To begin with, regarding (1), it is well known that a fierce, evenly balanced competition between many private companies has developed in each region, and the foundations of economic growth have been supported by the energy of the private sector. Expressions like "mass capitalism" (Marukawa 2013) and "primacy of competition" (Boyer 2012) capture this phenomenon well. It is referred to in Table 11.1 as "competitive régulation."

Regarding (2)'s "weight of state-owned corporations," China, along with Russia, is indisputably a country with a high ratio of value added by state-owned corporations and heavy government intervention in the economy compared to other nations around the world. If we look at the situation in China over time, while the share of the state-owned economy has indeed been continuously declining in the industrial sector, the important and strategic industries of telecommunications services, automobile manufacturing, electrical power, petrochemical production, and banking have been brought almost entirely under state ownership. On the policy front, too, in recent years a "state advances, the private sector retreats" approach has been clearly evident in initiatives such as the strengthening of macroeconomic control and support of state-owned corporations (Katō et al. 2013: Ch. 2). It is often noted that macroeconomic control by the central government, particularly through finance,

Table 11.1 State capitalism as a mode of régulation

	Era	Mode of régulation		Rent-seeking	Growth regime
		Fundamental compromise	Main route of régulation		
Chinese state capitalism	2000s-	Improvement in quality of life (job creation) ⇔ political monopoly of the Communist Party	<Multi-layered routes of régulation> - State régulation (macroeconomic management) - Local state corporatism (mutually beneficial coexistence between local states and corporations) - Competitive régulation (no-holds-barred, cutthroat competition)	Political rent-seeking centered around local state corporatism	Investment/ export-led model
Russian state capitalism	2000s-	-Guarantee of stability in daily life (for the general public) and acceptance of the freedom to pursue wealth (for the wealthy) ⇔ submission to political authority -Nationalism	Private markets cannot perform adequate régulation, and instead there is powerful guidance by the state	Political rent-seeking centered around Putin's circle	Resource export-led model
American Fordism	1950s–1960s	Productivity indexed wages ⇔ Taylorism	Collective bargaining between labor and management + market régulation	Lobbying of politicians by business interests emerges toward the end of this era	Wage/consumption-led model
Japanese Companyism	1950s–1980s	Guaranteed employment ⇔ acceptance of unlimited duties at work	Intra-corporate negotiation + inter-corporate cooperation	Corruption through the relationships between politicians, bureaucrats and business people exists, but is not structurally significant	Investment/ export-led model

Note: American Fordism and Japanese Companyism are also included for the sake of comparison
Source: Author

penetrates all aspects of the economy in China. This is the "state régulation" aspect of the Chinese economy (Yan 2011).

Next, (3) the "competition for growth among local governments" is a distinctly Chinese characteristic, and an important focal point when it comes to understanding the Chinese mode of régulation. According to Katō, "under China's unique central-local relationship, a competition for growth is observed that resembles a quasi-free market competition," and a system is formed in which the "central players in this competition among regions are bureaucrats, with bureaucrats at each level of local and central government sharing the same inclination toward growth, albeit of differing intensities, and those who succeed in creating economic growth being able to advance" (Katō et al. 2013: 26). In short, the local governments (bureaucrats, the party), seeking regional growth, invite and welcome businesses, and businesses, while earning high profits on this basis, pay taxes (and often bribes) to the local governments. With these funds the local government bureaucrats push ahead with local development (often while lining their own pockets), and bureaucrats who achieve good results are promoted and eventually selected for the central government. Under these incentives intense competition for growth arises between regions, and this in turn brings about a high rate of growth in China as a whole.

This kind of mutually beneficial symbiosis between local governments and corporations has also been called "local state corporatism" (Oi 1992; Boyer 2012), and described as "local governments as aggressive actors" and "local government-led economic development" by Kajitani (2011), who also defines it as a "decentralized system of development" (Kajitani 2012). Having confirmed the importance of state régulation and competitive régulation in China, it is "local state corporatism" or "local government-led economic development" as a unique system that coexists in profound interrelation with them that forms the central axis of the Chinese mode of régulation. This constitutes both the source of growth and at the same time also the hotbed of political rent-seeking.

We thus arrive at (4), "the formation of interest groups of bureaucrats/the party's ruling class," or, in other words, the question of state capitalism in Bremmer's sense of the term. According to Kajitani, even when it comes to local state-led development, while in the 1980s this took the positive form of "the local government promoting local business by intervening with local financial institutions," from the 1990s onwards it has acquired the negative form of "local governments or real-estate developers becoming rent beneficiaries through the monopolistic provision of land" (Kajitani 2011:187). In this struggle for the scarce resource of land (1990s onwards) rather than money (1980s), winners and losers are clearly distinguished. The winners are the bureaucrats/party ruling class and those connected to them, while the losers are the farmers (whose land is appropriated at low prices) and residents of large cities (who buy housing at high prices). The intense competition for growth among local governments exacerbates environmental problems, and at the same time through land market rent-seeking creates a super-wealthy class and gives rise to social inequality. If the word "state" can be interpreted in a broad sense to include "local governments," then here literal state capitalism in Bremmer's sense of rent-seeking through the control of the economy (wealth) by politics (political power) takes shape, and corruption spreads.

On this point, as Katō (2014) asserts, it may be more accurate to see corruption and economic growth as structurally coexisting in China, with corruption being "built in" to growth. According to data released in 2016, China's score of 40 out of 100 on the Corruption Perception Index, an index of the degree of corruption among public officials, placed it 79th out of 176 countries surveyed. For the sake of comparison, Russia placed 131st with a score of 29 (Transparency International 2016).

As we have seen, the characteristic route of mediation in the Chinese mode of régulation is thus an overlapping of "competitive régulation – local state corporatism – state régulation." There is room for the taking of private profits by politicians at various places within this overlapping structure. The question, therefore, is what exactly is being régulated through this route of régulation? In other words, what is the content of the (presumably tacit) compromise that is being struck among the Chinese people? It would appear to be an arrangement in which the general public accepts the communist party's political monopoly in exchange for the promise of the improvement of citizens' standard of living (including job creation) by the central and local governments. It can be posited that the Chinese export-led or export and investment-led growth regime exists on the basis of this fundamental compromise (See Table 11.1). But how does this Chinese capitalism or Chinese mode of régulation stimulate macroeconomic circuits, and what sort of virtuous cycle growth regime patterns are created as a result? A precise analysis of this question is a task that remains to be carried out.

It is also a fact that today's Chinese economy is grappling with a serious problem. Regarding the "improvement of the standard of living," while the per capita GDP has indeed increased, irregular income disparity has also emerged along with this growth, and China has become one of the most unequal societies in the world. The share of GDP comprised by individual consumption is also extremely low, as is the share comprised by wages. In other words, the reality of this nation's economy is quite far from an internal demand-led or consumption-led regime. Not only does this form a bottleneck to future growth, but in combination with the deepening environmental issues noted above may give rise to an explosion of popular discontent. In this sense China's state capitalist régulation has the potential to transform into factors detrimental to economic growth and the welfare of the population, and is facing severe challenges.

There isn't room here to discuss the state capitalism of Russia, the other major country with a transition economy, but I will say one thing before moving on. As a reaction of the citizenry to the "freedom" and confusion of the Yeltsin era, the general public's greatest demand of the Putin administration was the guarantee of stability in their daily lives. Putin was blessed with the good fortune of high prices of the export resources of oil and natural gas (although recently he has been put in a difficult position by low crude oil prices), and to a certain extent has been able to meet this demand of the public. In exchange for this, however, he has demanded the citizenry submit to his political authority. When it comes to the spheres of business and finance, too, to the extent that they submitted to Putin's political authority the freedom of actors in these fields to pursue wealth was accepted. These factors formed the foundation of the Putin administration's national compromise, and of its long-term rule. From this position Putin brought important industries such as oil and gas back under state ownership, installed members of his own faction (*siloviki* from his hometown of St. Petersburg or former agency the KGB) at the top of corporations, and constructed a system under which these individuals pursued rent-seeking and strengthened their political power (Hitai 2009; Kimura et al. 2010; Äslund 2013). By portraying a "strong state" and "strong leader" Putin has also increased the influence of nationalism in Russia, another source from which he draws popular support. This is Russian state capitalism, and compared to China's it forms a much more powerfully concentrated political authority. Through this kind of state-led route of régulation, 21st century Russia has established a resource export-led growth regime (see Table 11.1). The details of this process are a topic for future consideration.

11.7 Conclusion: The Market, the State, and Civil Society

More than a quarter of a century ago socialism began to collapse and transition to capitalism. The framework of "capitalism versus socialism" had disappeared, and the world of the future came to be seen as one covered entirely by the former. Right at that early stage Michel Albert published *Capitalisme contre capitalisme* (Albert 1991), in which he noted that capitalism comes in different forms and predicted that in the future these differing types of capitalism would vie for supremacy. These competing types were the "Anglo-Saxon type" (free market economies such as Britain and the U.S.) and the "Rhenish type" (institutionalized market economies such as Germany and Japan). And while the Rhenish type was superior both in terms of economic efficiency and social justice, it was not the Rhenish type but the Anglo-Saxon type that the former socialist countries – and other nations with emerging economies – were competing to emulate. He identified this as a great irony of history.

Several decades have now passed, and most of the former socialist nations have become neither Anglo-Saxon type nor Rhenish type capitalist economies. At least what China and Russia, the two largest transition economies, have arrived at is neither of these types of capitalism. With the progress of globalization many third world countries have also appeared on the world stage as emerging economies, but the form of capitalism found in these countries, too, does not fit neatly into either the Anglo-Saxon or Rhenish framework. Instead, today's Chinese, Russian, and emerging economies are often referred to as "state capitalist." Through Bremmer's emphatic portrayal of "state capitalism" as a threat to "free market capitalism," today's "capitalism versus capitalism" paradigm has come to be spoken of, de facto, as "free market capitalism versus state capitalism." Here Albert's Anglo-Saxon type and Rhenish type capitalism are both taken to be "free market capitalism."

Some complaints remain with Bremmer-like perspectives that seek to understand the global economy as a dichotomous confrontation between free market capitalism and state capitalism. On this point we should consider the seven type theory (Boyer 2011: Ch. 4) and the five type theory (Amable 2003) that have emerged from comparative economic system theory (see Chap. 9). If I were to look for something positive to say about the Bremmer approach, however, it would be that it accurately picks up on the global shift toward capitalism that has progressed alongside globalization and reflects its realities. Through developments such as the transition to capitalism of the former socialist nations and the shift toward emerging economies in the third world, the sphere of capitalism has come to encompass nearly every country on Earth. As is symbolized by the expansion of the G7 political economic summit to the G20, we have already entered in era in which the global economy can no longer be spoken of as including only so-called "developed nations" such as the OECD countries. Bremmer's argument is significant insofar as it raises questions about the 21st century "capitalism versus capitalism" showdown, including the countries that have newly become capitalist.

In addition, Bremmer also poses the contrast between free market capitalism and state capitalism more as a difference in the type of capitalism being employed than as a gap in the maturity or stage of development of the capitalist economies in question. This is presumably a valid approach. It does not seem that the countries called "state capitalist" today could easily become "free market capitalist," nor do they seem likely to have any inclination of their own to do so. The converse is also the case. What is lacking in Bremmer, however, is the following perspective.

Is "capitalism" slanted toward "the state" or toward "free markets"? A sharp inclination toward the state creates rent-seeking state capitalism, while a sharp inclination toward free markets creates market fundamentalism. The absence of a sound "civil society" gives rise to both of these extremes. Rent-seeking state capitalism is inseparable from the immaturity of civil society, and market fundamentalist capitalism is intimately connected to the weakening of civil society. Since there is no guarantee that civil society will develop automatically along with the development of capitalism, in every country the formation and maturation of civil society is called for and the régulation of capitalism by civil society is required. In this sense it is essential to add a third conceptual apparatus of "civil society" between "markets" and "the state" when we talk about the diversity and dynamism of capitalism. The problem of state capitalism in transition economics takes us beyond the framework of transition economics and presents us with a larger issue: "civil society."

References

Aglietta, Michel and Guo Bai (2013) *China's Development: Capitalism and Empire*, London and New York: Routledge.
Albert, Michel (1991) *Capitalisme contre capitalisme*, Paris: Edition du Seuil.
Aligica, Paul Dragos and Vlad Tarko (2012) 'State Capitalism and the Rent-seeking Conjecture,' *Constitutional Political Economy*, 23(4).
Amable, Bruno (2003) *The Diversity of Modern Capitalism*, Oxford: Oxford University Press.
Äslund, Anders (2013) 'Putin's Conservative State Capitalism,' *The Moscow Times*, Dec. 18.
Bergère, Marie-Claire (2013) *Chine: Le nouveau capitalisme d'Etat*, Paris: Fayard.
Boyer, Robert (2011) *Les financiers détruiront-ils le capitalisme?*, Paris: Economica.
——— (2012) 'The Chinese Growth Regime and the World Economy,' in Robert Boyer, Hiroyasu Uemura and Akinori Isogai eds., *Diversity and Transformations of Asian Capitalisms*, London and New York: Routledge.
Bremmer, Ian (2009a) 'State Capitalism Comes of Age,' *Foreign Affairs*, May/June.
——— (2009b) 'State Capitalism and the Crisis,' *Insights & Publications*, Jul.
——— (2010) *The End of the Free Market: Who Wins the War between States and Corporations?*, New York: Portfolio/Penguin.
Campbell, Keith (2012) 'Is It a Rival to Market Capitalism? And How Does It Affect the Natural Resources Industries?,' *Mining Weekly*, Mar. 30.
Chattopadhyay, Paresh (1994) *The Marxian Concept of Capital and the Soviet Experience: Essay in the Critique of Political Economy*, Westport: Praeger.
Cooper, Richard N. (2010) 'The End of the Free Market: Who Wins the War between States and Corporations?,' *Foreign Affairs*, Sep/Oct.
Dyer, Geoff (2010) 'State Capitalism: China's "Market-Leninism" Has Yet to Face Biggest Test,' *Financial Times*, Sep. 13.
Economist (2012) *The Economist*, 402 (8768), Jan. 21.
Ferguson, Niall (2012) 'We're All State Capitalists Now,' *Foreign Policy*, Feb. 9.
Gerschenkron, Alexander (1962) *Backwardness in Historical Perspective: A Book of Essays*, Cambridge MA: The Belknap Press of Harvard University.
Haley, Usha C. V. and George T. Haley (2013) *Subsidies to Chinese Industry: State Capitalism, Business Strategy, and Trade Policy*, Oxford: Oxford University Press.
Hitai, Takeo (2009) 'Pūchin no "Kokka Shihonshugi"' (Putin's "State Capitalism"), *Shūkan Ekonomisuto* (*Economist Weekly*), July 21.
Ikumi, Takuichi (1979) 'Gendai Shihonshugi no Rekishiteki Kōzō' (Historical Structure of Contemporary Capitalism), in Noriyoshi Imai et al. eds., *Gendai Keizai to Kokka* (*Contemporary Economy and the State*), vol.2, Tokyo: Nihon Hyōron-sha.
Janjigian, Vahan (2010) 'Communism Is Dead, But State Capitalism Thrives', *Forbes*, Mar. 22.
Kajitani, Kai (2011) *Gendai Chūgoku no Zaisei Kin'yū Shisutemu: Gurōbaruka to Chūō-Chihō Kankei no Keizaigaku* (*Public and Private Finance Systems in Modern China: Economics of Globalization and Center-Periphery Relationship*), Nagoya: The University of Nagoya Press.
——— (2012) 'Chūgoku no Keizai Seichō to "Bunsangata no Kaihatsu Taisei"' (Chinese Economic Growth and "Decentralized System of Development"), *Hikaku Keizai Kenkyū* (*Japanese Journal of Comparative Economics*), 49(1), Jan.
Katō, Hiroyuki (2014) '<Views on China> Chūgoku ha Huhai Bokumetsu ni Seikō suruka (<Views on China> Will China succeed in the Eradiction of Corruption?), [On line] http://www.tkfd.or.jp/research/project/news.php?id=1306
Katō, Hiroyuki et al. (2013) *21-seiki no Chūgoku: Kokka Shihonshugi no Hikari to Kage* (*China in the 21st Century: Light and Darkness of State Capitalism*), Tokyo: Asahi Shimbun Publications Inc.
Kimura, Hiroshi et al. (2010) *Gendai Roshia wo miru Me: "Pūchin no 10-nen" no Shōgeki* (*How to Watch Modern Russia?: The Impact of "Putin's Decade"*), Tokyo: NHK Books.

Kurlantzic, Joshua (2012) 'The Rise of Innovative State Capitalism,' *Bloomberg Businessweek*, June 28.

Lardy, Nicholas R. (2014) *Markets over Mao: The Rise of Private Business in China*, Washington D.C.: Institute for International Economics. (Book Reviews on *The Wall Street Journal*, Sep. 10, 2014; *Forbes*, Oct. 16, 2014)

Lenin, Vladimir Ilyich (1965) 'Report on the Immediate Tasks of the Soviet Government' (Originally published in 1918), in: *Collected Works*, vol.27, Moscow: Progress Publishers.

Levingston, Steven (2010) 'China's Authoritarian Capitalism Undermines Western Values, Argue Three New Books,' *Washington Post*, May 30.

Li, Xing and Thimothy M. Shaw (2013) 'The Political Economy of Chinese State Capitalism,' *Journal of China and International Relations*, 1(1).

Lubman, Stanley (2012) 'China's State Capitalism: The Real World Implications,' *The Wall Street Journal*, Mar. 1.

Marukawa, Tomoo (2013) *Chainīizu Dorīmu: Taishū Shihonshugi ga Sekai wo Kaeru* (*Chinese Dream: Mass Capitalism Changes the World*), Tokyo: Chikuma Shobō Ltd.

Mielants, Eric (2007) *The Origins of Capitalism and the 'Rise of the West,'* Philadelphia: Temple University Press.

Musacchio, Aldo and Sergio G. Lazzarini (2014) *Reinventing State Capitalism: Leviathan in Business, Brazil and Beyond*, Cambridge MA: Harvard University Press.

Nakagane, Katsuji (2010) *Taisei Ikō no Seiji-keizaigaku: Naze Shakaishugikoku ha Shihonshugi ni mukatte Dassō surunoka* (*The Political Economy of Transition: Farewell to Socialism*), Nagoya: The University of Nagoya Press.

Nölke, Andreas ed. (2014) *Multinational Corporations from Emerging Markets: State Capitalism 3.0*, Bassingstoke/New York: Palgrave Macmillan.

Oi, Jean C. (1992) 'Fiscal Reform and the Economic Foundations of Local State Corporatism in China,' *World Politics*, 45(1).

Ōtani, Teinosuke et al. eds. (1996) *Soren no "Shakaishugi" toha Nan dattanoka* (*What was the "Socialism" in Soviet Union?*), Tokyo: Ōtsuki-shoten.

Reich, Robert (2009) *Supercapitalism: The Battle for Democracy in an Age of Big Business*, new edition, London: Icon Books.

Rostow, Walt W. (1960) *The Stages of Economic Growth: A Non-communist Manifesto*, London and New York: Cambridge University Press.

Sapir, Jacques (2013) 'Le "capitalisme d'Etat" est-il l'horizon historique de la Russie?,' *RussEurope*, 22 nov. [En ligne] http://russeurope.hypotheses.org/1750

Schmidt, Vivien A. (2003) 'French Capitalism Transformed, yet Still a Third Variety of Capitalism,' *Economy and Society*, 32(4).

Schuman, Michael (2011) 'State Capitalism vs the Free Market: Which Performs Better?,' *Time*, Sept. 30. [Online] http://business.time.com/2011/09/30/state-capitalism-vs-the-free-market-which-performs-better/

Screpanti, Ernesto (2001) *The Fundamental Institutions of Capitalism*, London and New York: Routledge.

Stewart, Devin T. (2010) 'Book Review: "The End of the Free Market" by Ian Bremmer,' *Global Policy Innovations*, May 12.

Walter, Andrew and Xiaoke Zhang eds. (2012) *East Asian Capitalism: Diversity, Continuity, and Change*, Oxford: Oxford University Press.

Transparency International (2016) *Corruption Perceptions Index 2016*. [Online] http://www.transparency.org

Yan, Chengnam (2011) *Chūgoku no Keizai Hatten to Seido Henka* (*Economic Development and Institutional Change in China*), Kyoto: Kyoto University Press.